NEW TREATY, NEW TRADITION

CARWYN JONES

NEW TREATY, NEW TRADITION

Reconciling New Zealand and Māori Law

UBCPress · Vancouver · Toronto

25 24 23 22 21 20 19 18 17 16   5 4 3 2 1

Printed in Canada on FSC-certified ancient-forest-free paper (100% post-consumer recycled) that is processed chlorine- and acid-free.

Library and Archives Canada Cataloguing-in-Publication

Jones, Carwyn, author
New treaty, new tradition : reconciling New Zealand and Māori law / Carwyn Jones.

Includes bibliographical references and index.
Issued in print and electronic formats.
ISBN 978-0-7748-3168-0 (hardback). – ISBN 978-0-7748-3170-3 (pdf)
ISBN 978-0-7748-3171-0 (epub). – ISBN 978-0-7748-3172-7 (mobi)

1. Maori (New Zealand people) – Claims. 2. Maori (New Zealand people) – Land tenure. 3. Maori (New Zealand people) – Legal status, laws, etc. 4. Land tenure (Maori law). 5. Reconciliation (Law) – New Zealand. Title.

KUQ2568.J65 2016   346.9304'3208999442   C2016-902472-5
C2016-902473-3

Canadä

UBC Press gratefully acknowledges the financial support for our publishing program of the Government of Canada (through the Canada Book Fund) and the British Columbia Arts Council.

UBC Press
The University of British Columbia
2029 West Mall
Vancouver, BC V6T 1Z2
www.ubcpress.ca

To Chele and Evan – for everything

Contents

Preface

Stories play an important role in the construction and maintenance of legal systems. In his influential "*Nomos* and Narrative," Robert Cover explains that law is an institution built on the stories of a community's social life: "For every constitution there is an epic, for each decalogue a scripture."[1] Law must be understood in the context of these common narratives if it is to have relevance in our lives.

My use of Māori storytelling forms reflects Cover's view of law. By using *pūrākau* (Māori stories) throughout the book, I seek to reinforce the social, cultural, and political contexts of law. This is consistent with recent legal history scholarship of colonial societies, which views law as both a product and source of cultures of those societies.[2]

As a means of transmitting embedded norms and cultural values, storytelling is particularly relevant to research on Indigenous law.[3] Anishinabe legal scholar John Borrows has noted that "stories express the law in Aboriginal communities, since they represent the accumulated wisdom and experience of First Nations conflict resolution."[4] Borrows uses storytelling techniques throughout his own work to explain, explore, and discuss Indigenous law and legal issues.[5] Borrows has even used storytelling forms to explain the importance of stories.[6]

Stories not only play an important role in the production and maintenance of legal culture within communities, they are also employed to communicate legal rules and principles in various cultural communities. For example, Lumbee scholar Robert Williams Jr. illustrates the vital role of stories in establishing common understandings of legal rights and obligations within various American Indian cultural models of diplomacy.[7] In many American Indian societies, suggests Williams, stories have long been understood as an essential ingredient of successful diplomatic and treaty relationships.[8] In this context, stories might have many functions. They may be told to establish and facilitate communicative processes. They may be told to educate treaty partners about expected standards of behaviour and accepted legal norms. Some stories might also generate law.[9] One of the most significant aspects of stories within American Indian diplomacy is their integrative power to transcend cultural and social borders. Williams sees the creative potential of stories as crucial in this regard, empowering communities to imagine new connections and relationships: "In American Indian treaty visions of law and peace, a treaty itself was a special kind of story: a way of imagining a world of human solidarity where we regard others as our relatives."[10]

Williams also notes that many critical race and feminist legal scholars have employed storytelling techniques to assist in their analysis of legal issues and "to make connections with strange others in a world of human diversity and conflict."[11] Critical race theorist Derrick Bell explains various types of discrimination by constructing a series of separate narratives.[12] Feminist legal scholar Patricia A. Cain recounts the stories of lesbian women in order to ground her theoretical approach in the lived experiences of women.[13] Richard Delgado argues that storytelling can be employed as an academic technique to provide an appropriate and effective voice for those who might otherwise be marginalized within legal systems.[14]

Stories reflect traditional Indigenous forms of preserving and transmitting knowledge. Their re-telling at different times by different people helps to construct and maintain a sense of shared cultural values.[15] Pūrākau, therefore, provide a means of expressing the values, norms, rules, and processes that comprise the body of Māori legal traditions, within a context that maintains the integrity of the subject matter.

Linda Smith has noted the inextricable link between whakapapa and *te reo* (the Māori language) and pūrākau. She has pointed out that whakapapa is inherently connected to stories and events that involve ancestors. These stories are understood through *whakapapa* (genealogy), and knowledge captured in whakapapa is transmitted across generations by the re-telling of those stories.[16] The survival and revival of Māori language and culture is a key part of the reassertion of tino rangatiratanga.[17]

Māori educationalist Jenny Lee suggests that using pūrākau "creates the opportunity to write about culture as well as write culture into the text."[18] An example of how storytelling forms can enable Indigenous researchers to "write culture into the text" can be seen in Jo-ann Archibald's *Indigenous Storywork*.[19] Archibald considers the role of Indigenous storytelling in educational settings and uses Indigenous storytelling forms throughout the book to explore and develop her ideas. Her Stō:lo traditions and culture inflect these stories and her research as a whole. Her approach provides an opportunity to introduce many Indigenous cultural forms, to demonstrate practices, and to illustrate cultural values. Readers can see, for example, the book reveals the importance of dreams within Stō:lo culture and the way that dreams can be analysed in order to assist in our understanding of the world. The practical application of dreams is characteristic of many Indigenous cultures, as is also evident in John Borrows's *Drawing Out Law*, an exploration of Indigenous legal traditions through storytelling forms.[20]

Here I use the opportunity provided by pūrākau to weave *waiata* (songs), *karakia* (prayers), *whakatauki* (proverbs), and other Māori forms into the research. These performative opportunities help communicate Māori concepts across cultures. In addition to providing an appropriate cultural context in which to explore Māori concepts, pūrākau can help Māori researchers communicate with Māori communities. I use short narratives, in the pūrākau form, to illustrate my analysis and arguments. These stories are from my own community and about my own ancestors. They provide information about me as well as my interest in these issues. They tell the reader who I am and, specifically, who I am in a way that makes sense to the Māori world. Some of the stories are about ancestors from the time of the first arrival of Māori in Aotearoa. Others are more recent, with characters from the nineteenth and twentieth centuries. While these stories are based on histories recorded elsewhere in books or songs or other forms, I have retold them here to support the discussion in this book. The final story in the book is not based on a previously existing narrative. Although the character is prominent in Māori mythology, this story is based on my own experiences and engagement with issues relating to Indigenous legal traditions. It is, in that sense, a new story, intended to reflect the need for new stories about Māori legal traditions and the treaty settlement process.[21] Overall, the stories presented here provide examples of Māori law and explain Māori concepts, principles, and values within a culturally appropriate context.

These stories are not intended to be an authoritative or definitive history; rather, I have adapted them for the purpose of this book in order draw attention to the issues and arguments addressed here. Lee suggests that adopting a pūrākau approach "guides us to speak in a language that is not exclusive, but draws on our own ways of seeing, speaking and expressing ourselves in order to bring 'to life' the issues and complexities of our experiences that may be culture specific and local and/or more universal in nature."[22] This approach assists in situating the researcher in relation to the research, while at the same time leaving space for others to approach the research from their own locations. The conscious use of voice can also help to make transparent the researcher's own "ideologies, knowledge, subjectivities and politics."[23] I deliberately employ a storytelling voice to make clear that the stories and histories of my whānau and our ancestors are retold within the context of this book and for the purpose of communicating aspects of this research. They are all presented in the context of a father telling stories to his son. This grounds the discussion of the settlement process and Māori legal traditions in the reality of Māori lives. The figures of father and son remind the reader that these issues are relevant to the lives of real people and that the values and practices of Māori legal traditions continue to animate day-to-day Māori life. The stories also serve to remind the reader that law is a human and social phenomenon concerned with relationships among people; law influences how people interact with the world. Finally, the stories are intended to reflect a traditional way of preserving ancestral knowledge and transmitting that knowledge from one generation to the next.

The use of storytelling as a means of cultural reproduction and communication is, of course, not unique to Māori communities. Cherokee scholar Thomas King argues for the fundamental role of stories in our lives by quoting the Nigerian storyteller Ben Okri. Okri suggests that everyone is effectively part of one's own story, constructed by one's own actions. Thus, "If we change the stories we live by, quite possibly we change our lives."[24] Or, as King himself simply and elegantly suggests, "The truth about stories is that's all we are."[25]

The stories in this book provide a space for various forms of communication – for songs and prayers, legends and histories – and also for expressions of hope, aspiration, concern, care, and humour. They are Māori stories; they help to situate the ideas within a Māori space.

Acknowledgments

I would like to thank Hamar Foster, John McLaren, Christine O'Bonsawin, and David V. Williams, for all their comments and feedback on early drafts of work that formed the basis of this book. Each contributed enormously to my thinking, research, and writing, and each brought particular skills and knowledge to bear on this project. I would also like to thank Peter Cole, Brian Slattery, Linda Tuhiwai Smith, Susan Drummond, Pat O'Reilly, and Marlene Kadar, who helped me to find my voice as a Māori scholar and whose influence is reflected in this work.

My colleagues at Victoria University of Wellington have also provided feedback and comments in various seminar sessions, which have helped to shape my approach to matters addressed in this book. A number of people whom I have been lucky enough to work with have inspired and supported me in ways they may not always have been fully aware of. These include Indigenous scholars such as Māmari Stephens, Maria Bargh, Moana Jackson, Ani Mikaere, Jacinta Ruru, John Borrows, Val Napoleon, Gordon Christie, and Jeff Corntassel. Others include those who have been leading voices on Treaty of Waitangi issues, working tirelessly in this area for many years – in particular, Justice Joe Williams and Sir Edward Taihakurei Durie. I have also been privileged to work with a number of Indigenous students who have encouraged, provoked, and supported my thinking in various ways: Tai Ahu, Horiana Irwin, Te Rangimarie Williams, David Jones, Kiritapu Allan, Erin Carr, Julia Whaipooti, Ariana Reweti, Stevie-Rae Hart, Caleb Behn, and many others from Ngā Rangahautira and ILSA.

My thanks also go to Ngā Pae o te Maramatanga, New Zealand's Māori Centre of Research Excellence, for providing a grant to support the publication of this work; to the anonymous readers who engaged with this work so constructively to help improve the manuscript; and to the team at UBC Press for bringing the book to fruition.

Some portions of Chapters 1 and 3 were previously published as "Whakaeke i ngā Ngaru – Riding the Waves: Māori Legal Traditions in New Zealand Public Life," in *Between Indigenous and Settler Governance,* edited by Lisa Ford and Tim Rowse (New York: Routledge, 2013), 174-86. Some portions of the descriptions and explanations of Māori law that appear, especially in Chapter 3, also appear in "A Māori Constitutional Tradition," (2014) 12 NZ Jnl. Pub. and Itn'l. L 187. Some portions of Chapters 1 and 6 are drawn from "Tāwhaki And Te Tiriti: A Principled Approach to the Constitutional Future of the Treaty of Waitangi," (2013) 25 NZULR 703. Material relating to the dispute between Ngāti Maniapoto and Ngāti Tama that appears in Chapter 5 was previously published as "Māori Dispute Resolution: Traditional Conceptual Regulators and Contemporary Indigenous Processes." In *Mediating across Difference: Indigenous, Oceanic and Asian Approaches to Conflict Resolution,* edited by M. Brigg and R. Bleiker (Honolulu: University of Hawaii Press, 2010). The Epilogue was originally published as "Māui and the People of the North," (2013) 44 VUWLR 535.

The friendship and support of a number of people helped to keep me grounded while I was in Canada, working on my PhD and researching material that would eventually form the basis of this book. These people also made this a really special time for me and my whānau. In particular, I would like to acknowledge Racquel Fraser, Jen Smith, Kerry Sloan, Danika Littlechild, Connie Nisbet, Lorne Underwood and his family, and Boardo and Shelly and their family.

A special thank you to my Ngāti Kahungunu tīpuna and my Ngai Te Apatu relations for trusting me with our stories, especially Pat Katene and Lena Kaui; to Chele and Evan, who have always encouraged me; to Kohurangi, Ruaariki, and Te Rauhina, who amaze and inspire me every day, and to Nikki for her support and love.

Glossary of Māori Terms

Note: Plurals in Māori: plurals of nouns are indicated by a preceding article or determiner, such as "ngā" or "te," while the plural form of the noun will often be the same as the singular (e.g., ngā waka – the canoes; te waka – the canoe). In some cases, the first vowel sound will be lengthened in the plural form of the noun (e.g., tangata – person; tāngata – people).

āe	yes
Aotearoa	New Zealand
aria	form
aroha	love
atua	god
ea	state of equilibrium
e Tama	son/boy
hapū	Māori kin community
hara	wrongs
Hawaiki	traditional homeland of Māori
iwi	Māori nation/people
kai	food
kaitiaki	guardian/steward
kaitiakitanga	guardianship/stewardship
kanohi ki te kanohi	face to face
karakia	prayer/incantation
kauhanga	passageway

kaupapa	principle/foundation
kāwanatanga	government
kōrero	talk/stories
kōrero rangatira	chiefly discussion
kotahitanga	unity
kuia	grandmother/female elder
mamae	injury/hurt
mana	spiritually sanctioned authority
mana whenua	authority in relation to land
manaakitanga	nurturing relationships
marae	central community space/complex
mauri	life force
moana	sea
motuhake	special, distinct
muru	ritualized confiscation of property
noa	profane/everyday/flipside of tapu
Pākehā	New Zealander of European descent
Pāpā	father/Dad
pāua	abalone
pōwhiri	welcome ceremony
pūrākau	Māori story/stories
rangatira	chief/leader
rangatiratanga	chiefly authority
taihoa	slow down
take	reason for action
Tāne	one of the *atua* (Māori gods)
tangata	person
tāngata	people
tangata whenua	Indigenous/"people of the land"
taonga	treasured possession
tapu	spiritual character of all things
tātau	we – you (two or more) and I
tawhito	ancient (noun or adjective)
te maramatanga o ngā tikanga	philosophy of Māori law
te reo	the Māori language
tikanga	the right, correct, or just way of doing things
tikanga Māori	Māori law and practice
tino rangatiratanga	self-determination/chiefly authority
tipua	demon/supernatural being

tipuna, tupuna/tīpuna, tūpuna	ancestor/ancestors
tohunga	expert/priest
ture	law
utu	balance and reciprocity
waiata	song(s)
waka	canoe
Waka Umanga	"vehicle for community undertaking"
whakahaere	management
whakapapa	genealogy
whānau	extended family
whanaunga	relation
whanaungatanga	relationships
whare wānanga	traditional university/house of learning
whenua	land

Pronunciation Guide

Note: This Pronunciation Guide is a reproduction of the Te Reo Māori pronunciation guide that appears on the Victoria University of Wellington website, http://www.victoria.ac.nz/maori-at-victoria/ako/te-reo-at-victoria/te-reo-pronunciation-guide.

Sounds

There are fifteen distinct sounds within the Māori alphabet:

- five vowels: "a," "e," "i," "o," and "u"
- eight consonants: "h," "k," "m," "n," "p," "r," "t," and "w"
- two digraphs (two letters that combine to form one sound): "wh" and "ng."

Vowels

While there are only five vowels, combinations of vowels (diphthongs) are common, e.g., "au," "ao," "ea," "oi," and "ua."

A vowel can also have a long or short sound. A long sound is usually denoted by a macron (a bar appearing over a vowel to indicate it is lengthened during pronunciation, e.g., "ā" as in "wāhi").

Pronunciation

Vowels are pronounced as follows:

Short

"A" as in "aloud"
"E" as in "entry"
"I" as in "eat"
"O" as in "ordinary"
"U" as in "to"

Long

"A" as in "car"
"E" as in "led"
"I" as in "peep"
"O" as in "pork"
"U" as in "loot"

Consonants

Pronounce consonants as you would in English, with two key exceptions:

The "t" sound depends on which vowel appears after it. When it follows an "a," "e," or "o," pronounce it with as little sibilant sound as possible (almost like a "d"). When it follows an "i" or "u," it includes a slight sibilant sound, but not nearly as much as an English "t."

"R" is pronounced as a soft "rolled" "r."

Digraphs

The "ng" digraph is pronounced as it sounds in the English word "singer."

The "wh" digraph originally sounded like the "wh" in "whisper," but in most dialects has evolved to be more like the English "f" sound.

NEW TREATY, NEW TRADITION

1

Tino Rangatiratanga and Māori Legal History

TAMATEA

"What story are we going to have tonight, Pāpā?"

"What story would you like, e Tama?"

"Maybe the one about Rātā?"

"That's a good one, isn't it? Do you remember what happens in that story?"

"Rātā tries to cut down a tree, Pāpā. He wants to make a canoe. But the spirits of the forest keep putting the tree back together again every night when Rātā goes home."

"That's right, e Tama."

"Why don't they let him build his waka, Pāpā?"

"Because he didn't follow the proper process. He didn't say a karakia to Tāne before he chopped down the tree. He didn't follow tikanga."

"What is 'tikanga,' Pāpā?"

"It is just the right way of doing things, e Tama. Like when we say karakia before we have our kai. Or when we have a pōwhiri to welcome visitors. In some ways, tikanga is a bit like the Pākehā idea of 'law.'"

"But Rātā was able to build his waka in the end, wasn't he?"

"Yes, but only after he had acknowledged Tāne and the spirits of the forest appropriately. That was very important. Just like when our ancestor, Tamatea, was careful to acknowledge the great tree that Tāne provided to build the waka Takitimu. On the voyage to Aotearoa, Tamatea would chant:[1]

Ko wai te waka e takoto nei,
Ko Takitimu, Ko Takitimu.
Pā atu ra taku hoe,
Ki te riu tapu nui o te waka e takoto nei
Rei kura, rei ora.
Rei ora te mauri-e.
Ka turuturua, ka poupoua,
Ki tawhito o te rangi-e.
Rurukutia,
Rurukutia te waka e takoto nei.
Rurukutia te kei Matapupuni,
Rurukutia te ihu matapupuni a Tāne.
Rurukutia i te kowhao tapu a Tāne,
Rurukutia i te mata tapu a Tāne.
Rurukutia i te rauawa tapu a Tāne,
O te waka e takoto nei.

Who is the sacred canoe that lays here in rest?
It is Takitimu, it is Takitimu.
As I rest my paddle on
the sacred hull of this ancestral canoe that lays here in rest.
This canoe is a cherished treasure with its everlasting life force,
The life force that is the vital essence of this canoe.
It is to be firm, it is to be fixed and connect us
to our ancestors of the higher realm.
Bind together,
Bind together this canoe that lays here in rest.
Bind together the lashings from the stern and
Bind together the lashings to the bow of the sacred canoe, created by Tāne.
Bind together the sacred timber of Tāne and
Bind together the sacred embodiment of Tāne.
Bind together the sacred sides of the canoe of Tāne to be as one,
to the sacred canoe that lays here in rest.

"Did that keep the waka safe, Pāpā?"
"Ae, e Tama. Tamatea and the others on board Takitimu safely completed their journey to Aotearoa."
"What happened to Tamatea and the others after they got to Aotearoa?

"Tamatea made a home for himself at a place called Kawhai-nui. But some people say that he wasn't entirely happy in Aotearoa."

"Why not, Pāpā?"

"Well, Tamatea had been a great leader of his people back in Hawaiki. He had a deep knowledge and understanding of the tikanga in that place and so was able to fulfill the role of a chief. But things were different in Aotearoa. There was already a community at Kawhai-nui and they had their own leaders – people who knew about the local way of doing things and the way that tikanga had developed in response to this new land and new circumstances. Tamatea was still highly respected, but he found it difficult to find a role for himself in his new home. Nobody disputed Tamatea's knowledge and power, but the means of expressing knowledge and power had changed. The tikanga had changed."

"Has tikanga changed again since that time, Pāpā?

"Many times, e Tama. Tikanga must constantly adapt to new situations and different contexts, adjust to meet challenges that arise, and grow along with the hopes and dreams of our people."

"And what about the others who came with Tamatea, Pāpā? What did our other ancestors do? Did they know that tikanga had changed? Did they try to do anything about it? Did they try to change things themselves, like Māui did?"

"So many questions! And very good questions they are too. We'll get to their stories soon, e Tama."

Tikanga, Change, and Māori Legal Tradition

Change and adaptation are important aspects of any dynamic legal culture. Legal cultures, like other features of social life, adapt and develop in response to changes in matters such as community values, technology, and the environment. Flexibility and dynamism are often identified as defining characteristics of common law systems. This book is concerned with another flexible and dynamic legal culture – that of the Māori peoples of Aotearoa/New Zealand.[2] In particular, it examines the ways in which Māori legal traditions have changed in response to the process of the negotiated settlement of historical claims against the state. The settlements stemming from the 1840 Treaty of Waitangi and agreed between Māori groups and the state provide significant opportunities and challenges for Māori communities and, inevitably, force those communities to confront questions relating to the application of their own legal traditions within these changing circumstances. These questions are especially pertinent in the context of establishing post-settlement governance entities, a process that unavoidably touches on issues of identity, authority, rights, and resource management. This book focuses specifically on Māori legal traditions and post-settlement governance entities. However, the intention is not simply to record changes to Māori legal traditions but also to offer some assessment of whether these changes and adaptations support or, alternatively, detract from two key goals of the settlement process: reconciliation and Māori self-determination, or *tino rangatiratanga*.

Background to the Treaty Settlement Process

The treaty settlement process unfolds against a broader historical and political backdrop. This book does not provide a comprehensive analysis of the history of race relations in New Zealand or even a comprehensive history of Māori-Crown relations. The section that follows instead paints in broad brushstrokes an outline of the political and historical context of the treaty settlement process in order to provide the context for an explanation of the dynamics of that process. I wish to avoid the stadial approach to history or the suggestion that New Zealand political history has moved in a linear fashion from a uniform Māori-Crown relationship to the heterogenous intricacies of the treaty settlement era. The reality is inevitably even messier and more complex. Here I provide a small number of key reference points in order to give a flavour of the Māori-Crown relationship over time.

Official British government involvement in Aotearoa did not begin with the signing of the Treaty of Waitangi on February 6, 1840. As a result of increasing settler activity in Aotearoa, including an established missionary presence, itinerant whalers and sealers, and growing numbers of permanent settlers, the British government had appointed James Busby as Resident of New Zealand in 1832. Busby's role was to try to establish some measure of law and order over a settler population that was often lawless. He was not provided with any resources or practical powers to achieve this, however, and was famously described as "a man-o-war without guns."[3] Busby encouraged the Māori peoples of the northern New Zealand to adopt some of the institutions of Western government. In 1834, a group of northern chiefs adopted a national flag, which was important for shipping and trading purposes. The following year, this northern group, referred to as "He Wakaminenga on Nga Hapū o Niu Tireni" (The Confederation of the United Tribes of New Zealand) adopted a Declaration of Independence. The declaration states that "all sovereign power and authority" within New Zealand resides with the chiefs of the various tribes. It includes provision for the chiefs to meet in congress each year to pass laws for the good governance of the country, and it asks the king of England to protect the independence of the chiefs. The relationship between the Declaration of Independence and the Treaty of Waitangi is worthy of its own study. In its report on Stage 1 of the Northland inquiry, the Waitangi Tribunal undertakes a comprehensive examination of both the Declaration of Independence and the Treaty of Waitangi, considering the likely meaning of those two documents for those who signed them.[4] The tribunal's view of the declaration was that it did not radically alter Māori political organization. That is, the declaration's intention that chiefs would come together in congress to pass laws did not override the authority of individual *rangatira* (chief/leader) and *hapū* (Māori kin community). It appears that the congress envisioned by the declaration may not ever officially have met. Nevertheless, the Declaration of Independence is important to the context of the Treaty of Waitangi, signed less than five years later.

The Treaty of Waitangi

The Treaty of Waitangi has been described as "simply the most important document in New Zealand's history."[5] At its heart the treaty provides a framework for the relationship between Māori and the New Zealand government. Consequently, the Treaty of Waitangi informs discussions in New Zealand public life that relate to constitutional powers and limitations, race relations, justice, identity, and reconciliation. It is a legal instrument, a political tool, and a historical document.

The treaty was signed in 1840 between representatives of the British Crown and a group of Māori chiefs, initially, at Waitangi in the Bay of Islands. There is still debate about the Treaty's precise legal status and its role in the British Crown's acquisition of sovereignty over New Zealand.[6] There is an English-language version and a Māori-language version of the treaty.[7] The vast majority of the Māori signatories signed the Māori version. Although there are significant differences between the two, the essential agreement, in both the English and Māori versions of the treaty, is that the Crown has the authority to establish some form of government in New Zealand and that Māori property and other rights and the authority of the chiefs is protected.[8] The concepts of self-determination and reconciliation underpin the treaty and infuse the discussion (legal and otherwise) about the relationship between Māori and the state.[9] These two important concepts consequently shape the contemporary discussions that take place between Māori and the Crown in the context of Treaty of Waitangi claims and the settlement of those claims. The fact that these formal interactions between the state and the Māori leadership began with the mutual recognition of these two important concepts is an important reference for the Treaty of Waitangi settlement process if that process is to contribute towards sustainable Māori self-determination and effective reconciliation.

The precise nature and scope of the governmental authority that was ceded and the Māori authority that was guaranteed by the Treaty of Waitangi has been the subject of considerable discussion. The orthodox view is that, while the treaty may have been an important part of the establishment of the Crown's sovereignty in New Zealand, it cannot have been the mechanism by which that sovereignty was practically effected. Prominent New Zealand legal scholar F.M. Brookfield uses Hans Kelsen's theory of a hierarchy of norms to suggest that the Crown's acquisition of sovereignty was a revolutionary act in constitutional terms.[10] He argues that the assertion of Crown sovereignty and the replacement of the Māori legal order with a new governing constitution had no validity within the pre-existing legal order.[11] The Treaty of Waitangi may have provided partial legitimisation for such a constitutional revolution, though only so far as the Crown's assumption of authority was consistent with treaty guarantees.[12] According to that model, New Zealand has effectively been undergoing a constitutional revolution since 1840, with various factors contributing to the legitimisation of the current constitutional arrangements.[13]

Constitutional lawyer and author Matthew Palmer has published similar views.[14] Palmer sees the Treaty of Waitangi as part of the establishment of Crown sovereignty rather than the instrument that technically transferred sovereignty from Māori to the British Crown. Palmer suggests that the Treaty of Waitangi was necessary as a political step more than a legal requirement and that the treaty is not an international treaty of cession but instead a treaty of protection. It provided protections and guarantees to the Māori chiefs so that the British Crown was able to assert sovereignty. While Palmer sees the treaty's strict legal role as rather limited, he goes on to consider the ways the Treaty of Waitangi can have legal effects within the New Zealand legal system.

Palmer primarily addresses the treaty's place within the colonial legal system. He acknowledges that the treaty also has a place within Māori legal systems and suggests ways in which the Treaty of Waitangi might have been viewed within Māori legal systems. His analysis in this area is somewhat limited, however. For a greater understanding of the meaning and effect of the treaty according to the legal rules and constitutional principles of Māori legal traditions, we must turn to other treaty scholars. Māori authors such as Ani Mikaere and Moana Jackson provide analyses of the Treaty of Waitangi that consider not only Māori perspectives on the Treaty but the constitutional impact of the treaty according to Māori legal traditions.[15]

Māori legal scholar Ani Mikaere argues that it is the Māori legal concepts in the Māori text that indicate the intent of the treaty agreement. She points to the consistency between the Māori text and the 1835 Declaration of Independence, and the political reality of the time, to suggest that the only reasonable meaning of the treaty is that, in signing, the Māori signatories declared and cemented their own authority, while acknowledging and defining the presence of the Crown and its citizens in their midst.[16] Mikaere compares this to a *pōwhiri,* a ceremony of welcome and encounter that acknowledges and recognizes a visiting group and provides space for them, but always takes place according to the traditions of the hosts, the *tangata whenua.*[17] One of New Zealand's foremost Indigenous rights advocates, Moana Jackson, has also pointed to rules of treaty interpretation that suggest greater reliance ought to be placed on the Māori text when seeking to ascertain the meaning of the Treaty of Waitangi.[18]

Mikaere also describes Māori legal systems as "the first law of Aotearoa," suggesting that they are the only legal systems upon which New Zealand's constitution could legitimately have been based.[19] This perspective supports the view that the treaty was signed within the context of Māori legal systems. Jackson further argues that the Treaty of Waitangi must be seen in the light of what was in 1840 already a long line of inter-*iwi* agreements that regulated political relations between *iwi* (Māori nation/people). Understood in this Indigenous context, the treaty does not talk about a shift in absolute sovereignty because, as Jackson has pointed out, this would have been inconceivable to Māori.[20] Giving up one's *mana* (spiritually sanctioned authority) or rangatiratanga was simply not possible under Māori law. Mana and rangatiratanga, Jackson notes, were part of the whakapapa (genealogy) of the community. The rights and obligations that are inherent within those concepts cannot then be transferred, at the stroke of a pen, to others who have different whakapapa and descend from different ancestors.

In 2014, the Waitangi Tribunal, the body charged with hearing claims based on the principles of the Treaty of Waitangi, released a report that supports the view that the treaty did not transfer sovereignty. This report addressed the first stage of inquiry into claims in the Northland region. Titled *He Whakaputanga me te Tiriti – The Declaration and the Treaty,* it focuses on the meaning and effect of the Māori-language texts of He Whakaputanga o te Rangatiratanga o Nu Tireni and Te Tiriti or Waitangi alongside their English-language counterparts: the Declaration of Independence and the Treaty of Waitangi. The central finding made by the tribunal was that the rangatira, the Māori leaders, who signed the Treaty of Waitangi in February 1840 did not cede their sovereignty in doing so. However, the tribunal makes clear that this report on the first stage of the inquiry does not contain findings in respect of claims, nor does it draw any conclusions about the sovereignty the Crown exercises today or how the treaty relationship should operate in a modern context.

The special significance of He Whakaputanga (the 1835 Declaration of Independence) in the Northland region was one of the reasons the tribunal was required to produce a thorough analysis of evidence about the treaty's meaning and effects in 1840. In coming to its conclusions, the tribunal considered, among other things, statements from previous tribunal reports about the effects of the treaty. There is considerable variation among those earlier reports as to how the authority of the parties was affected by the treaty. In this report, the tribunal places particular emphasis on the *Report on the Orakei Claim* (1987) and the *Muriwhenua Land Report* (1997). The Orakei Tribunal took the view that the text of the treaty would not have conveyed the cession of the English concept of sovereignty, but that contemporary statements by Māori suggested that Māori accepted "the Crown's higher authority." The Muriwhenua Land Tribunal pointed out that, while the British might have assumed they had obtained sovereignty through the treaty, the guarantee of tino rangatiratanga meant that the Māori perspective would have been quite different. Consequently, the Muriwhenua Land Tribunal concluded that the best way to understand the treaty is as an expression of the parties' "honest intention that Maori and Pakeha relationships would be based on mutual respect and the protection of each other."[21]

Alongside earlier tribunal reports, relevant court rulings, and existing scholarship relating to the treaty, the Waitangi Tribunal also heard evidence from claimants and a number of eminent historians. Dame Anne Salmond dismissed the possibility that the rangatira had ceded sovereignty to the Crown, arguing that *kāwanatanga* (government) would have been understood as "a subordinate and delegated power."[22] Don Loveridge thought the rangatira would have understood they would become subject to a higher authority and to British law under the treaty,[23] and Paul McHugh described the treaty signing as part of "the process by which Māori agreement to British sovereignty over New Zealand was obtained."[24]

After assessing the evidence presented at the inquiry, the Waitangi Tribunal stated:

> We think it likely that the rangatira viewed their agreement with Hobson at Waitangi as a kind of strategic alliance. It followed on from and extended the alliance that they saw as dating back at least to 1820, and which had been

> advanced since then by important developments in the 1830s ... They had chosen a powerful ally, with what they considered good reason. At the same time, they would have regarded the relationship as subject to further and ongoing negotiation as the two peoples came increasingly into everyday contact.[25]

The tribunal noted the divergence between British understanding and rangatira understanding but concludes, as the Muriwhenua Land Tribunal had done, that an agreement had been reached in the treaty. According to the tribunal, this agreement can be discerned from the Māori text, which mirrors the oral agreement and the explanation to the rangatira of Hobson's assurances. The tribunal states:[26]

> Our essential conclusion, therefore, is that the rangatira did not cede their sovereignty in February 1840; that is, they did not cede their authority to make and enforce law over their own people and within their territories. Rather, they agreed to share power and authority with the Governor. They and Hobson were to be equal, although of course they had different roles and different spheres of influence. The detail of how this relationship would work in practice, especially where the Māori and European populations intermingled, remained to be negotiated over time on a case-by-case basis.

After the Treaty

The mid- to late nineteenth century saw significant developments in the Māori-Crown relationship. The Kīngitanga, or Māori King Movement, which evolved through the 1850s, eventually resulted in the crowning of a Māori king. While the movement was not universally supported by Māori, the Kīngitanga represented an attempt to form a pan-Māori movement. It was intended to mirror the British monarchy and put forward a Māori leader who could engage with the British sovereign on equal terms. The Kīngitanga continues to this day and remains especially important to the peoples of the Waikato region.

One of the key objectives of the Kīngitanga when it was established was to bring traditional Māori lands under the authority of the Māori king and halt the rapid acquisition of Māori land by the British Crown. Land and sovereignty issues were at the heart of a series of major nineteenth-century military conflicts between Crown forces and Māori in various regions. Land confiscations often followed these conflicts, with regions such as the Bay of Plenty, the Waikato, and Taranaki being particularly hard-hit. These confiscations, or *raupatu,* are the basis of many historical claims.

Along with confiscations, a significant amount of land passed out of Māori ownership in this period through the operation of the Native Land Court. The first *Native Land Act* was passed in 1862, but the court was not fully established until the revised act passed in 1865. The primary function of the Native Land Court was to identify the customary owners of Māori land and transform the customary title to a fee simple title that could be freely bought and sold. The court was extremely successful at facilitating Māori land sales. The existence of this specialist court from relatively early in the contact period goes some way towards explaining why New Zealand has not experienced the landmark Aboriginal-title cases that have been a feature of Indigenous–State relationships in some other common law jurisdictions such as Canada and Australia.[27] Native land law in New Zealand has largely been governed by statute. The Native Land Court is now known as the Māori Land Court. Many aspects of its original functions continue, such as determining succession of interests in Māori land. However, the purpose of the court has effectively been reversed. The *Te Ture Whenua Māori Act* (1993) is the court's current governing legislation; its two key objectives are identified as the retention of Māori land in the hands of its owners and the better utilization of the land. There are now significant restrictions on sale and ownership of Māori land.

Also in this period, four seats were set aside for Māori in the House of Representatives. Māori were not formally excluded from voting prior to the establishment of these seats. However, because only land-owners were entitled to vote and because Māori land was primarily communally held, very few Māori were qualified to vote before the Māori seats were established in 1867. The Māori Representation Act 1867 removed the property ownership criteria and extended the franchise to all Māori males over the age of 21.[28] Since that time, there have always been Māori Members of Parliament from a range of political parties (primarily the Labour Party for most of the twentieth century). Sir James Carroll, one of the early Māori parliamentarians was acting prime minister for periods of time. The Māori seats remain an important part of Māori political representation. Māori have the option of choosing to vote on the Māori electoral roll or choosing to vote on the general roll; since the introduction of proportional representation in 1996, the number of Māori seats is determined by the number of Māori who choose to register on the Māori roll as compared to numbers registered on the general roll. The Māori Party has won at least one of the Māori seats in each of the four most recent general elections (2005, 2008, 2011, and 2014). Following the last three elections, the Māori Party has entered into confidence and supply agreements with the governing centre-right National Party.

Māori politics has always been vibrant outside of Parliament, too. The Māori Party itself was formed largely following a large-scale march (a *hikoi,* literally "walk") protesting the Crown's foreshore and seabed policy, which would eventually be implemented through the *Foreshore and Seabed Act* of 2004. That act effectively removed Māori customary rights to areas of the foreshore. The *Foreshore and Seabed Act* was repealed in 2011 and replaced with the *Marine and Coastal Area Act,* though many of the changes in the new legislation are either purely symbolic or merely cosmetic. The protest action relating to the foreshore and seabed was part of a history of similar activity. The *hikoi* itself followed on the concept of the famous "land march" of 1975. The land march is now generally seen as contributing to the political pressure that resulted in the establishment of the Waitangi Tribunal.

Another important community-led initiative was the Kohanga Reo movement. *Kohanga reo* means "language nest." The term is used to describe Māori-language immersion early-childhood education. The first kohanga were set up in the early 1980s and quickly became popular with Māori. They are often credited as having a huge impact on the revitalization of Māori language, culture, and identity. Subsequently, Māori immersion schools were established, as were Māori universities, or *wānanga*. In addition to being important for the revitalization of Māori language, the Kohanga Reo movement is identified by Linda Smith as central to the development of study tools such as Kaupapa Māori research (a Māori-centred research methodology), described in more detail below.

Māori make up a politically significant proportion of the electorate (15 percent). They have managed to use the Treaty of Waitangi as a political instrument reasonably successfully. The reports of the Waitangi Tribunal and the establishment of the settlement process have also helped to secure the support of non-Māori and the political will of successive governments to provide at least some redress for some widely recognized breaches of the treaty (land confiscations, for example). As political instruments with no direct legal enforceability, however, the treaty rights are always in a slightly precarious position. This precariousness was illustrated in 2003 and 2004, when the government decided it would be better to appropriate Māori property rights to the foreshore and seabed than to risk upsetting non-Māori voters, who make up the vast majority of the population. Whether or not recognizing Māori rights to the foreshore would have upset a significant number of non-Māori voters is debatable. In another example, what had appeared to be a consensus about treaty claims and the settlement process being a mechanism for redressing historical injustices was shattered in 2004 by then leader of the National Party Don Brash, in what is now known as the Orewa Speech. In that speech, delivered at the Orewa Rotary Club, Brash railed against what he saw as Māori privilege. He gained immediate and widespread popular support for his views. Though the National Party lost the general election the following year, and Brash was deposed as party leader, this incident revealed the fragile nature of political support for the treaty settlement process.

During this period, the courts also engaged with the treaty, and their decisions often mirrored the political context of the time. A key aspect of the development of constitutional recognition of the Treaty of Waitangi, and the establishment and refinement of the treaty settlement process, has been the recognition, interpretation, and application of the treaty in the courts. The courts' approach to the treaty has changed considerably since the 1840s, mirroring, and often influencing, public perceptions of the treaty and the political imperatives of the day. Below is a brief overview of some of the important cases and trends in treaty jurisprudence, from decisions in the nineteenth century to the inclusion of treaty principles in legislation, to more recent cases that focus on treaty claims and the settlement process.

Early case law does not engage with the interpretation of the treaty in any great detail. Instead it draws on international law and precedents from other parts of the common-law world. The New Zealand courts first directly addressed the application of the Treaty of Waitangi in the 1847 decision *R. v. Symonds*.[29] This case related to the pre-emption clause in Article 2 of the treaty, which states that Māori cannot sell land to any purchaser other than the Crown. The governor had purportedly waived the Crown's right of pre-emption to allow Māori to sell land to whomsoever they wished and so facilitate settlement through freer land sales. This case was brought forward in order to test the validity of the governor's waiver. The facts of the case, simply stated, were that there existed two competing claims to title, each asserted by a Pākehā settler (that is, there was no Māori party in the case). The plaintiff claimed to have purchased the land directly and had a certificate that he claimed waived the Crown's right of pre-emption. The defendant held a Crown grant of title to the same land. The court found that the plaintiff's direct purchase and the certificate of waiver could not displace title obtained by Crown grant. While this was consistent with the pre-emption clause in the Treaty of Waitangi, the court found that the clause simply reflected and affirmed long-standing common-law principles of Aboriginal title. Ultimately, the court did not need to address the interpretation of the treaty or any questions of its legal enforceability, relying instead on the common law. The court generally referred to the treaty in positive terms, however, emphasizing its affirmation of common law rights.

The Supreme Court did not use such positive language in reference to the treaty thirty years later in its judgment in *Wi Parata v Bishop of Wellington*.[30] This case also turned on the validity of a Crown grant. In this instance, the Crown grant had been made in favour of the Bishop of Wellington. It was issued in 1850, two years after the local iwi, Ngāti Toa, had agreed to set aside a piece of land upon which a school was to be built. The grant was then made, allegedly without the consent of Ngāti Toa. Twenty-seven years passed, and still no school had been built on the land; Ngāti Toa sought the return of the land on the basis that the school had not been built and that no consent had been given for the Crown grant. The chief justice ruled in favour of the defendant, reasoning that the existence of the Crown grant was evidence that the Crown had exercised its sovereign powers to extinguish any Native title to the land. Thus, any obligations that the Crown had to Māori were not legal obligations but moral obligations, which the courts had no role in enforcing. The judgment refers to many of the same authorities cited in *R. v. Symonds*, but Chief Justice Prendergast here arrives at quite different conclusions, relying on the doctrine of discovery and finding that, as Māori had no civilized system of law that could be recognized and that, as an uncivilized people, they were not capable of holding sovereignty, consequently they could not be said to have ceded sovereignty via the Treaty of Waitangi. This led to Chief Justice Prendergast's infamous description of the Treaty of Waitangi as "a simple nullity."[31]

One other early case ought to be noted in this brief overview. In *Hoani Te Heuheu Tukino v Aotea District Maori Land Board*, decided by the privy council in 1941,[32] the privy council applied to the Treaty of Waitangi the principle that international treaties cannot be enforced in the domestic courts unless they are incorporated into legislation. In one sense this could be seen to reinforce the decision in *Wi Parata*, which held that the Treaty of Waitangi does not, by itself, create legally enforceable obligations on the Crown in the domestic courts. On the other hand, the *Hoani Te Heuheu* decision reverses the assumption of Chief Justice Prendergast in *Wi Parata* that the treaty cannot be a valid international law instrument. In fact, the privy council appears to proceed on the assumption that the Treaty of Waitangi is a valid international treaty, although the court does address that issue directly.

The courts' engagement with the treaty begins in earnest in the late 1980s. In landmark cases from 1987 through the 1990s, the higher courts began to give some teeth to the principles of the Treaty of Waitangi. One obvious factor in the courts' interest in treaty principles was the inclusion of principle provisions in major pieces of reforming legislation. The *State-Owned Enterprises Act* (1986), the *Conservation Act* (1987), and the *Resource Management Act* and *Crown Minerals Act* (both 1991) each represented significant re-structuring of the public sector, and each contained a section protecting the principles of the Treaty of Waitangi (to a greater or lesser degree). One view might be that the courts were then only doing as the legislature directed. The number of treaty-related cases over this period can be explained by new legislative provisions that provide a basis for litigation. However, there is another contributing factor that should not be overlooked. The recognition of the treaty in the courts follows the establishment of the Waitangi Tribunal in 1975 and the extension of the tribunal's jurisdiction in 1985 to enable it to hear historical claims. The establishment of the tribunal and the increasing number of claims it was addressing form an important part of the context within which the courts were considering treaty issues. The seminal Court of Appeal decision in *New Zealand Maori Council v Attorney-General* (1987) makes explicit reference to the Waitangi Tribunal. Not only do the judgments refer to the substantive content of tribunal reports, which the Court of Appeal considers in determining how to interpret and apply the treaty itself, but the fact of the tribunal's creation is seen as significant. Several judges in the Court of Appeal note the enhanced constitutional status of the treaty, which Parliament clearly intended when it established a standing commission of inquiry to hear claims based upon treaty principles.

In the latter part of the twentieth century, the courts, the parliament, and the cabinet recognized various obligations of the Crown. Aside from direct statutory incorporation, the Treaty of Waitangi influences New Zealand law in much the same way as a valid international law treaty does, despite some debate as to whether or not the Treaty of Waitangi is such an instrument. Palmer suggests that, were the issue put directly to the New Zealand Supreme Court, it is likely the Treaty of Waitangi would be found to be a valid treaty for international law purposes and therefore binding on the Crown.[33] At this point, the New Zealand courts have shown a willingness to recognize the Treaty of Waitangi as an extrinsic aid to statutory interpretation, and a factor to be considered in applications for judicial review of government action.[34]

The judgment in *Huakina Development Trust v Waikato Valley Authority* illustrates the readiness of the High Court in 1987 to take notice of the principles of the treaty against the backdrop of the tribunal's activities, even in cases where there is no express statutory reference to the treaty or its principles. In that case, the central question was whether metaphysical considerations based on Māori cultural understandings ought to be taken into account in environmental planning decisions relating to the Waikato River. After using the treaty as an extrinsic aid to interpret the applicable legislation, the High Court found that these considerations were relevant. The judgment noted that the treaty was "part of the fabric of New Zealand society" and could therefore be deployed as an interpretive aid wherever there was ambiguity in a statute and the subject-matter was such that treaty interests would likely be affected.[35]

The *Huakina Development Trust* case actually preceded the 1987 *New Zealand Maori Council* case (sometimes referred to as the *Lands* case or the *SOE* [state-owned enterprises] case), though the latter has come to be seen as the beginning of the modern treaty jurisprudence. In that case, the New Zealand Court of Appeal had to face for the first time the task of implementing the principles of the Treaty of Waitangi. The case arose out of the re-structuring of the state sector that took place in New Zealand through the mid- to late 1980s. One of the key components of that re-structuring was the corporatization and privatization of many government departments. In order to begin this process, legislation was passed that would enable government departments to be transformed into "state-owned enterprises." This raised the possibility that significant land and other assets, which may have been the subject of Waitangi Tribunal claims, passing out of Crown control and ownership. If this happened, these assets would be effectively unavailable for use as redress of those claims. The enabling legislation includes a provision that "[n]othing in this Act shall permit the Crown to act in a manner that is inconsistent with the principles of the Treaty of Waitangi."[36] The New Zealand Māori Council argued that the Crown's proposal to transfer land and assets out of Crown ownership before claims to that land could be heard was in breach of the principles of the Treaty of Waitangi and therefore outside of the powers conferred by the state-owned enterprises legislation. Despite agreement on the outcome and approach, separate judgments were written by each of the five judges who heard this case in the Court of Appeal (which, at that time, was New Zealand's highest locally based court, with only the privy council above it in the hierarchy). The Court drew heavily on the work produced by the Waitangi Tribunal up to that point and characterised the treaty as a partnership. The Crown and Māori were the treaty partners, each with obligations to the other, similar to the obligations entailed in a private law partnership. Acting towards each other reasonably and with utmost good faith were central principles of the treaty partnership. The court described the Crown's obligations as similar to those that exist within a fiduciary relationship. Treaty principles involve a duty of active protection to reflect the Crown's promises in Article 2, which are expressed as positive guarantees. Furthermore, the court found that where treaty principles have been breached, some form of redress ought to be provided.

The basic principles as articulated in the *Lands* case were applied in a string of cases through the late 1980s and 1990s, many of them brought by the New Zealand Māori Council against the Attorney-General. The *Forests* case,[37] which follows directly from the *Lands* case, led to the establishment of the Crown Forestry Rental Trust, a major funder of treaty claims research, as part of an agreement that allowed the deregulation of the forestry sector to take place while protecting the ability of Māori to seek the return of Crown forest land as redress for well-founded treaty claims. The return of Crown forest land remains one of the few areas in which the Waitangi Tribunal has binding powers.

Over this period, the Court of Appeal also addressed treaty principles in the context of broadcasting, and the Crown's obligations in relation to the Māori language. In the *Radio Frequencies* case,[38] the Crown was required to wait for a relevant Waitangi Tribunal report, so that it could be fully appraised of the treaty interest, before completing a tender process for the allocation of radio frequencies. In the *Broadcasting Assets* case,[39] the privy council confirmed the general approach that the Court of Appeal had taken to the application of treaty principles up to that point and noted that the particular circumstances, such as the state of the subject-matter to be protected, would determine the action required by a reasonable treaty partner acting in good faith. For example, if the Māori language was in a fragile state and past Crown action had contributed to this, then there would be greater obligations on the Crown to take action to redress this.

Primarily, the courts treated these cases as orthodox judicial review applications. The reasoning generally rested on established principles of administrative law, addressing procedural issues such as whether all relevant considerations had been taken into account or whether a decision-maker had acted outside the scope of his or her powers. There are some suggestions that the president of the Court of Appeal at the time, Robin Cooke, viewed the treaty as creating something more like an independent constitutional ground of judicial review, but this was never fully supported by the majority of the court, though the privy council did suggest that a statutory incorporation of treaty principles required a heightened level of court scrutiny of administrative action.[40] In one case, however, the Court of Appeal did make a decision relating to the substance of an administrative decision. The *Ngai Tahu* or

Whale-watching case related to the grant of concessions under the *Conservation Act,* which would permit a commercial whale-watching enterprise to operate off the east coast of the South Island. The court found that, all other things being equal, treaty principles required that the local *iwi* be given "a substantial degree of preference" when the Crown is determining whether or not to grant applications for whale-watching concessions in that area.[41]

Most of the leading treaty cases during this period focused on large-scale action by the Crown, often as a result of the massive re-organization of the state undertaken by the fourth Labour government. The decision in *Barton-Prescott v Director-General of Social Welfare* shows how treaty principles can affect rights as between individuals.[42] This case related to the custody of a child; the issue was whether the director-general of social welfare had exercised its powers appropriately in determining that the child ought to be placed outside of the family rather than with the child's grandmother. The Treaty of Waitangi was cited because the child was Māori; the grandmother argued that the child should have the opportunity to be raised among the culture of the family. Drawing on the same principle as *Huakina Development Trust,* the High Court found in this case that treaty principles were relevant, despite no explicit statutory reference. Because the treaty was so fundamental to New Zealand society, the court found that treaty principles ought to shape the interpretation of legislation that impacts upon treaty interests.[43]

Since the turn of the century, the focus of cases brought before the courts appears to have shifted to procedural aspects of the claims and the settlement process itself. A number of judicial review proceedings brought in recent years have challenged procedural determinations made by the Waitangi Tribunal.[44] In *Haronga v Waitangi Tribunal* (2011),[45] the Supreme Court took the unusual step of substituting its own decision on a matter relating to the tribunal's procedure, rather than simply returning the issue to the tribunal in order for it to decide the matter again. The key issue in the *Haronga* case was whether the tribunal had correctly exercised its powers when it declined to grant an urgent hearing into claims that a specific block of Crown forest land must be returned to a specific claimant group. Generally, the tribunal would have discretion as to whether it granted an urgent hearing into a particular claim. In this instance, the Supreme Court found that, because the substantive claim to the land had already been determined to be well-founded, and the exercise of the tribunal's binding powers was sought, the tribunal could not be said to have concluded its functions in relation to the claim until it had made a decision about whether it would issue binding orders for the resumption of the relevant land. After assessing the case, the Supreme Court decided that the Tribunal had no choice but to grant an urgent inquiry to address the question. The focus on the claims and settlement process is mirrored in the increasing number of Waitangi Tribunal reports that assess aspects of the Crown's policy and practice in this area against treaty principles.[46]

The most recent Supreme Court decision that addresses the application of treaty principles provides an interesting bookend to this line of cases. The *Mighty River Power* case effectively addresses the same issues that arose in the *Lands* case, only this time in relation to how Māori rights to water would be affected by the partial privatization of state-owned power-generation companies. The Crown had taken steps to sell its shares in these companies. Mighty River Power was to be the first company transformed from a wholly state-owned company to the new mixed-ownership model. The company used significant volumes of water for hydro-electric generation (as did other companies put forward for partial privatization). The New Zealand Māori Council raised concerns about how partial privatization might constrain the Crown's ability to provide appropriate recognition of Māori water rights. The council submitted a claim to the Waitangi Tribunal on this basis. The tribunal granted an urgent hearing into that claim and recommended that the Crown halt its partial privatization process until Māori interests and treaty rights in water could be properly explored. When the Crown proceeded to sell shares in Mighty River Power, the New Zealand Māori Council made an application to the High Court for judicial review.

The High Court comprehensively rejected the Māori Council's submissions, finding that the Crown's actions in this situation were not even required to be consistent with the treaty principles. Leave was sought to appeal this decision directly to the Supreme Court (leap-frogging the Court of Appeal). While the Supreme Court also found no grounds for judicial review, it did find, importantly, that treaty principles were relevant. This finding lent further support to the approach articulated in the 1987 *Lands* case. Significantly, a key part of the court's reasoning was that the Crown had given evidence that it was engaging with Māori to identify and recognize Māori water rights. The court suggested that the legal and political context in relation to the treaty had changed sufficiently since 1987 for Māori to now be confident that their treaty claims would be appropriately addressed. It is debatable whether such a change has in fact taken place, but in making such a statement, the court signalled that Māori could rely on the expectation that the Crown would not remove its ability to provide redress for treaty claims without ensuring a full understanding of the Māori rights that might be affected, and that there would be in place an appropriate protection mechanism.

The Settlement Era

Since the 1990s, the Crown has been engaged in a comprehensive process of negotiations with Māori groups over redress for the settlement of historical claims.[47] For more than forty years, the Waitangi Tribunal has provided a forum in which claims under the Treaty of Waitangi can be heard. However, the systematic, comprehensive settlement of historical claims is a much younger process. In 1992, the New Zealand government agreed that officials should develop a set of principles to govern the settlement of historical treaty claims. These principles were developed in the context of the national settlement of all Māori claims to commercial fishing interests and, after being roundly rejected by Māori, were amended slightly and became official Crown policy in 1995. Settlements agreed to between the Crown and the major tribal groupings Ngāi Tahu and Waikato-Tainui in the mid-1990s further established the framework for the modern settlement process. The Crown had commenced negotiations with both Ngāi Tahu and Waikato-Tainui before the comprehensive settlement policy was formalised. Both settlements provided key benchmarks for all subsequent settlement negotiations. In 1994, the government established the Office of Treaty Settlements (OTS) within the Ministry of Justice. OTS grew out of the Ministry's Treaty of Waitangi Policy Unit, and its officials are the ones who engage in settlement negotiations with claimant groups. While there is a significant body of literature that examines the Waitangi Tribunal claims process, there is surprisingly little that addresses the mechanics of the settlement process. The relative lack of settlement process literature may be explained by the fact that the process is relatively young: arguably, too little time has elapsed to pass any insightful judgments on the settlement process itself. Perhaps, too, the private and essentially confidential nature of settlement negotiations has not resulted in the same sort of raw materials generated by the highly public Waitangi Tribunal hearings and reports. Or perhaps the Waitangi Tribunal is perceived to be a more innovative mechanism than the internationally tried and true process of pragmatic and political government deal-making that characterises the settlement process. Whatever the case, the Waitangi Tribunal has been the subject of significantly greater comment and analysis than has the settlement process.

Key issues identified in the settlement process relate to definitions of Māori identity and appropriate models of Māori social and corporate organization,[48] the importance of viewing treaty claims and settlement as merely part of a wider process of reconciliation and constitutional evolution (albeit an important part),[49] and the need to encourage mechanisms of law and policy that positively contribute to the relationships that underlie, and are articulated by, the Treaty of Waitangi.[50] Each of these has continued to be significant in the development and implementation of the treaty settlement process. Each also highlights some of the pressures exerted on Māori legal traditions by the settlement process.

Māori groups experience many frustrations with the settlement process, including the lack of genuine negotiation in many areas; the view that Crown policies relating to matters such as group identification and mandate are unnecessarily rigid; and the lack of attention paid to actual grievances and matters of justice, such as the particular circumstances of the community concerned and the nature of reparations necessary in their unique case.

Post-settlement governance has also proved to be a complex issue. Despite the fact that many Māori groups have already progressed through the settlement process and others are currently moving towards a settlement with the Crown, there is no uniform governance model for receiving and managing settlement assets – a model that could carry out the core responsibilities required and also be easily adapted to the particular needs of specific settling communities. Neither is there a standard mechanism for the resolution of disputes arising within settling groups (either between members or between members of the community and those charged with managing settlement assets) that would address the specific cultural practices and values of the settling community.

Overview of the Book

The first part of this book lays out important historical, theoretical, and conceptual background to the analysis of Māori law in the settlement process and also examines the nature of Māori legal traditions. This provides the context of the research and explores several fundamental principles that guide Māori legal traditions, offering a brief overview of Māori social organization as the foundation on which Māori legal traditions are based. It also outlines some important aspects of the operation of the system of tikanga, which encompasses Māori customary law. Five concepts central to the operation of Māori legal traditions have been identified in the work of anthropologists, legal writers, and Māori scholars:[51] These concepts are *whanaungatanga, manaakitanga, mana, tapu, and utu.* Detailed explanations of these concepts are set out in Chapter 2, but it is sufficient to note at this point that, collectively, these concepts speak to the nature of relationships, spirituality, and authority in the Māori world. These five central concepts and the key processes that derive from them together form the foundation of Māori legal traditions. This foundation has changed over time and continues to develop as a result of key tensions in Māori legal history.

I have used the idea of tension to capture the complexity and diversity of the development of Māori legal traditions, and to provide an analytical framework that suggests the broad shape (if not the precise detail) of the nature of Māori legal traditions over the period of the Treaty of Waitangi settlements. These tensions are not bound by chronological periods; in using them as a framework I avoid some of the more problematic aspects of periodization of histories of Indigenous peoples.

The idea of tension also avoids the appearance of uniformity (or near uniformity) that might be suggested in a discussion of Māori legal traditions according to theme. The existence of a tension implies that there is more than one perspective, strategy, or approach vying for attention at any given time. My intention is to convey the fact that there will always be a diversity of the types of change to which legal traditions are subject. By using the idea of tension to analyse Māori legal traditions, we see that the development of these traditions has not been – and is not currently – linear or uniform. Tensions are creative and produce dynamic change. By focusing on the tensions themselves, I hope to reveal some of the central concerns, strategies and modes of operation of Māori law. Once we understand something of the pressures placed on Māori legal traditions and the way those legal systems have developed in response, we can begin to understand the Māori legal context in which issues of post-settlement governance arise at the start of the twenty-first century.

The three tensions applicable to an examination of Treaty of Waitangi settlements are 1) adaptation (self-determined change vs. reactive change); 2) relationship to the treaty partner (engagement vs. disengagement with the state legal system); and 3) renewal (reinvigorating tikanga vs. losing relevance). These tensions are not completely separate from one another but, rather, coexist and overlap.

Alongside the tensions in Māori legal history, several key terms are used throughout this book to describe aspects and levels of Māori law and legal practice. The following definitions are employed:

- *tikanga* describes the right or correct way of doing things within Māori society. It is a system comprising practice, principles, process and procedures, and traditional knowledge. It encompasses Māori law but also includes ritual, custom, and spiritual and socio-political dimensions that go well beyond the legal domain.

- "Māori legal tradition" is an aspect of tikanga that has a legal quality. This term includes Māori legal practice, Māori legal principles, Māori legal process and procedures, and Māori legal knowledge.
- "Māori legal systems" refer to the coherent systems that comprise Māori legal traditions. The plural form is used in order to reflect the existence of variations among different Māori communities.
- "Māori legal order" describes the fundamental values, institutions, and philosophical perspectives that underlie all Māori legal systems.

This terminology is consistent with that deployed by Harold Berman in his study of the Western legal tradition.[52] Like this book, Berman's study has a strong pluralist foundation. In the introduction to *Law and Revolution*, Berman argues that "[p]erhaps the most distinctive characteristic of the Western legal tradition is the coexistence and competition within the same community of diverse jurisdictions and diverse legal systems." He also notes that "[t]he same person might be subject to the ecclesiastical courts in one type of case, the king's court in another, his lord's court in a third, the manorial court in a fourth, a town court in a fifth, a merchants' court in a sixth."[53] Berman's terminology is particularly helpful in examining legal traditions in this pluralistic context. In *Legal Traditions of the World*, Patrick Glenn explores the concept and theory of "tradition" as it applies in a legal context. Glenn suggests that tradition can be seen as a means of capturing information from the past in a way that is meaningful for the present. Once understood in this way, traditions are not simply habitually repeated actions that remain fixed and unchanging.[54] When I write of Māori legal traditions, or use the term "traditional" in this book, I am establishing a link with practices and ideas that have been handed down from the ancestors; I do not intend to imply that anything "traditional" is static or somehow frozen in the past.

The second part of the book focuses on the treaty settlement process. Engagement in the settlement process has a significant impact on Māori communities. It can result in changes in leadership. Those in traditional leadership positions are not always the people chosen to speak for the community in the settlement process. The Crown conducts negotiations with only those representatives of the claimant community who can demonstrate that they hold a mandate from the community to engage in those negotiations. However, the Crown also requires that the mandate to negotiate be conferred through mechanisms such as a universal ballot of adult community members, a mechanism that owes more to Western liberal democratic processes than to any Māori legal traditions. The way leaders are chosen, as well as the means by which their authority is maintained, is also likely to differ from past practice. Collective community identity can also be affected. Community identity is often strengthened as community histories are researched, made more widely accessible, and validated through the settlement process. Choices about how to engage in the settlement process can sometimes change inter-iwi and intra-iwi relationships. Such matters are particularly significant in the New Zealand context, where there has been no history of state-imposed tribal registers, and where community affiliation has largely been a matter of self-identification coupled with recognition by the community itself. Despite this, experience to date indicates that iwi and hapū have continued to express their traditional ways of doing things, their customary law, both within the substance of settlement packages negotiated with the Crown and also within the constitutions of corporate governance entities established to manage settlement assets on behalf of the community. These changes to community identity and relationships, and other areas, have had significant effects on Māori legal traditions.

The very real danger for Māori and Māori legal traditions in interactions with the treaty settlement process is that the effects may represent an ongoing colonization of tikanga Māori rather than a healthy expression of tino rangatiratanga as part of a dynamic, living, legal culture. This book considers whether the effects of the settlement process on Māori legal traditions are consistent with the aims of the process and the aspirations of the iwi and hapū.

Key Tensions in Māori Legal History

The study of legal history has developed considerably in Aotearoa in recent years, but very little study has been done of Māori legal history, by historians, legal academics, or lawyers. Many people consider Māori legal history to be the study of the historical development of laws that relate to Māori. This approach derives primarily from the twin assumptions that Māori have had no distinct legal system historically and have no such system currently. As a consequence, the majority of New Zealand's legal-historical work does not take account of Māori law or Māori legal traditions. Neither do the majority of Māori histories engage in a legal-historical analysis. But a study confined to legislation and case law that affects Māori is in fact just a small part of this field. There are some notable exceptions to the norm: The research centre Te Mātāhauariki has done some excellent work on Māori customary law concepts, including the development of such concepts;[55] there has also been some very good legal-historical work on significant cases involving Māori or issues that particularly affect Māori.[56] Nevertheless, this work still only skirts the edges of the field of Māori legal history. An analytical framework structured around the three key tensions enables us to examine broad developments in Māori legal traditions.

Adaptation: Self-determined change vs. reactive change

It is difficult to distinguish between changes in Māori legal traditions that are self-determined and those forced upon the Māori legal order. All changes are responses to pressures on the Māori legal order; it can be challenging to discern precisely which pressures are due to the self-determining actions of Māori communities and which are due to external forces – and which are due to a mixture of both of these. Arguably, every change to Māori legal traditions is intended to maximize the self-determination of Māori communities. Nevertheless, it is useful to consider the range of adaptive changes that can occur and the tensions that exist between different types of adaptive change. How Māori legal traditions adapt is determined by the nature of the pressures exerted upon them, including whether such pressures are internally or externally generated. The clearest example of the divide between internally generated pressures and externally generated pressures can be seen in 1) the changes in Māori legal traditions that resulted from Māori migration to Aotearoa and settlement there and 2) the changes to Māori legal traditions that are primarily responses to later colonization. This tension is not simply about pre-contact and post-contact developments, however. Māori legal traditions respond to changes to Māori society initiated by Māori communities themselves, even as they experience change in response to external variables. Conversely, pre-contact Māori society was forced to respond reactively to a range of factors (including environmental conditions) beyond its control, which resulted in significant changes to Māori legal traditions. This tension is an important consideration in the context of this book because self-determination is a central concern of Māori involved in the treaty settlement process. It will be helpful to identify the types of changes that indicate that communities are in control of the development of their legal traditions. In particular, our attention should be focused on the following two questions:

a) Are the changes to Māori legal traditions resulting from the treaty settlement process self-determined changes or reactive changes?
b) What does this tell us about the effectiveness of the settlement process in reaching goals of tino rangatiratanga and reconciliation?

Relationship to the Treaty Partner: Engagement vs. disengagement

The relationship between Māori legal traditions and the state legal system has been reasonably well documented. Strategies of engagement and disengagement have been employed by Māori communities, for as long as the treaty relationship has existed, in their attempts to retain the authority to regulate themselves. Over the history of the treaty relationship, one can see Māori engagement (and sometimes disengagement) with the specific institutions of the colonial parliament and government.[57] Various models of engagement have been deployed by Māori legal institutions at various points in time.[58] The common law has responded (though not always positively) to Māori engagement whenever it has occurred.[59]

Renewal: Reinvigorating tikanga vs. losing relevance

There is also tension between the desire on the part of some to reinvigorate Māori legal traditions and the wish on the part of others to set aside Māori legal traditions, based on the view that they are irrelevant to public life. This tension is perhaps most obvious in the deliberate choices made by Māori communities as they move through the treaty settlement process and establish post-settlement governance entities. Designing a constitution for a post-settlement governance entity requires that the settling community consider how and to what extent it wishes to see its legal traditions reflected in that constitution. In some instances, Māori legal traditions are reasserted, perhaps adapted to ensure they are relevant when confronted by the challenges of governance in the twenty-first century. In some cases, a deliberate choice is made to discard a particular legal tradition when it is seen to be no longer relevant, or perhaps when other options are perceived to better serve the needs of the settling community.

Tino Rangatiratanga and Māori-centred Research

Another important part of the framework of this research is the concept of tino rangatiratanga and its relevance for Māori-centred research. Tino rangatiratanga is the Māori concept of self-determination and autonomy; it has been described as comparable to the Western concept of sovereignty.[60] The idea of tino rangatiratanga is not only at the heart of the treaty settlement process but infuses Māori-centred scholarship. Although tino rangatiratanga is a distinctively Māori concept, self-determination is recognized as an important political objective by many Indigenous scholars who have articulated Indigenous approaches to research. Taiaiake Alfred, for example, has described an ethic of "warrior scholarship" that aims to contend with instances of colonial power expressed in academic or scholarly sites.[61] Indigenous self-determination underlies the ethic of warrior scholarship, which, according to Alfred, requires Indigenous scholars to honour Indigenous knowledge, confront false claims of legitimacy, and "fight for political independences in the face of state sovereignty."[62] Similarly, Dale Turner draws a philosophical connection between research/scholarship and "the legal and political discourses of the state."[63] Turner goes on to suggest that a "critical Indigenous philosophy must unpack the colonial framework of these discourses, assert and defend our 'indigeneity' within the dominant culture, and defend the legal and political integrity of Indigenous communities."[64]

The political objective of self-determination, which scholars such as Alfred and Turner perceive to be an inherent part of Indigenous-centred research, is expressed in the Māori worldview as tino rangatiratanga. Tino rangatiratanga is the concept used in the 1840 Treaty of Waitangi to reflect the authority of the Māori signatories, which the British Crown guaranteed would be recognized, notwithstanding the establishment of colonial government. The concept has a long history in the structure of the political relationship between Māori and the Crown.

As the Treaty of Waitangi settlement process and the treaty itself frame the subject of this book, the political objectives of tino rangatiratanga are central to the theme. When we consider how the settlement process has shaped Maori legal traditions, we also consider how these changes have contributed to or compromised tino rangatiratanga. The underlying aim of this book is to prompt changes in the political and legal discourse to open up space for the expression of tino rangatiratanga through the recognition of Māori legal systems in a way that is meaningful to Māori communities.

Within the Māori worldview, kinship relations animate tino rangatiratanga. The fundamental organizing principle of Māori philosophy is whakapapa (genealogy), supported by the associated concepts of *whānau* (extended families) and *whanaungatanga* (relationships). Māori theologian and philosopher Māori Marsden has described the importance of whakapapa to Māori philosophy and knowledge systems. He notes that all peoples create maps and models as a means of understanding and representing the world. Māori use whakapapa as the organizing model. That is to say that the symbols used by Māori to label, identify, and represent phenomena are based on genealogical forms, which are the basis for Māori philosophy and understanding of the world.[65]

Whakapapa is fundamentally about connections[66]: "Whakapapa turns the universe into a moral space where all things great and small are interconnected, including science and research."[67] Ultimately, whakapapa establishes the relationships between each person and the world around him or her.[68] Māori businesswoman and former politician Donna Awatere states that, in the Māori world, all one's relationships with others are dependent on one's own identity and whakapapa. One's relationships with one's ancestors are understood as being ongoing, and the source of how one defines one's place in the world.[69]

As a consequence of the centrality of whakapapa within Māori philosophy, the associated concepts of whānau and whanaungatanga also require careful consideration. For example, my identity as a member of the iwi Ngāti Kahungunu is reflected in the stories woven throughout this book. Ngāti Kahungunu is the third largest iwi by population. The 2013 census figures show that a little more than 60,000 people identify as members of Ngāti Kahungunu, which is approximately 9 per cent of the total Māori population. Ngāti Kahungunu also has a relatively large traditional territory, covering the southern half of the east coast of the North Island of New Zealand. My family is from the northern part of this territory; our *marae* (central community space/complex), named Takitimu after the great canoe, is in the small town of Wairoa, which lies between the cities of Napier and Gisborne. My hapū is Ngai Te Apatu, and we describe where we come from with reference to the river Te Wairoa Hōpūpū Hōnengenenge Matangirau and the mountain Whakapūnake. We also see ourselves as intrinsically connected to these important landscape features.

This introductory chapter has outlined some of the important background to the Treaty settlement process. Some key terms and concepts that are central to the analysis in this book have also been introduced here. This chapter has also addressed the way in which political aspirations of tino rangatiratanga have informed my approach to this research.

The next chapter builds on the foundations laid out in Chapter 1, developing the framework for an analysis of Māori legal traditions in the treaty settlement process. It explores concepts from legal pluralism and Indigenous legal theory, as well as concepts in Māori philosophy of law, and then constructs a theoretical platform for further research. I discuss the nature of Indigenous self-determination and reconciliation, which can be seen as the two underlying objectives of the treaty settlement process.

Chapter 3 provides a brief historical overview of the development of Māori legal traditions. First, I provide the reader with a sense of the way that Māori law operates – how it "channels behaviour by regulation, prevention and 'cleaning up social mess.'"[70] Second, I draw attention to the three key tensions in Māori legal history that have contributed to significant developments within Māori legal traditions. Here, I discuss some of the effects on Māori legal traditions of Māori encounters with the New Zealand state. My intention is to provide a picture, albeit one painted with a relatively broad brush, of Māori legal traditions at the end of the twentieth century, as the comprehensive treaty settlement process takes shape.

The implementation of a comprehensive treaty settlement policy introduces a new set of challenges as Māori legal traditions move into the new millennium. Chapter 4 provides a detailed account of the treaty settlement process, the types of settlement agreements that have been reached, and the models of Māori governance emerging out of this process. I identify the governance aspect of settlement as a key issue because it reflects the process of re-grouping that is being undertaken by Māori communities as they strengthen themselves, build their capacity for self-determination, and develop modern Indigenous solutions and institutions.

Chapter 5 considers more directly the effects of the treaty settlement process on Māori legal traditions. Engagement in the settlement process has a significant impact on Māori communities, particularly around issues related to community governance. The chapter focuses on the effects of the Treaty of Waitangi settlement process in three broad categories: 1) Māori law-making, 2) Māori dispute resolution processes, and 3) the content of Māori law. I re-identify key tensions in Māori legal history and then examine the effects of the settlement process on each of these three aspects of Māori legal traditions.

Finally, Chapter 6 evaluates the changes to Māori legal traditions that have resulted from the treaty settlement process in terms of how these changes have contributed – or not – towards reconciliation and tino rangatiratanga. I argue that the treaty settlement process is undermining goals of self-determination/tino rangatiratanga and reconciliation, at least with respect to Māori legal traditions. I also suggest, however, that it is possible to change that narrative. By focusing on Māori legal traditions in the settlement process, we can re-story the process and move towards tino rangatiratanga and reconciliation, with the vision of realizing the mutually beneficial relationships expressed in the Treaty of Waitangi.

2

Reconciling Legal Systems

RUAWHARO

"Pāpā, have our ancestors always lived here?"

"Since the time of Tamatea, when our people came to Aotearoa on the great canoe called 'Takitimu.'"

"How did they find their way here, Pāpā? Did Tamatea show them the way?"

"Tamatea was their leader, yes, but Ruawharo was the tohunga of Takitimu, the expert with the knowledge of the gods of the earth and the oceans."

"He must have been a very wise man, Pāpā."

"Ae, Ruawharo was a man of great learning."

"But how did he know to come to this place, Pāpā? How did he know this would be the home of our people?"

"Well, e Tama, let me tell you the story of Ruawharo."

"Like Tamatea, Ruawharo came to Aotearoa from Hawaiki aboard the waka Takitimu. And like Tamatea, Ruawharo was one of the leaders on that voyage. Back in Hawaiki, he had studied at the whare wānanga, the house of learning. There he had gained knowledge about the natural world and the spiritual world. He gained particular expertise in those matters relating to the earth and the oceans. Ruawharo's story is closely bound to the story of the waka Takitimu. Some say that it was Ruawharo's axe that felled the tree from which the great canoe was made. And it was his knowledge of ritual, ceremony, and karakia that enabled the canoe to be brought to its launching place. So you see, even before he could chart a course for Aotearoa, Ruawharo had to understand the wider landscape. He learned about the journeys that others had taken before him. He studied their techniques for reading the land, sky, and seas. He followed the protocols and pathways laid down by his ancestors. Only then was he able to set off on his journey with Tamatea and the others who travelled aboard Takitimu. And as the mighty canoe crossed the oceans from Hawaiki, Ruawharo was able to use the skills and knowledge that had been passed down to him to help guide Takitimu to Aotearoa. When our ancestors arrived at this place, Ruawharo, with his knowledge of the natural world, was able to recognize features of the land that were similar to Hawaiki, and after they made landfall, Ruawharo spread on this new land earth and sand brought from Hawaiki. The way of life and the knowledge that came out of the lands of our ancestors thus became the foundation of a new home here. It is said that Ruawharo then placed his three sons at different points along the coast to be the mauri, the life force, of this new home. And so, e Tama, that is how this came to be the home of our people – through the understanding that Ruawharo and others had of the landscape that surrounded them and the way they built on the knowledge of their ancestors to create a new path and a new home."

Building on the Knowledge of Ancestors

This chapter builds the framework for the analysis of Māori legal traditions within the context of the treaty settlement process. Specifically, I consider the importance of Indigenous legal theory and legal pluralism in issues relating to Māori legal traditions, focusing on concepts from Māori law and Māori legal philosophy. I also review influential ideas relating to two key objectives of the treaty settlement process – tino rangatiratanga/self-determination and reconciliation. Using these concepts as reference points and the theoretical approaches for guidance, my framework builds on the knowledge of those who have gone before.

A Theoretical Framework for Examining Treaty Settlements

Legal theories rooted in Indigenous philosophies are essential for a robust and healthy theoretical discourse about Indigenous legal issues.[1] Each theorist employs a particular conceptual apparatus in establishing his or her theories; this apparatus sustains implicit ideological and political positions.[2] These positions are especially significant within law, a socially constructed and contested realm of human culture. Theoretical perspectives that reflect Indigenous communities' understandings and experiences of law, therefore, provide a distinctive contribution to legal theory.[3] Gordon Christie, whose work has directly addressed the concept of Indigenous legal theory, suggests that such theoretical perspectives may provide insights into the operation of particular legal systems (whether they be Indigenous or non-Indigenous systems), as well as assisting in our understanding of law at a more abstract level.[4] Christie's view of Indigenous legal theory does not reflect a single, uniform, pan-Indigenous view of law but, rather, allows for a diverse range of legal theories. The one characteristic these theories have in common is that they are in some way connected to an Indigenous worldview. Christie describes this characteristic as cultural and experiential grounding. This kind of conceptualization of legal culture is also recognized in much non-Indigenous legal theory.[5] A grounding in Indigenous culture and experience directly affects how Indigenous theorists conceptualize law and "how the world of legal phenomena comes to be perceived and studied" within Indigenous legal theories.[6] The writing of Indigenous legal scholars such as Patricia Monture-Angus, Sakej Henderson, and John Borrows provides some helpful examples of the way these cultural and experiential groundings affect analyses of law and legal systems.

In *Journeying Forward: Dreaming First Nations Independence,* Monture-Angus explicitly frames her examination of Indigenous legal issues within the culture and experience of her own community: "In order to understand the way I have processed the recognition and affirmation of existing Aboriginal (and treaty) rights in Canada's constitution, the basics of Haudenosaunee political thought must be briefly established."[7] *Journeying Forward* is focused primarily on the conceptualization of Aboriginal rights. It describes a vision of Aboriginal rights that reflects an Indigenous worldview. Monture-Angus's objective is to begin to articulate "what a theory of Aboriginal rights looks like from one Aboriginal location."[8] She provides a forceful critique of Canadian rights discourse as exemplified by decisions of the Supreme Court of Canada and associated scholarly writing.[9] She notes that the categorization of rights as either "individual rights" or "collective rights" not only diminishes the value of rights characterized as "collective" but also misrepresents the concepts of rights and obligations within Indigenous communities.[10] *Journeying Forward* examines Aboriginal rights cases from the perspective of the communities involved. In relation to the Supreme Court of Canada's decision in *R. v. Sparrow,*[11] a case that addressed Aboriginal fishing rights, Monture-Angus explores the personal and community background of Ronald Sparrow and the cultural understandings and practices that led him to exercise his traditional fishing rights.[12] She explains how this analysis leads to a different view of rights, obligations, and relationships than the narrower and *narrowing* examination evident in the Supreme Court's judgments.[13] Her approach thus infuses the concept of human rights with Indigenous values and understandings. For example, she suggests that First Nations' relationships with the land form an important component of any Indigenous conceptualization of human rights.[14] Christie contends that this type of conceptualization in Monture-Angus's work represents "a lived experience passing through the lens of her cultural grounding as a Mohawk woman."[15]

Sakej Henderson's work also illustrates the way in which cultural and experiential grounding affects Indigenous understandings of law and legal theory. Henderson sees Indigenous legal traditions and philosophies as inextricably connected to other aspects of the lives of Indigenous communities. Henderson notes that Indigenous legal systems develop from the particular relationships within a community, and the community's history and experiences. They reflect the community's shared philosophy, values, and beliefs. Law is thus not merely a set of rules or practices but instead a dynamic and self-sustaining system that both expresses a community's shared understanding of how social life should operate and continues to respond to the lived experiences of the community.[16]

Henderson uses Indigenous legal and philosophical concepts to build a theoretical framework to consider Indigenous legal issues. He suggests that "First Nations knowledge and jurisprudence are organized around four insights: the insights of covenants of creation, embodied spirits, implicate order,[17] and dynamic transformation."[18] These insights form the basis of Henderson's conceptualization of law.[19] He applies this theoretical framework to his analysis of Indigenous legal issues, as they are addressed not only within Indigenous legal systems but also within the Canadian state legal system.[20] To illustrate this point, it may be helpful to consider how Henderson's articulation of legal communication and reasoning in Indigenous traditions has implications for understanding the substance of *sui generis* Aboriginal rights in the Canadian legal system. Henderson explains that "First Nations jurisprudence and law are very much embedded in the heritage of societies of sound and ceremonies."[21] Consequently, much Indigenous legal procedure is based in performance, or has a performative aspect.[22] Forms of legal reasoning that have developed from common law traditions, centred around precedent and legislation, have limited application to the substance of Indigenous law. Henderson describes Indigenous performative jurisprudence as "open-textured,"[23] "dynamic,"[24] and "transformational,"[25] and notes that this type of jurisprudence tends to define wrongs in "relational rather than in purely physical or economic terms."[26] Approaches to legal reasoning derived from legal conceptualism or legal positivism, prevalent within common law systems, are based on assumptions about the use of language and the operation of legal processes that do not take account of a more performative jurisprudence. Ultimately, Henderson argues, this renders such approaches "incapable of doing justice to *sui generis* Aboriginal rights."[27]

John Borrows also acknowledges the cultural and experiential groundings of Indigenous legal traditions, noting that the "underpinnings of Indigenous law are entwined with the social, historical, political, biological, economic, and spiritual circumstances of each group."[28] The theoretical framework applied by Borrows reflects these cultural and experiential groundings and can be seen in the way that Borrows constructs his analysis of Indigenous law in *Canada's Indigenous Constitution*. Borrows first explores the sources of Indigenous law in order to illustrate the complexity of these systems and the choices Indigenous peoples may face in developing law.[29] The various sources of Indigenous law, identified by Borrows as including "sacred teachings, naturalistic observations, positivistic proclamations, deliberative practices, and local and national customs,"[30] become key organizing principles for the analysis of Indigenous legal traditions.

Borrows then turns to the lived experiences of Indigenous communities. He considers specific examples of Indigenous legal traditions, paying careful attention to the specific social, historical, and cultural experiences of particular communities.[31] He then uses these specific examples to "develop an understanding of Indigenous law in a more applied context and attempt to show how Indigenous law channels behaviour by regulation, prevention and 'cleaning up social mess.'"[32] This allows Borrows to advance the argument for the recognition of Indigenous legal traditions as part of a multi-juridical constitution. Features of Indigenous legal theory, as described by Christie, enable Borrows to address "questions related to the intelligibility, accessibility, equality, applicability, and legitimacy of Indigenous laws."[33]

Being grounded in the culture and experience of Indigenous communities is a defining characteristic of theories that fall within the rubric of Indigenous legal theory. There is also scope for the application of non-Indigenous theoretical tools within Indigenous legal theory, but Christie warns that Indigenous legal theorists should engage with non-Indigenous theoretical tools carefully and deliberately.[34] After all, such tools have been developed with conceptual apparatus grounded in other cultures and experiences and will sometimes reflect ideological or political foundations that are antithetical to Indigenous aspirations.[35]

Christie does acknowledge, however, the utility of deploying non-Indigenous theoretical tools in some circumstances and notes that this need not undermine Indigenous theorizing. For example, Indigenous legal theorists may find it helpful to consider various strands of critical legal theory in order to interrogate assumptions relating to objectivity and neutrality of laws and legal processes, while at the same time relying on Indigenous understandings of what objectivity and neutrality mean and require in the context of law and social relations, in order to support the revitalization of Indigenous legal traditions.[36] Christie suggests that the two positions are not mutually exclusive; both approaches may sometimes be required.[37] Indigenous legal theory enables Indigenous scholars to present innovative frameworks for examining law, which can lead to new insights about the way law and legal systems operate. At the same time, there is an urgent need to ensure that Indigenous law is not undermined by the perpetuation of assumptions based on Eurocentric understandings of law. To address these assumptions, it may be necessary to use conceptual tools that derive from Western ideas about law. But, says Christie, this ought not to preclude Indigenous scholars from also continuing to develop theoretical frameworks better suited to working with Indigenous law. If carefully deployed, these two perspectives ought to be complementary.

Indigenous legal scholars such as John Borrows, Val Napoleon, and Robert Williams Jr., demonstrate ways in which non-Indigenous theoretical tools may be put to use safely and fruitfully. In *Canada's Indigenous Constitution*, Borrows draws on non-Indigenous theoretical tools, in particular, building on strands of legal pluralism.[38] In an extended example, Borrows considers the possibility of an approach to constitutional law that draws on both Canadian state law and Indigenous law.[39] Borrows does not seek to step outside the Canadian legal system but instead forcefully argues that the system, as it stands, is incomplete. The central argument of *Canada's Indigenous Constitution* is not that law ought to be rejected as a mechanism for governing relationships within Canadian society but, rather, that the rule of law can be strengthened in Canada if Indigenous legal traditions are recognized as a source of Canadian law.[40] Borrows incorporates ideas from law and anthropology literature to construct a pluralist framework for his analysis.[41] This allows Borrows to situate Indigenous legal traditions "within interpretive communities in which those who are affected by them are able to participate in their continued construction."[42] This is an important theoretical turn because one of Borrows's key arguments is that Indigenous and non-Indigenous legal traditions in Canada may be strengthened if interpretive legal communities are widened by more people engaging with Indigenous norms.[43] An excellent example of the way

Borrows uses aspects of non-Indigenous legal theory is his exploration of how Anishinabek legal traditions could "stand beside the Canadian Constitution to organize and structure society's relationships." That exploration relies heavily on legal pluralist theories at the same time that it is rooted in the culture and experiences of the Anishinabek community.[44]

Indigenous legal scholar Val Napoleon, whose PhD dissertation begins to articulate a Gitksan theory of law, also makes use of what she calls the "resources" provided by non-Indigenous legal theories.[45] In particular, she finds helpful conceptual tools within the positivist legal theory of H.L.A. Hart and the work of Lon Fuller.[46] Napoleon draws comparisons between Hart's model of primary and secondary rules and identifiable categories of Gitksan law.[47] She suggests that Gitksan legal processes also "fulfill Hart's characterization of the rules of obligation because people were acting on a belief that the rules are necessary to the maintenance of social life, and may require sacrifice or renunciation."[48] Though Napoleon uses aspects of Hart's theoretical framework, she is careful to identify the "cultural-boundedness" of Hart's theories and the distinctive features of the cultural context of Gitksan law, which makes an uncritical application of those theories inappropriate[49] Napoleon is also careful to disconnect Hart's framework from the concept of a centralized state legal system.[50] In order to explore the Gitksan legal order, a decentralized, non-state legal system, Napoleon turns to Lon Fuller's theory of law as social interaction.[51] She analyses Gitksan law using Fuller's idea that law derives from human interaction over time. She introduces the concept of "implicit Gitksan law," exploring how informal law becomes formalized within the Gitksan legal order and how human agency plays a role in this process.[52] As in the case of Hart's theories, Napoleon is careful to disconnect aspects of Fuller's work from some of its culture-specific assumptions.[53] This enables her to extract the tools that are helpful for her analysis without taking on board the features of Fuller's work that are not applicable to Gitksan law. This is consistent with the cautious and critical approach to the use of non-Indigenous legal theories that is urged by Christie.[54]

Prominent Lumbee academic Robert Williams, Jr., also makes use of both Indigenous and non-Indigenous theoretical frameworks. Williams uses the conceptual tools of critical race theory (CRT) throughout his work. In particular, Williams assumes that meaning ascribed to words or terms is not stable but, rather, socially constructed.[55] This non-essentialist stance in relation to language is a characteristic feature of CRT (as well as a number of other critical theories).[56] Critical race theory, along with the work of various non-Indigenous theorists, such as Derrick Bell and Richard Delgado, provides Williams with the theoretical tools he has used to critique United States law and its legal discourse, which has arguably operated to subjugate Indigenous peoples in that country.[57] Williams also brings aspects of Lumbee philosophy to his CRT framework, including the Lumbee cultural imperative to "think independently and act for others." Throughout his work, Williams foregrounds his personal responsibilities to family and community.[58] As Christie notes, Williams's adoption of non-Indigenous theory neither removes the need for Indigenous legal theory nor precludes its use. Christie suggests that, while Williams uses the tools of CRT to critique American law and policy, Williams's Lumbee identity means that the scholar must also embed the values of his community, learned from his own experiences, in his scholarship and in other aspects of his life.[59]

Māori Philosophy of Law

Understanding the key features of the underlying philosophy of Māori legal traditions is central to constructing the analysis of the development of those traditions.[60] Māori legal traditions are based on a system of tikanga (the right, correct, or just way of doing things).[61] The system of tikanga is in turn founded on a set of underlying values. There is some debate about what these values are. As noted in Chapter 1, the following five values are considered foundational by leading scholars in the field:[62]

1. *Whanaungatanga* – "the centrality of relationships to Māori life."[63]
2. *Manaakitanga* – "nurturing relationships, looking after people, and being very careful how others are treated."[64]
3. *Mana* – "the importance of spiritually sanctioned authority and the limits on Māori leadership."[65]
4. *Tapu* – "respect for the spiritual character of all things."[66]
5. *Utu* – "the principle of balance and reciprocity."[67]

As a whole, these values reflect the importance of recognizing and reinforcing the interconnectedness of all living things and maintaining balance within communities.[68] Together they also recall the importance of whakapapa as an organizing principle in Māori society.

In developing models that are appropriately grounded in Māori community life, we can take guidance from Māori scholars active in the wider social sciences. A Ngāti Awa leader and scholar of Māori language and culture, Hirini Moko Mead has suggested a tikanga framework that can be applied to any given set of circumstances to ascertain a viewpoint or a position grounded in Māori philosophy and reflective of the core values of the system of tikanga.[69] Mead may be thinking of tikanga as a broader cultural system rather than strictly a legal system, but the framework he suggests provides clear direction for the development of theories that address Māori legal traditions. In part, this reflects the fact that tikanga comprises social as well as legal norms. Tikanga includes community-backed sanctions for actions that cause serious imbalance but also includes "approaches or ways of doing things which would be considered to be morally appropriate, courteous or advisable, but which are not rules that entail punitive sanctions when broken."[70] For example, tikanga dictates that one should purify oneself with a sprinkling of water and by washing one's hands after having been in a cemetery or close to a dead body, but there are no legal sanctions for failing to do so.[71] There is no distinction between criminal and civil law within tikanga, because all "offences" are understood to upset the balance of the same basic social, religious, and legal order.[72] In any case, Mead's framework outlines general concepts and normative principles within Māori law, points to a coherent picture of law as it is understood within a Māori worldview, and indicates aspects of the general workings of law, all areas one would expect a legal theory to address.[73]

According to Mead's framework, the basic purpose of the system of tikanga is to maintain balance, particularly where tapu may have been affected.[74] How maintaining balance in these crucial areas of life drives the development of Māori legal processes can be seen in the practice of *muru*, the ritualized confiscation (and sometimes destruction) of property as compensation for an offence. An eyewitness account of a relatively large-scale, nineteenth-century muru serves as an example.[75] A young couple had eloped, despite the fact that their relationship was considered adulterous according to the practices of their communities. Both the man and woman were of high rank, which elevated the seriousness of the situation. Under tikanga, those wronged by the couple's actions included not only the partners and immediate families of the couple but the communities as well. At the same time, the offence was seen as the responsibility of the young man but also the responsibility of his entire community. The process for restoring balance among the parties had to provide some form of restitution to the communities wronged. In this instance, a ritualized confiscation and destruction of the property of the young man's community was seen to be the appropriate course of action. All the affected communities were entitled to take property as compensation. Once the appropriate compensation had been made, balance was deemed to have been restored, the previously existing marriage and betrothal were annulled, and the young couple's new marriage, originally in breach of tikanga, was now deemed to have been confirmed in accordance with the community's law.

Mead's framework suggests that Māori legal traditions develop as Māori communities determine the most appropriate mechanisms for maintaining balance and for redressing imbalance when it occurs. Such determinations may be made by reference to various sources of law, including models previously developed, and the key underlying values discussed above. The example above may be an extreme case, but it demonstrates how the process addresses the central values of tikanga. The sense of reciprocity and the need to restore balance, integral to the concept of utu, are perhaps the most obvious elements of the example. But it also demonstrates the importance of assessing the seriousness of the breach of tapu and/or the offence to mana. Whanaungatanga also plays a role in regulating this process, because muru is primarily a process for dealing with disputes among close kin. Avoiding full-scale conflict is most important when all parties are related. Without kinship connections, a serious offence may very well lead to physical conflict.

The use of precedent as a source of tikanga indicates that Mead's framework, though rooted in cultural values, also uses community experience as a point of reference. This is consistent with the view of Māori legal traditions expressed by Moana Jackson.[76] Jackson sees the philosophy of Māori law as sourced not only within the basic values of Māori culture but also within the histories and lived experiences of Māori communities. Jackson notes that Māori philosophy of law, or "te maramatanga o ngā tikanga," is bound up with Māori cosmology. It has connections to the gods and understandings of the natural and spiritual worlds and of Māori knowledge systems. According to Jackson, this philosophy of law is transmitted from generation to generation through examples of practice, which are employed as precedent. He describes the interconnection between values and experience as "an intricate tāniko pattern," which reflects dynamic movement back and forth from principles and values to the reality of social life. This interaction, Jackson says, leads to a clear set of rules and practices that maintain balance within relationships, provide the means for appropriate sanctions and mechanisms for resolving disputes, and lead to internal processes for changing and adapting law to new circumstances.[77]

When we seek to explore, understand, and explain Māori legal traditions, it is important to employ philosophical tools and conceptual frameworks from within Māori society.[78] Jackson's recent discussion of a Māori form of title, the rights and obligations in relation to the land that stems from Māori legal traditions, provides a useful illustration of this. What is significant about the description that follows is not the particular substance of this "tipuna title." Of greater interest for our purposes are the conceptual tools that Jackson calls upon to articulate this form of title. "Tipuna title" makes sense only when it is understood in the context of the Māori world. The basis of the title stems from forms of social organization such as the whānau, hapū, and iwi. Whakapapa structures the networks of relationships between people and the natural world, and thus helps determine rights and responsibilities. Jackson reinforces the importance of these kin-based relationships by using the term *tipuna* (ancestor) to describe this form of title. Māori forms of personal, collective, and political authority, expressed in the concepts of mana and rangatiratanga, are also central to the nature of this title.[79] Jackson also uses Māori approaches to conceptualizing the natural environment when he explicitly sets the term whenua in the context of a relationship with people and the identity of Indigenous communities: *tangata whenua* (literally, people of the land). Explains Jackson:

> Tipuna title may be described as the physical and spiritual interests that collectively vested in Iwi or Hapū as part of their mana or rangatiratanga in regard to the whenua. It is a title that exists within what may be termed "relational interests," that is[,] the interests that inhered in the relationships of a particular whakapapa and the willingness of our people to develop existing or potential relationships with others.[80]

Tipuna title is an absolute title in the sense that rangatiratanga and whakapapa create inalienable ties to the land. Being tangata whenua implies having whenua to be tangata upon, and tipuna title presupposes a continuing authority in relation to the land.

Jackson's explanation highlights the importance of using concepts from within Māori legal traditions as points of reference. Jackson is careful to explain that while this title may have similar features to property rights that arise out of common law traditions,[81] tipuna title derives from a quite different "cultural and legal paradigm."[82] Tipuna title is sourced in whakapapa, that is, a network of kinship connections. The rights and entitlements associated with tipuna title are, therefore, also defined by whakapapa. Individual rights to land exist within this framework, though they are ultimately relational, constrained by collective interests and obligations to the land itself. This framework also allows for various use rights to be allocated to others outside of the kin group. For example, Jackson notes that within the Ngāti Kahungunu community, "a notion of *kauhanga* or 'passageways' developed as the means to facilitate access by others on approved and negotiated terms."[83] However, because the tipuna title depends on whakapapa, it can never be permanently alienated. The exercise of rights that derive from tipuna title may be affected by factors such as defeat in battle or by a group member moving away from the area, but the notional title is based on the genealogical connection to the land and could not, therefore, be extinguished.[84]

Māori legal traditions must be understood as part of Māori culture, reflecting Māori systems of social organization and political authority, aimed at reinforcing values that stem from a Māori worldview. I take the view that concepts from within Māori philosophies ought to underlie any discussion of Māori legal issues. Mana, utu, tapu (and *noa,* the profane or ordinary, in juxtaposition to tapu), whanaungatanga, and manaakitanga are important guides. These concepts drive the development of Māori legal traditions and must frame our analysis of the changes to those traditions over time.

The Treaty of Waitangi and Legal Pluralism

The Treaty of Waitangi acts as another important reference point for analysis. The treaty is central to the substantive issues of the settlement process, but it also suggests important theoretical directions for this analysis. The relationship between Māori and the New Zealand government is framed by the treaty, signed in 1840 by Māori chiefs and representatives of the British Crown.[85] This instrument paved the way for the introduction of a colonial government in New Zealand in return for British guarantees that Māori interests would be protected.[86] In the English text, the Māori chiefs cede sovereignty to the British Crown in exchange for a broad-ranging guarantee of property rights. In the Māori text, the chiefs cede a form of governmental authority (expressed as *kāwanatanga*) and retain their tino rangatiratanga (usually translated in this context as "unqualified exercise of their chieftainship").[87] While there continues to be debate about the scope of the Crown's kāwanatanga in relation to Māori tino rangatiratanga, it is clear that the treaty envisaged a framework within which the two forms of political and legal authority would co-exist. The treaty provides an important link between Māori legal traditions and a legal pluralist framework.

The Treaty of Waitangi discourse affects how Māori law is received and applied by Māori and non-Māori alike. Ani Mikaere, a Māori legal scholar who has sought to promote a discussion of Māori law that is "free from the constraints of colonised and colonising attitudes" and that "acknowledges tikanga as the first law of Aotearoa," has commented on the relevance of the treaty to discussions of Māori law.[88] Mikaere notes that how the treaty is interpreted has an impact on perceptions of tikanga. She suggests that attitudes to tikanga often reflect prevailing views of the treaty and its role in public life.[89]

The Treaty of Waitangi also provides an important expression of Māori legal norms. It reflects the cultural and experiential groundings that are critical for understanding the operation of Māori law. Moana Jackson has argued that the treaty, at least in its Māori-language version, should be understood within the context of the Māori legal system. Jackson points out that the treaty gives expression to rights and obligations that are sourced in Māori law. The guarantees reflect ancestral practice. What is more, the form of the treaty is also consistent with Māori law, as the agreement was discussed and debated by the representatives of hapū and iwi and ultimately signed by rangatira who were authorized to commit their people to such an agreement.[90]

This view is similar to that expressed by John Borrows, who suggests that treaties between First Nations and the Crown in Canada were entered into within an Indigenous legal framework.[91] The Treaty of Waitangi can, therefore, be seen as a Māori legal mechanism, which protects Māori rights that were sourced in Māori legal traditions. It is inextricably connected to Māori communities' experiences of law in Aotearoa.

The treaty establishes a pluralist framework within Aotearoa. Theories of legal pluralism have played an important role in developing understanding about the various forms of law and the existence of multiple legal orders within a single political entity. Such theories have been central to the identification of Indigenous legal systems and the recognition of Indigenous law – as law – by scholars, lawyers, even state legal systems. By challenging legal centralism, pluralist theories have also contributed to the advancement of the broader project of Indigenous self-determination. Nevertheless, there are still questions about whether the framework of legal pluralism can accommodate the particular claims of Indigenous legal systems.

In recent years, some legal pluralist theories have incorporated aspects of the conceptual framework of critical legal studies, which has seen the establishment of critical legal pluralist theories. The development of critical legal pluralism, although not directly aimed at recognizing the self-determining character of Indigenous legal orders, may be able to move the legal pluralist discourse closer to addressing the concerns of the Indigenous self-determination project. There are, however, some conceptual difficulties with the critical legal pluralist model when considered in light of the objectives of the Indigenous self-determination project. At the same time, it is important to remain focused on the complex interactions between legal systems and legal subjects, which the critical legal pluralists draw to our attention. If that theoretical balance can be achieved, there is potential within the legal pluralist framework to create a space for Indigenous law that takes into account the culture and experiences of Indigenous communities and is consistent with Indigenous self-determination.

One of the most significant aspects of legal pluralism for Indigenous peoples is the move away from legal centralism. This has been a key driver in the development of the legal pluralist discourse and creates a theoretical space in which Indigenous law can be recognized. However, there is considerable variation among legal pluralist theories in terms of the degree to which state law is de-centred and non-official law is recognized.

In an influential article published in 1986, John Griffiths addresses the variations in legal pluralist theories and distinguishes between "strong" and "weak" legal pluralism.[92] Strong legal pluralism is concerned with the interaction between two or more distinct legal systems; weak legal pluralism focuses on pluralism within the state legal system. According to Griffiths, there cannot be pluralism within a state legal order: even when state law employs different rules for different groups of people, this is only because the system itself has determined that these different categories should be treated differently. Griffiths argues that this is legal diversity, not legal pluralism.[93] In other words, in this example one cannot say that different legal mechanisms are being applied in the same situation because the "sameness" of the situation is determined not by any empirical measure but by the legal order's own rules.[94]

Griffith's analysis suggests that the de-centring of state law must be part of any genuinely pluralist legal theory (that is, a "strong" legal pluralism as opposed to a "weak" legal pluralism). This analysis is consistent with the self-determination objectives of Indigenous communities. Woodman agrees that to advance the project of de-centring state law, the concepts of legal pluralism must be addressed across, not just within, legal orders.[95] But it does not follow that legal pluralism must *always* address pluralism across legal orders or that legal pluralism must *necessarily* advance the project of de-centring state law. Many legal pluralist theories recognize the existence of law that sits outside of the state legal system but still maintain that state law has qualities that are distinct from other legal and normative orders. Sally Engle Merry argues that "it is essential to see state law as fundamentally different in that it exercises the coercive power of the state and monopolizes the symbolic power associated with state authority."[96] Similarly, Boaventura de Sousa Santos recognizes that the state is not the sole source of law and that supra-state law and infra-state law operate upon and within national legal systems; nevertheless, these other legal orders all exist in the orbit of a central state legal order.[97] These conceptualizations of legal pluralism, even while challenging legal centralism, do not completely de-centre state law. They certainly do not provide for the kind of de-centring of state law that would be consistent with Indigenous self-determination.

While the development of legal pluralism and its challenge to legal centralism has led to wide acknowledgment that Indigenous law can be understood and recognized *as law*, this acknowledgment goes only part-way towards addressing Indigenous peoples' concerns about the relationship between Indigenous law and state law. These concerns are not limited to the recognition of Indigenous law; they may also include matters relating to Indigenous self-determination, such as the sources of legitimacy, authority, and political power within official legal systems. Reflecting on these matters in the New Zealand context, Paul Havemann argues that legal pluralism cannot accommodate the aspirations of Indigenous self-determination simply by incorporating aspects of Indigenous law in the procedural and substantive law of the state or by adapting state institutions.[98] For those who aspire to Indigenous self-determination, such adaptations are purely cosmetic and serve only to disguise the central and oppressive role of state law.[99] Moana Jackson, who aspires to Indigenous self-determination, argues that forms of legal pluralism which do not take account of the "dialectic of colonization" cannot deliver justice for Indigenous peoples[100] because they do not link "cultural and philosophical perceptions of justice and political power."[101] Historically, the legal pluralist discourse has not concentrated on such issues. However, the arguments advanced by Havemann and Jackson should not be interpreted to mean that scholars concerned about Indigenous self-determination should reject legal pluralist theories outright. Rather, not all legal pluralist theories will provide a satisfactory framework for the appropriate recognition of Indigenous law, even though some form of legal pluralism may be necessary for the appropriate recognition of non-state law.

Recent legal pluralist scholarship has moved in the direction that scholars such as Jackson suggest is necessary to address Indigenous peoples' aspirations. This scholarship has shifted the discourse some way towards an arguably more effective, de-centring of state law.

Critical legal pluralism re-conceptualizes the legal pluralist approach, focusing more directly on the individualized construction of legal orders. Critical legal pluralist theories look to legal subjects to consider how legal orders regulate the behaviour of individuals within societies. This emphasis on legal subjects means there is scope to explore the types of cultural and philosophical perceptions of justice that Jackson argues are necessary to further Indigenous self-determination. As Jeremy Webber has pointed out, however, this framework does not fully account for the fundamentally social nature of the establishment of norms.[102] Nevertheless, critical legal pluralism's attention to the legal subject (and to the intersection of multiple legal orders in which that subject participates) expands the legal pluralist discourse to allow space for a project of Indigenous peoples' self-determination.

One of the aims of the critical legal pluralists is to challenge the privileged position that state law has effectively maintained in the legal pluralist discourse.[103] Melissaris suggests that to concede that "legal pluralism exists in the shadow of an ultimate law of laws" is to undermine the whole project of legal pluralism.[104] This insistence on a genuinely non-hierarchical theory of interacting legal orders is of benefit to the Indigenous self-determination project, a fundamental requirement of which is that Indigenous legal orders are not dependent upon, or in any way subordinate to, the state legal order.

The complete de-centring of state law is not the only aspect of critical legal pluralism that may be attractive to advocates of Indigenous self-determination. To construct a theory of normative ordering that is truly non-hierarchical, critical legal pluralists focus on legal subjects and their ability to create legal orders.[105] Within this theoretical framework, emphasis is placed on the transformative capacity of legal subjects, which "enables them to produce legal knowledge and to fashion the very structures of law that contribute to constituting their legal subjectivity."[106] Melissaris explains this focus on the legal subject by reference to the role that personal narratives play in the construction of law.[107] Melissaris's explanation builds on Robert Cover's assertion that for a law to exist, those who are affected by it must have some level of commitment to it. According to Cover, "commitment" is established by legal subjects participating in instances of legal discourse.[108] Melissaris supports Cover's assertion that such discourse must be part of the legal subject's "world- or juris-generative narrative."[109] However, Melissaris provides a critical legal pluralist gloss to argue that these narratives need not be shared by whole communities but may be personal to the legal subject.[110] The recognition of how legal subjects construct subjective legal spaces by reference to multiple normative orders suggests that critical legal pluralism may be able to take account of Indigenous perceptions of justice that underlie Indigenous legal orders – in a way that other forms of legal pluralism cannot. However, while emphasis on the legal subject appears to provide space to address the self-determination objectives of Indigenous communities, this emphasis has been criticized for failing to adequately take into account the inherently social nature of legal orders.

Jeremy Webber has criticized the critical legal pluralists' focus on the legal subject, arguing that the fundamental framework of critical legal pluralism places too great an emphasis on each individual's assessment of the particular norms that regulate his or her behaviour.[111] Under such a conceptualization, institutions (state and otherwise) are pushed to the margins. Webber argues that this "leaves out the hard truth that norms always involve a kind of imposition, where parties submit ... to norms that would not be the ones they would choose if left to their own devices."[112] According to Webber, what critical legal pluralists are really focused on are asserted or proposed norms and the social interactions that construct those norms. But the establishment of norms takes place only once these assertions of norms are settled by "some emphatically social, non-individual process."[113] In essence, Webber argues, this is the "legal" quality of "legal pluralism." Law is concerned with the emergence of norms and the ways that disagreement is managed.

Webber also argues that critical legal pluralists take the idea of de-centring the state too far, by "treating every one of individuals' manifold normative relationships as presumptively equal, thereby definitively shifting the focus from the relationships to the individual's decision among them as the determinant of normative obligation."[114] Webber suggests a model in which contending normative orders encounter each other and engage in a negotiation. Importantly, to understand the appropriate relationship between normative orders, one must consider the perspective from each side. For example, what type of relationship between state and Indigenous systems does each party (that is, the state and the Indigenous people) see as appropriate and/or legitimate?[115] In the end, which normative order is determinative in a particular situation (whether it is the normative order of the state or the normative order of another entity) should be subject to inquiry, as to which order is best equipped to manage the specific disagreements at issue. In other words, the legitimacy of any normative order should not be assumed but, rather, must always be justified.[116] This negotiated, perspectival approach to the construction of normative ordering may be compatible with the Indigenous self-determination framework.

Webber's approach has not been universally accepted by legal pluralists. David Schneiderman, for example, disputes the need for a common normative order to manage disagreement.[117] Echoing Melissaris and the critical legal pluralists, Schneiderman contends that Webber's position is more in line with legal positivism than legal pluralism.[118] It may be, however, that Schneiderman is more concerned about Webber's confidence in the institutions of state law. Schneiderman acknowledges that the need for some form of common normative order is consistent with pluralist concepts such as Moore's "symbolic consensus."[119] If Webber's conceptualization returns state law to a central and privileged position, as Schneiderman argues,[120] then that conceptualization would certainly be inconsistent with the requirements of Indigenous self-determination.

I contend, however, that Webber's "friendly critique" of critical legal pluralism is actually of assistance to the Indigenous self-determination project. Like the critical legal pluralists, Webber recognizes the complex and fluid way that individuals, groups, and normative orders interact within the social milieu.[121] Furthermore, the Indigenous self-determination project requires not only a de-centring of state law, but also a re-centring of Indigenous legal orders. The former is certainly consistent with critical legal pluralism. The latter is more difficult to address within that framework because critical legal pluralism tends to de-centre *all* legal institutions in deference to the legal subject. Webber's re-centring of the social aspect of the construction of normative orders to manage disagreement is, therefore, entirely consistent with Indigenous self-determination. Such an approach need not necessarily privilege state law. Webber explicitly recognizes that the legitimacy of any normative order (which presumably includes state law) cannot be assumed and must always be justified. So, although Webber appears to see considerable merit in the democratic institutions of state law, this preference does not necessarily translate into a re-centring of state law. New Zealand legal scholar Nicole Roughan suggests a similar, deliberate approach in her model of "legal association," which she suggests could be developed in Aotearoa.[122]

Further support for this type of legal pluralism can be found in the writings of Brian Tamanaha. Tamanaha's version of legal pluralism is also helpful to the Indigenous self-determination project in that it is consistent with the type of individual agency evident in Webber's conceptualization and among the critical legal pluralists. Tamanaha, like Webber and the critical legal pluralists, recognizes the hybridity and fluidity of groups and individuals in heterogeneous societies.[123]

Within Tamanaha's model of legal pluralism, normative orders are not completely independent of each other. In any conflict between normative orders, Tamanaha argues, strategic actors will make strategic decisions about which legal system to invoke and how to invoke that system.[124] Critical legal pluralists might suggest that it is the availability of these choices, and the inherently "biographical" nature of the factors, that leads to particular decisions; in effect, individuals construct their own normative system, which reflects their personal understanding of the norms they are obliged to follow in any given situation.[125] But Tamanaha's argument does not necessarily lead to that type of individualized construction of legal orders. On the contrary, Tamanaha refers to strategic choices determined by structural factors rather than by individual characteristics or preferences.[126]

Tamanaha's conceptualization is, therefore, closer to Webber's view of legal pluralism and the role of official law in resolving conflict between clashing normative orders. Arguably, Tamanaha goes even further than Webber in privileging state law. The strategic choices made by strategic actors in Tamanaha's conceptualization are always made "to enlist the endorsement or support of existing *official legal systems,* to, if possible, lend legitimacy, resources and coercion to their cause."[127] This might well be construed as an unexpected re-centring of state law, which would run counter to the aims of the Indigenous self-determination project.

The language Tamanaha uses becomes highly significant in this context. Tamanaha's use of the term "official legal systems" is not equivalent to his use of "state law." Certainly state law forms part of official law, and the state legal system can be considered as *one of many* official legal systems, but they are by no means the same thing. Tamanaha's recognition that there are multiple official legal systems shows that he does not equate state law with official law. The implication is that there are other forms of official law that strategic actors might invoke. These official legal orders might conflict with each other, as well as with non-official law. Tamanaha also warns that "one must not assume that strategic actors pursuing their aims in situations of legal pluralism will consistently invoke or support the same official legal system or normative system over time."[128] Thus, while Tamanaha's conceptualization clearly privileges *official* law, it does not necessarily privilege *state* law.

Challenging legal centralism and the state's perceived monopoly on the creation of law has always been a key element of the legal pluralist discourse. Nevertheless, many legal pluralist theories privilege the state legal order. This continued deference to state law has been one of the reasons that scholars who seek to advance an Indigenous self-determination project have not seen legal pluralism as helpful to, or even compatible with, their aims. By shifting the focus of legal pluralist inquiry to the legal subject, critical legal pluralism provides a conceptual framework that is genuinely non-hierarchical. Such a framework has considerable potential to reconcile the Indigenous self-determination project with legal pluralist discourse. However, as Webber and Tamanaha argue, the inherent legal subjectivity of critical legal pluralism does not take sufficient account of the social process by which normative orders are constructed. This is problematic for the Indigenous self-determination project because, although crticial legal pluralist scholarship provides support for the de-centring of state law, it does not provide a theoretical or analytical framework that re-centres Indigenous legal orders. Therefore, the approaches of scholars such as Webber and Tamanaha – approaches which recognize and address the role of legal subjects as well as legal institutions in the creation of normative orders – may be more consistent with the aims of Indigenous self-determination and the cultures and experiences of Indigenous communities. This raises the possibility of a form of reconciliation between legal systems as envisaged by the Treaty of Waitangi. The final two parts of this chapter begin to explore this possibility by examining the two fundamental concepts of tino rangatiratanga and reconciliation.

Tino Rangatiratanga and Indigenous Self-Determination

Much has been written on the subject of self-determination and Indigenous peoples. Often the discussion focuses on the institutions of international law[129] and on liberal egalitarian conceptions of rights.[130] More recently, Cherokee scholar Jeff Corntassel has advocated a move away from a rights-based discourse of self-determination, towards what he suggests is "sustainable self-determination."[131] Corntassel argues persuasively that there are many problems with a rights-based discussion of Indigenous self-determination. The benchmarks he outlines for sustainable self-determination appear to be more consistent with Māori ideas of autonomy, independence, and self-determination that are bound up in the concept of tino rangatiratanga.

Corntassel's central thesis is that governments, individually and collectively, have constructed a discourse around self-determination that pushes key relationships within the Indigenous worldview to the periphery. In this discourse, relationships with, and responsibilities to, community and the natural world have become secondary considerations at best. A more holistic approach would be more consistent with an Indigenous worldview. Corntassel articulates this approach as "sustainable self-determination."[132]

Corntassel suggests that framing Indigenous self-determination within a state-centred rights discourse is problematic for the future development of Indigenous peoples in four distinct ways.[133] First, the rights discourse has "compartmentalized" Indigenous self-determination, so that issues such as the control and ownership of lands and natural resources are disconnected from forms of political and legal recognition that are compatible with the existing constitutional apparatus of the state.[134] Two examples illustrate this reality within the New Zealand context. The *Resource Management Act* (1991) was drafted so as to deliberately disconnect issues of ownership from issues of management and environmental decision-making. Throughout the drafting process, however, Māori argued that before the government enacted legislation such as the *Resource Management Act*, which comprehensively details the mechanisms of control over environmental planning, questions of Māori customary ownership interests ought to be addressed. That did not happen, which is one of the reasons Māori have continued to argue that, despite several provisions directed at Māori values, this legislation does not appropriately address their interests, especially their tino rangatiratanga, or self-determination. The Treaty of Waitangi settlement process also demonstrates this split between economic self-determination and political self-determination. The New Zealand government is now reasonably comfortable with providing financial redress for historical breaches of the principles of the Treaty of Waitangi; it appears to be less at ease with an ongoing recognition of the distinctiveness of Indigenous communities.

The second way in which the rights discourse is problematic for Indigenous peoples, according to Corntassel, is that it has encouraged states to deny Indigenous peoples' status as Indigenous peoples. In particular, Corntassel points to the actions of the Botswana government in classifying their Indigenous populations as "tribes," "races," or "communities" in order to avoid having to meet international human rights standards for Indigenous peoples. The New Zealand state has not explicitly denied that Māori are Indigenous peoples; however, there remains a disturbingly strong element of the political discourse in New Zealand that suggests Māori should not be considered in this way. It is also worth noting the qualifications that the New Zealand government placed on its eventual acceptance of the United Nations Declaration on the Rights of Indigenous Peoples.[135] Arguably, the qualifications reflect a government view that the full rights of Indigenous peoples as they have been recognized by the international community do not apply to Māori, which perhaps comes close in substance to the more brazen denial by the Botswana government.

Corntassel's third concern is the focus on legal and political rights, at the expense of cultural responsibilities and the relationships that exist within Indigenous communities. This concern is directly relevant to Māori communities. Māori legal traditions, social structures, and the foundational ideas within Māori philosophy are all centred on relationships and kinship connections. Concepts such as whanaungatanga and whakapapa are basic organizing principles of the Māori world; like many other Indigenous peoples, Māori perceive real kinship relations between people and the natural world. Once more, the Treaty of Waitangi settlement process provides an excellent illustration of the way that self-determination as a concept framed by the state can be dangerous for Māori communities. In 2007, the Waitangi Tribunal released its report on the operation of the government's treaty settlement process in the Auckland area.[136] The *Tāmaki Makaurau Settlement Process Report* was a scathing indictment of the government's approach. The report addressed the central claim that the proposed settlement with one of the iwi of Tāmaki Makaurau (Auckland) would prejudice other iwi in the area. The tribunal noted that there were approximately ten iwi that could claim they exercised traditional authority and customary rights within the area.[137] The tribunal found that the ability of these groups to exercise their rights and obligations as *kaitiaki* (guardians/stewards) in Tāmaki Makaurau had been diminished by the Crown's approach to settlement negotiations in the area, and that they would be further prejudiced if the settlement was to proceed unaltered.[138] The report was particularly critical of the fact that government action had damaged relationships between the various iwi of the Auckland area, with the tribunal noting that "[i]nstead of supporting the whanaungatanga that underpins rangatiratanga, the Crown's actions have undermined it."[139] The tribunal found that the principles of the Treaty of Waitangi required the Crown not to take actions that undermine relationships between iwi, in part because whanaungatanga is of such central importance to Māori social interactions. The settlement of Māori claims to commercial fishing interests can also be seen to be damaging to relationships between Māori groups. That settlement led to significant litigation, which pitted coastal iwi against inland iwi and traditional iwi against more recent urban Māori groupings. The commercial fishing settlement was supposed to provide for a measure of Māori self-determination, but the characteristic of those rights as political and legal (and, in this instance, economic) entitlements actually undermined the relationships that are fundamentally important in the Māori world and for the operation of tino rangatiratanga.

Finally, Corntassel argues, Indigenous peoples' self-determination is limited when framed within the rights discourse because it becomes subject to ad hoc restrictions imposed by states. Here Corntassel is referring to matters such as UN General Assembly resolution 1514 (1960), which stipulates that only territories that were geographically separate from the colonizing power could invoke the right of self-determination. In the New Zealand context, the qualifications surrounding the United Nations Declaration on the Rights of Indigenous Peoples may be seen to constitute such a limitation. The settlement process is rife with examples of ad hoc limitations on the way that self-determination can be exercised. For example, the Crown effectively has complete control over the selection of groups with which it will enter negotiations, thereby granting itself the role as the final arbiter of who is entitled to self-determination, in whatever form the treaty settlement process recognizes. The Crown has also set a number of limits on the content of redress packages available in the treaty settlement process.

Building on the work of James Anaya, Taiaiake Alfred, James Tully, and others, Corntassel suggests that the most effective approach for Indigenous peoples is to move away from the state-centred rights discourse of self-determination and move towards sustainable self-determination.[140] Corntassel argues that the limitations of conceptualizations of self-determination derived from a rights discourse inevitably constrain the practice of self-determination, in particular the ability on the part of Indigenous peoples to maintain self-determining communities. This is why he advocates using sustainability as the key benchmark. Self-determination that is not sustainable is not effective self-determination because, by definition, it results in Indigenous communities (sooner or later) losing the means to govern themselves. Corntassel describes sustainable self-determination as a process that rejects "colonial strategies founded on economic dependency as the main avenues to meaningful self-determination" and that rejects also "the compartmentalization of standard political/legal definitions of self-determination by taking social, economic, cultural, and political factors of shared governance and relational accountability into consideration."[141] Corntassel stresses the importance of addressing self-determination at a regional and local level. Ultimately, for practices of self-determination to be sustainable, Corntassel argues that they must operate at a community level "as a process to perpetuate Indigenous livelihoods locally via the regeneration of family, clan, and individual roles and responsibilities to their homelands."[142] According to Corntassel, sustainable self-determination for Indigenous peoples will not be fully realized until Indigenous peoples play a more influential role in shaping the global political economy. The most effective means of achieving this influence is for Indigenous peoples to focus on rebuilding and re-strengthening local and regional Indigenous economies.[143] This enables Indigenous peoples to engage in the global political economy from a position of strength, with stable foundations established according to their own principles of social, political, and economic organization. That engagement in the global economy then becomes sustainable, as it is not dependent on the goodwill of state actors or the prevailing political or economic climate.

It is important to note that Corntassel is not suggesting that rights-based arguments and strategies for Indigenous self-determination be completely abandoned.[144] He recognizes explicitly that the rights discourse can provide useful tools for Indigenous communities. His point is that this framework can take Indigenous self-determination only so far, and that in order to develop a durable and sustainable self-determination the discourse needs to be shaped by Indigenous communities and the state needs to be removed from the centre of discussions of Indigenous self-determination. Ultimately, Corntassel argues that authentic and long-lasting self-determination for Indigenous peoples will be achieved only if the benchmarks of self-determination are set by Indigenous communities themselves, with reference to the network of relationships and responsibilities that organize those communities, rather than being grounded in a system of individualized rights consistent with the structures of colonial state parties and a colonizing global political economy.

In discussion, the concept of tino rangatiratanga has been approached in many ways. As Mason Durie points out, various people ascribe various levels of Māori authority to the concept of tino rangatiratanga.[145] For some it means a level of self-government. To others it is full authority, closely connected to the concept of mana. At times it has been equated with the English concept of "sovereignty" or "sovereign rights." In all cases, the concept implies a high degree of Māori autonomy and speaks to the distribution of political authority, both within Māori society and between Māori and the state.[146] A national debate about tino rangatiratanga led by the National Māori Congress in the mid-1990s (incidentally, as part of a response to the government's proposals for the settlement of Treaty of Waitangi claims)[147] generated consensus on the three key principles that underlie tino rangatiratanga: Ngā Matatini Māori (Māori diversity), Whakakotahi Māori (Māori unity), and Mana Motuhake Māori (Māori autonomy and control).[148] In the context of the Treaty of Waitangi, Ngāti Kahu leader and scholar Margaret Mutu has noted the important spiritual aspect of tino rangatiratanga. While some aspects of the authority encapsulated in tino rangatiratanga might seem comparable to the powers of a land "owner" in the English system, the centrality of the spiritually sanctioned authority invested in the Māori term make its meaning quite different.[149]

The Waitangi Tribunal and the New Zealand courts generally have had to address the concept of tino rangatiratanga when applying the principles of the Treaty of Waitangi. They are constrained in how they define the concept; as they are part of the state legal system, their definitions must be consistent with Crown sovereignty. Nevertheless, it is helpful to examine how this concept is being applied within the state legal system, especially in the context of treaty claims and settlement.

In *Taiaroa v Attorney-General,* Justice McGechan made some general comments about the content of tino rangatiratanga, accepting that "it encompassed a claim to an ongoing distinctive existence as a people, albeit adapting as time passed and the combined society developed."[150] Addressing the same subject matter in the *Māori Electoral Option Report,* the Waitangi Tribunal elaborated the meaning of tino rangatiratanga in relation to kāwanatanga, granted to the Crown in the Treaty of Waitangi. The tribunal noted that the central difficulty in describing tino rangatiratanga is that no one single English concept effectively captures the full meaning of the term. The term certainly includes aspects of self-determination, self-management, and even sovereignty, though any one of those terms, by itself, falls short of describing the concept of tino rangatiratanga. However, the tribunal also notes that the term must be understood in the context of the nation-state that was created via the Treaty of Waitangi.[151]

In this we can see some of the key aspects of how the courts and the tribunal have perceived tino rangatiratanga. First, the courts and the tribunal are required to define the concept in a very specific context, that is, in their interpretation and application of the principles of the Treaty of Waitangi within the parameters of their respective jurisdictions. The concept has consequently become a term of legal art and has been given a legal meaning that is not precisely the same as its practical, everyday meaning. Moreover, the term is defined in relation to kāwanatanga. Moana Jackson has argued forcefully that the application of the legal construct of treaty principles has led to a distortion of the Māori concepts involved, especially tino rangatiratanga.[152] This disjuncture further illustrates why it is important to set the tino rangatiratanga discourse within a broader conversation about Indigenous self-determination, especially building in some of the ideas of sustainable self-determination addressed by Corntassel.

In the context of the principles of the Treaty of Waitangi, tino rangatiratanga is defined as being qualified by the Crown's kāwanatanga; likewise, the treaty qualifies the Crown's authority by reference to the guarantee of tino rangatiratanga. The tribunal has found that any cession of authority by Māori to the Crown in Article 1 of the Treaty of Waitangi must be understood within the context of the Article 2 guarantees, especially the retention of tino rangatiratanga. The tribunal has therefore described the Crown's right to govern as "a qualified right."[153] The co-existence of two independent polities within the same territory is not impossible, however.

While the tribunal does not view the guaranteed protection of tino rangatiratanga as requiring Māori independence outside of the New Zealand state, the tribunal describes tino rangatiratanga as comprising quite substantial authority and autonomy. In the *Ngāwhā Geothermal Resources Report,* the tribunal states that "[t]he tribal right of self-regulation or self-management is an inherent element of tino rangatiratanga."[154] The tribunal has further found that tino rangatiratanga includes not only a right to manage resources but also an authority to regulate the behaviour of people across a range of areas of public life. In the *Te Arawa Representatives Geothermal Resources Report,* the tribunal found that the guarantee of tino rangatiratanga included "tribal control of Māori matters, including the right to regulate access to tribal members and others to tribal resources,"[155] and in the *Te Whānau o Waipareira Report,* the tribunal explained that tino rangatiratanga "applies to much more than the customary ownership of lands, estates, forests, fisheries and other taonga [treasured possessions]. It describes a value that is basic to the Māori way of life, that permeates the essence of being Māori."[156] Similarities can be seen in tino rangatiratanga as identified by the Waitangi Tribunal in the *Muriwhenua Fishing Claim Report.* In that report, the tribunal found that there were three key elements to the Crown's guarantee of tino rangatiratanga. The first element is recognizing why exercising the authority of tino rangatiratanga is important to the community: if a community is not able to exercise tino rangatiratanga, then its tribal estate becomes insecure. The second element is the importance of the spiritual aspect. This also reflects the purpose of the right being to enable Māori to exercise their obligations to nurture aspects of the natural world so that the taonga in question can be transmitted across generations.[157]

The third element that the tribunal noted is the close connection between mana and tino rangatiratanga, making this link in the context of understanding the principles of the Treaty of Waitangi. According to the tribunal, it is not possible to separate mana from rangatiratanga. Therefore, the treaty guarantee of tino rangatiratanga not only ensured that Māori would retain their landholdings but also the mana and authority to hold those lands in accordance with tikanga.[158]

At times the tribunal has also sought to locate tino rangatiratanga within the broader discourse of Indigenous self-determination, which is described as an inherent right of all Indigenous peoples. The tribunal views Aboriginal autonomy as being an essential component of the special constitutional status of First Peoples. This autonomy includes rights of self-government and the rights of Indigenous peoples to manage their own "policy, resources, and affairs" to the fullest extent possible within the wider state government. The tribunal has also found that the Māori term *tino rangatiratanga* expresses the same meaning as Aboriginal autonomy.[159]

Tino rangatiratanga reflects the concept of Māori self-determination and is an important objective of treaty settlements. It also provides the foundation for tensions and developments in Māori legal history and Māori-centred research.

Reconciliation

Reconciliation is a complex concept, cross-cultural reconciliation even more so. In order to assess the contribution of the Treaty of Waitangi settlement process to reconciliation between Māori and the New Zealand state, we must tease out some of this complexity.

Reconciliation can be a problematic concept for Indigenous peoples. The concept seems often deployed to encourage Indigenous peoples to "forgive and forget." Even some of the more recent and sophisticated work on reconciliation still has undertones of this.

For example, Susan Dwyer has suggested that human reconciliation is most usefully understood in terms of tensions ("tensions between two or more beliefs; tensions between two or more differing interpretations of events; or tensions between two or more apparently incommensurable sets of values") and how those tensions are countered and otherwise managed.[160] These tensions, suggests Dwyer, can cause "disruptions," which might affect an individual personally or, in the case of larger-scale disruptions, can have a significant impact on public life in a community. Dwyer contends that reconciliation is not about undoing the disruption but about finding ways to make sense of the disruption so that it does not threaten people's self-understanding and identity. Notably, this does not require forgiveness. Dwyer conceptualizes reconciliation as independent of forgiveness. The process of integrating a disruption or a new or difficult understanding into one's own story may sometimes be facilitated by an apology, atonement, and forgiveness, but these are not always necessary factors for reconciliation.[161]

Dwyer also notes that reconciliation is not the same as justice. Even when reconciliation is pursued in good faith, the process does not necessarily lead to justice. In any case, justice may be only one of a number of social and political objectives.[162]

While Dwyer distances reconciliation from forgiveness, her view of reconciliation's relationship with justice is of some concern. Dwyer suggests that coming to terms with social disruption is a process distinct from measures that might be necessary to deliver justice. My concern is that this argument implies that effective reconciliation can occur while injustices continue. I argue that a different vision of reconciliation is possible, and indeed preferable, for reconciliation between Indigenous peoples and settler polities.

Some Indigenous scholars have suggested that reconciliation is a Western concept, steeped in Christianity, and therefore should not be a primary objective of Indigenous peoples.[163] Reconciliation in this sense certainly has problematic connotations; however, Canadian political philosopher James Tully provides an account of reconciliation that creates space for both Indigenous and Western understandings. Tully's account accords with Corntassel's view that reconciliation processes need not be about restoring "an asymmetrical relationship with the state" but instead can be used to "restory our communities toward justice" through truth-telling and other Indigenous approaches to reconciliation.[164] I contend that reconciliation can be conceptualized in a way that is consistent with Indigenous perspectives of justice.

In her book *What Does Justice Look Like? The Struggle for Liberation in Dakota Homeland*, Waziyatawin provides a Dakota perspective on the steps necessary for her people to achieve justice.[165] Waziyatawin describes these four steps as 1) "Initiating an Era of Truth Telling," 2) "Taking Down the Fort," 3) "Making Reparations," and 4) "Creating an Oppression-Free Society." Truth-telling is often suggested by Indigenous scholars as a first and important step towards achieving justice vis-à-vis the settler state.[166] Similarly, Paulette Regan views truth-telling and the re-storying of public history as an important component of the process of decolonization, which is ultimately necessary if Native and non-Native peoples are to move towards reconciliation.[167] "Taking Down the Fort" is used by Waziyatawin as a metaphor for dismantling the imperial and/or colonial apparatus of the state.[168] Once truth-telling has taken place, the state ought to stop perpetuating the practices that have injured Indigenous peoples in the past and that continue to cause harm to Indigenous peoples. The next step is to make reparations and to provide redress for past wrongs.[169] The final stage is to negotiate and agree on arrangements for peaceful coexistence.[170] This entire process can be understood as a process of reconciliation, and is consistent with Tully's view of state–Indigenous relations. Tully's carefully articulated vision of reconciliation between Indigenous peoples and states such as Canada and New Zealand is founded on liberal democratic theory and takes into account Indigenous understandings of self-determination and reconciliation.

Though Tully is concerned primarily with the situation in Canada, the philosophical basis of his work is equally applicable to the New Zealand context. Tully describes two types of relationships between Indigenous peoples and the state.[171] The first is a treaty relationship in which the Indigenous nation is recognized as being self-determining and engages with the state in a nation-to-nation relationship. The Treaty of Waitangi is an expression of this type of relationship. The second type of relationship is what Tully characterizes as a colonial relationship. When a colonial relationship becomes the dominant narrative, it overwhelms the treaty relationships that exist, and even transforms the interpretation of those treaty relationships.[172] Tully's concept of reconciliation requires the rejection of the colonial relationship and the strengthening of treaty relationships.

Tully identifies five essential principles underlying the treaty relationship: mutual recognition, intercultural negotiation, mutual respect, sharing, and mutual responsibility.[173] The basic components of mutual recognition are "equality, coexistence and self-government."[174] Coexistence signifies a relationship that values political diversity and in which Indigenous peoples and settler populations retain distinctive and independent identities.[175] Such a relationship does not denote separation; Tully notes centuries of interactions between Indigenous communities and *arrivistes,* who, over time, developed shared histories and a network of intercultural relations.[176] Equality in the context of mutual recognition has two important aspects: first, that Indigenous and non-Indigenous peoples recognize each other as equal peoples who operate according to their own legal traditions; second, and crucially, that Indigenous and non-Indigenous peoples, as equals, "govern their common relations in accordance with the five principles [of the treaty relationship] on equal footing."[177] The final component of mutual recognition, self-government, is firmly rooted in liberal political theory. Tully notes that the Aboriginal peoples in Canada were clearly independent nations at the point of the initial contact with European settlers. Aboriginal peoples demonstrated their self-governing status in the same way that European peoples demonstrated their independence at international law: through exercising self-government over time within a defined territory and engaging in international relations. Tully points out that, in the modern world, these are the basic factors used to demonstrate the right to self-government.[178]

Exactly the same principle applies to the Māori iwi of Aotearoa. In fact, Tully's characterization of the process by which settler polities legitimized their presence in North America is startlingly reminiscent of the arrangements entered into in Waitangi in 1840. Tully suggests that treaty relationships reflect Indigenous peoples' recognition of the coexistence of settler communities as distinct and independent polities. According to this recognition, settlers would have the right to acquire territory and exercise self-government in the territory, and from there develop further nation-to-nation agreements.[179]

The first interactions between Indigenous peoples and settlers in Canada and in Aotearoa/New Zealand were framed by this type of treaty relationship, with its inherent mutual recognition. Since those first interactions, however, the growth of state power has enabled the state to re-frame the relationship, to superimpose a colonial relationship onto the treaty relationship. This type of relationship, based not on mutual recognition and equality but on the subordination and dependency of Indigenous peoples and Indigenous systems of governance, now affects how those first interactions are understood.[180] One central aspect of reconciliation, then, is to re-establish the treaty relationship and recognize that the legitimacy of the state depends on the consent of Indigenous peoples. This consent is conditional on the acknowledgment of Indigenous peoples' "equal yet prior status as nations."[181]

Relationships, through the process of reconciliation, must therefore be negotiated. Within the framework of a treaty relationship, those negotiations must be understood to be intercultural. As Tully notes, there is "no place for the injustice of non-Aboriginal people speaking for Aboriginal people, either in the imperial monologue of command and obedience or in the more subtle injustice of permitting Aboriginal people to speak, but only in the languages, traditions and institutions of the dominant society."[182]

Paul Nadasdy has also pointed to the difficulties that arise if reconciliation processes are not an intercultural negotiation but, rather, framed in the language of state law and the political institutions of the state government.[183] Nadasdy's account of land negotiations between Kluane First Nation and government parties in the Yukon from 1994 to 1998 illustrates the way that the colonial relationship can divert the process away from the underlying theory of reconciliation. Nadasdy suggests that asymmetrical power relationships in these negotiations resulted in the process being re-framed as one in which the government parties were giving land to the First Nation as opposed to one which recognized the First Nation's authority to determine which lands it ceded to federal and territorial governments. This further reinforced the power imbalance by focusing on the authority and control exercised by the government parties.[184]

If the relationship between Indigenous peoples and the state is to be a treaty relationship rather than a colonial one, negotiations between the parties must be genuinely intercultural. In this way, a dialogue takes place in an intercultural middle ground. Tully warns that this middle ground is not perfect, that it still contains inequalities, power imbalances, distrust, and other things that make dialogue and negotiation difficult. But despite its flaws and distortions, Tully argues, the middle ground is "a starting ground for a new dialogue of equality."[185] It is a space that has been constructed and tested over centuries by the many sites of positive interaction between Indigenous and non-Indigenous peoples. It may not be perfect, but there is no perfect space for the negotiation of reconciliation between Indigenous peoples and settler states.[186]

Tully also suggests that the process of reconciliation requires a form of mutual cultural respect.[187] It is only with this respect of peoples and cultures that mutual recognition of distinctive and equal legal orders and systems of governance can occur. Tully points out that a fundamental ethic of respect underlies Western political philosophy as well as the political philosophy of North America's Aboriginal peoples. The parallel with Māori philosophical perspectives is relatively straightforward: the concept of mana incorporates a similar ethic of respect for the inherent dignity of all people. Not only is this culture of respect deeply rooted in both Western and Indigenous philosophies, but there are significant advantages to fostering a public attitude of mutual cultural respect. Tully argues that there are two major benefits. First, mutual cultural respect is empowering for the parties involved: it engenders an environment in which communities are able to "live free and responsible lives." A further benefit to all citizens comes from living and participating in a vibrant and diverse society.[188]

The fourth principle that Tully sees as undergirding a treaty relationship is a principle of sharing.[189] Again, Tully notes that this principle is consistent with both Indigenous and Western philosophical foundations.[190] Similar ideas can be identified within tikanga, especially in relation to the concept of manaakitanga (nurturing relationships). A necessary part of the reconciliation process will be the return of lands and resources that were unjustly taken from Indigenous peoples. As an "act of reciprocal justice," mutually agreeable policies must be implemented in order to address the social and economic inequalities experienced by Indigenous peoples.[191] Indigenous peoples may be willing to accept alternative remedies, as long as there is recognition that lands were unjustly taken and the option of land returns has not been taken off the table. In Aotearoa/New Zealand, the ongoing presence of a settler population was clearly anticipated by those who signed the Treaty of Waitangi. Another important dimension of sharing in the context of reconciliation is "a just means of sharing legal and political powers."[192] For the sharing of legal and political power to be just, argues Tully, the exercise of legal and political power must be based on the principles that underlie the treaty relationship – "intercultural dialogue, negotiation between equals, based on mutual consent, recorded in treaty-like agreements, and open to review and amendment in the future."[193]

The final principle of the treaty relationship is mutual responsibility, where "the partners act responsibly towards one another and towards the habitat they share."[194] Mutual responsibility is also embedded in the fundamental tikanga principles of whanaungatanga and manaakitanga.

There are significant similarities between the principles that Tully identifies as necessary for a treaty relationship and the principles of the Treaty of Waitangi as articulated by the Waitangi Tribunal and the courts. Though there is no definitive list of the principles of the Treaty of Waitangi, the principle of partnership is well established and can perhaps be seen as a central concept from which other key principles flow. The New Zealand Court of Appeal has found that the Treaty of Waitangi established a relationship between Māori and the Crown that is akin to a partnership, the characteristic obligation of which is that each party must act towards the other with utmost good faith.[195] In a subsequent decision, the president of the Court of Appeal described this principle of partnership as "each party accepting a positive duty to act in good faith, fairly, reasonably, and honourably towards the other."[196] The Waitangi Tribunal has also identified principles of reciprocity and mutual benefit as part of the principle of partnership. Building on these principles, the tribunal states in its *Te Whānau o Waipareira Report,* "Partnership thus serves to describe a relationship where one party is not subordinate to the other but where each must respect the other's status and authority in all walks of life."[197]

The principles of the Treaty of Waitangi that have been identified and constructed through legal processes in Aotearoa/New Zealand incorporate key elements of Tully's principles of mutual recognition, intercultural negotiation, mutual respect, sharing, and mutual responsibility. It is therefore appropriate to consider those principles of reconciliation that are articulated by Tully in our discussion of the Treaty of Waitangi settlement process and its implications for Māori legal traditions.

Conclusion

My research is framed by the broad themes of Indigenous legal theory, as articulated by Gordon Christie and other Indigenous scholars, a discourse that is closely connected to critical Indigenous methodologies such as Kaupapa Māori research. In particular, Indigenous legal theory, like Kaupapa Māori research, places great importance on using conceptual tools that derive from Indigenous worldviews – though this does not mean that the use of non-Indigenous conceptual tools is necessarily inconsistent with Indigenous legal theory. Throughout the book, I employ conceptual and theoretical tools from both Māori legal philosophy and legal pluralism. Using this theoretical framework grounds the research in the lived experiences of Māori communities.

This chapter has also set this research in relation to discourses on tino rangatiratanga and self-determination, and reconciliation. This discussion provides the foundation for an analysis of the effects of the Treaty of Waitangi claims settlement process on Māori legal traditions.

3

Māori Law Today

KAHUNGUNU AND RONGOMAIWAHINE

"Pāpā, lots of our stories are about rangatira, people who are chiefs or leaders, aren't they?"

"Ae, I suppose they are, e Tama."

"Tamatea was a rangatira, wasn't he?"

"Yes, he was a very great rangatira."

"And Kahungunu? Our iwi is named after him, so he must have been a great rangatira too, eh?"

"Yes, that's right."

"Pāpā, how does someone get to be a rangatira? Do they have to fight someone else to show how strong they are?"

"There are many ways you can show you have the qualities of a rangatira. Sometimes our leaders were great warriors, that is true, but that is not the only way to show strength and leadership. Our tipuna Kahungunu, for example, was well known for being able to provide food for our people. That was partly how he convinced Rongomaiwahine's people that he was worthy of marrying her."

"Was Rongomaiwahine a rangatira too?"

"Yes. She was directly descended from Ruawharo of the waka Takitimu and also Popoto, the commander of the waka Kurahaupo. So she had whakapapa connections to the important rangatira of both those waka. Her beauty, strength of character, and nobility were known throughout the island."

"Why do we call ourselves Ngāti Kahungunu then and not Ngāti Rongomaiwahine?"

"The people of Mahia keep the name of Ngāti Rongomaiwahine. They are descendants of Rongomaiwahine's daughters, Rapuaiterangi and Hinerauiri. These two daughters were not the children of Kahungunu. Their father was Rongomaiwahine's first husband, Tamatakutai. But, even though we use the name Ngāti Kahungunu for our iwi, we still remember the rangatiratanga of Rongomaiwahine. It is her mana that was so important in establishing the authority of our people in this part of the country. Because while Kahungungu was born and raised up north, only settling here as an adult, Rongomaiwahine lived here all her life."

"But what was so great about Kahungunu? Why did Rongomaiwahine want to marry him? How did he get to be a rangatira?"

"Well, he was from a very famous family, too. And he was said to be very handsome, though Rongomaiwahine was not impressed by all the talk of what a fine man he was. He really had to show Rongomaiwahine and her people how skilled he was at gathering food. In those days, being able to provide for your people was a prized skill for a rangatira."

"So, what did he do?"

"Well, to begin with he gathered up huge quantities of fern root. It is said that he gathered so much that when he tied it together in bundles and rolled the bundles down the hill to the village, they piled up and blocked the doors to the houses."

"Whoah!"

"But that wasn't all. He also gathered huge quantities of the shellfish we call pāua. More than anyone else could."

"How did he do that?"

"He closely watched the shags diving for shellfish and counted to see how long they were under the water. Then he dived for the shellfish, holding his breath as long as the seabirds had done. He filled baskets of shellfish – enough for the whole village. And when he came up from his last dive he had covered his whole body with shellfish! Rongomaiwahine's people were again greatly impressed with his talent and his generosity."

"Is that why carvings of Kahungunu often have pāua shells on them?"

"Yes, that's right, e Tama. Although there is another story about Kahungunu and pāua, but I'll tell you that one another time."

Māori Legal Traditions

The story of Kahungunu and Rongomaiwahine illustrates a number of key values in Māori society. In particular, it shows that there are different types of leadership in Māori communities; being able to provide for the wellbeing of a community can be at least as important a leadership quality as exhibiting skill in battle, for example. The importance of caring for others, the value of kin relationships, and the motivating force of mana and status are also all evident from the narrative. This chapter provides a more detailed analysis of the foundational concepts of Māori legal traditions within the context of the wider system of tikanga. My aim is to identify and explain the legal framework that produces and maintains Māori law. Understanding this framework enables us to perceive how Māori legal traditions influence the legislative and treaty settlement processes, and in turn how those traditions are influenced by iwi and hapū engagement with the legal and constitutional machinery of the state.

The five central concepts underlying Māori philosophy have already been identified. These are:

- *whanaungatanga* – the centrality of relationships to Māori life
- *mana* – the importance of spiritually sanctioned authority and the limits on Māori leadership
- *tapu/noa* – respect for the spiritual character of all things
- *utu* – the principle of balance and reciprocity, and
- *manaakitanga* – nurturing relationships, looking after people, and being very careful about how others are treated.

Whanaungatanga – Relationships

Relationships are central to Māori society. They define rights and obligations between:

- individuals
- communities
- the individual and the collective
- past, present, and future generations
- people and *atua* (gods), and
- people and the natural world.

Relationships are thus also central to Māori legal traditions; Māori legal traditions should be understood through this relational lens.[1] How relationships are formed, maintained, changed, and dissolved are all key concerns of Māori legal traditions.

Some general observations can be made about how Māori legal traditions operate in order to illustrate how they prioritize the maintenance of relationships. For example, there is significant flexibility in the application of Māori legal traditions. Although precedents and past actions are important sources of Māori law, precedent within Māori law is used to identify important values rather than to suggest rules to follow when a particular set of facts arises. It has been observed that narratives of past behaviour, proverbs, and other sources of Māori law come together as an ethical system that "provides a wide and rich range of traditional focal points, and leaves it to the good sense and mana of those involved to arrive at reasonable solutions to their problems."[2] This approach results in a flexibility that differs from that within the common law. While the common law can adapt to changing socio-cultural values,[3] the practice of interpreting and applying established legal rules in light of current legal principles and models of justice (perhaps informed by human rights considerations)[4] is quite different from identifying the values of the ancestors and determining how to best express those values. Mead explains the role that precedent plays in determining the appropriate tikanga for a *tangihanga* (funeral) ceremony.[5] In some circumstances, one must recognize that the practice of tikanga may not always be a perfect expression of the values that underlie that tikanga.[6] While precedent is an important reference point, it is only part of the framework for interpreting and applying tikanga. In the case of the tangihanga ceremony, the tikanga applied and practiced is derived from background knowledge of the community (including past practice, but also knowledge of the broader history of the community and its environment), concepts of death and relationships with the spirit world, and wider principles and values that govern Māori life.[7] This approach allows for significant variation and flexibility in the tikanga of the ceremony. The flexibility of Māori law allows various factors to be weighted differently in determining the correct course of action in a given situation. In this way, relationships can be, and often are, prioritised.[8]

Processes for making legal decisions also reflect an emphasis on relationships. The relatively limited executive authority granted to leaders within Māori society requires that relationships among members of the community be constantly maintained and nurtured. Law-making and dispute resolution are undertaken with consideration of how relationships will be affected by both the process and the substantive outcome.[9] An analysis of Māori legal traditions must consider how those traditions structure relationships and what outcomes they prescribe for the apportionment of rights and obligations within those relationships.

The concept of whanaungatanga encapsulates the centrality of relationships within Māori legal traditions. Margaret Mutu, a professor of Māori studies at Auckland University, has described whanaungtanga as "[o]ne of the most fundamental values that holds any Māori community together."[10] Grounded in genealogical connections, whanaungatanga is central to individual and community identity and the rights and obligations associated with that identity.[11]

The importance of relationships in terms of identity, rights, and obligations is also evident in the story Māui's reunion with his family.[12] Māui had been abandoned at birth and was raised by one of his ancestors. When he returns to his mother and brothers many years later, he asserts his identity; his mother does not believe him until he recites the genealogical connections (whakapapa) that he had heard while in the womb. The story illustrates how important kinship connections are in establishing relationships, rights, and duties.[13]

The concept of whanaungatanga may be grounded in genealogical connections, but today the term is applied to other types of relationships where reciprocal obligations apply. Eminent anthropologist Dame Joan Metge has described how the root concept of *whānau* (extended family) has acquired new meaning over the course of the twentieth century: it is now widely applied to various types of communities and groups and no longer only to those with actual blood ties.[14]

The changing nature of whānau and whanaungatanga is an example of how expressions of fundamental elements of tikanga change and adapt to new environmental challenges.[15] Metge notes that the term whānau now has many meanings, traditional as well as more recent. For most Māori, the traditional understanding of whānau – a group defined by descent – is still primary. However, the term is now commonly used to extrapolate from, or extend, the primary meaning to include the collective relationships involved in non-kin groupings.[16] Evidence given in the Waitangi tribunal supports this understanding of whānau and whanaungatanga. Heitia Hiha emphasized the importance of kinship, marriage, and other relationships in describing the whanaungatanga of various hapū of Ngāti Kahungunu.[17]

A separate Waitangi tribunal inquiry related to the operation of an urban Māori organization, members of which were not all linked by genealogical connections. The organization, however, had adopted the name Te Whānau o Waipareira Trust. During the course of the Waitangi Tribunal inquiry, one member of Te Whānau o Waipareira explained that the organization had chosen to use "whānau" in its name in order to reflect the way members of the organization act towards each other, the existence of a common set of values, and the desire to act for the collective good in a uniform way, albeit in an environment that differs from that in which traditional whānau operates.[18]

Mana – Authority

Mana is the central concept underlying Māori leadership and accountability. It embodies spiritually sanctioned authority as well as democratically sanctioned authority. Māori scholar and theologian Māori Marsden has suggested that there are two related aspects of the spiritual dimension of mana.[19] First, there is a delegation of authority from the gods. Second, the gods imbue their human agents with the spiritual power to exercise that authority. The concept of mana also includes notions of influence, prestige, power, force, and vitality. The term dervies from an ancient Oceanic concept of mana used to describe supernatural power.[20] A description of the concept in the context of rights and obligations in relation to the Mohaka River is set out in evidence given by members of the Ngāti Pahauwera nation in their Waitangi Tribunal claim.[21] This evidence described the control of the river as "our mana from way back." Witnesses noted that this authority had been passed down from ancestors over many generations and that the essential element of the mana of Ngāti Pahauwera is the fact that it comes from the river itself. Thus, their mana is bound up in the joint history of the community and the river, and is reflected in the central role the river has in the identity of the people.

There are many different types of mana. Māori linguist Margaret Mutu has categorised the different types of mana that she has identified as relevant to her people, Te Whanau Moana: mana atua, mana tupuna, mana whenua, mana tangata, and mana moana.[22] *Mana atua* is the authority that derives from the gods. *Mana tupuna* is that authority that comes from one's whakapapa and is passed down from one's ancestors. *Mana whenua* is the authority sourced in the land itself. A community that maintains its connection to the land through occupation and the exercise of rights and obligations in respect of the land might be said to hold, or even to be, the mana whenua. *Mana tangata* is the status, power, and authority that one achieves through one's own actions that demonstrate expertise, wisdom, or other leadership qualities. *Mana moana* is authority that derives from and may be exercised in relation to the ocean. It is effectively the marine equivalent of mana whenua.

The different types of mana are extremely important for maintaining a relatively low level of executive authority among Māori leaders and a relatively high level of accountability of the leader to the community. In particular, the concept of mana tangata requires that leaders must continually demonstrate the qualities of leadership; their position as leader can never be taken for granted. Traditionally, Māori leaders did not command obedience but instead led by persuasion. Many Indigenous peoples of North America have similarly decentralized structures of leadership and authority.[23] This structure not only affects the substance of decisions made but also means that the decision-making process must be one that the people feel has legitimacy and provides the opportunity for their voice to be heard.[24] Eddie Taihakurei Durie has pointed out that mana is therefore both ascribed and achieved.[25] Durie notes that mana tupuna reflects the idea that all things are passed down from the ancestors. This is consistent with the Māori philosophy, which has whanaungatanga at its centre. However, Durie suggests that the attribution of mana often includes a retrospective aspect. For example, it might be cast in the following terms: "he is brave, caring, etc. for he is the descendant of so and so."

Anthropologist Elsdon Best has described what this meant for the practical operation of Māori leadership.[26] That is, one's lineage was important in terms of authority and leadership, but much depended on a leader's personal attributes and abilities. Demonstrating leadership ability might increase one's influence. On the other hand, failure to uphold the standards of leadership lessened one's mana and, along with it, one's authority and influence.

The demi-god Māui was the archetype of the Māori leader who established his position through ability, irrespective of position in the family. Māui was the youngest of five brothers; the expectation would have been that his elder brothers would take up positions of leadership ahead of him. However, Māui showed resourcefulness, imagination, and creativity, demonstrating that he was a much more capable leader than his brothers. Consequently, the elders identified him as someone worthy or receiving special knowledge and expertise; by his actions Māui takes on important leadership roles. The Māui story cycle reminds us that, no matter one's family position, mana and the authority to lead can be determined by one's own actions and abilities.[27]

Closely connected to mana, the concept of rangatiratanga is also of central importance in Māori understandings of leadership and authority.

The term has particular resonance in the context of the Treaty of Waitangi because of the guarantee of tino rangatiratanga, noted above.[28] Hugh Kawharu's modern English translation of the Māori text of the Treaty of Waitangi is referenced frequently. He translates the guarantee of tino rangatiratanga as "unqualified exercise of [Māori] chieftainship."[29] Kawharu has also suggested how rangatiratanga would have been understood by Māori in 1840 at the signing of the Treaty of Waitangi, identifying twin criteria as evidence of chiefly status: "breeding and greatness."[30] This reflects the importance of the different strands of mana. A rangatira would be expected to demonstrate through his or her actions that he or she is exercising spiritually sanctioned power authority.

The various strands of mana inherently limit the authority of rangatira. Māori politician Shane Jones has noted that the authority of the rangatira is subject to internal constraints.[31] Power and authority is granted for the purpose of benefiting the community. A leader who exercises power selfishly or in an unprincipled manner is effectively acting beyond the scope of the power granted to them. Rangatiratanga then can be seen as reflecting the autonomy and self-determination of the community itself rather than the absolute authority of an individual leader.[32]

Manaakitanga and Kaitiakitanga – Nurturing and Stewardship

Manaakitanga and kaitiakitanga reflect the importance of nurturing and the responsibility of looking after those in your care. They are distinct concepts – kaitiakitanga embodies the ethic of stewardship and guardianship (particularly in relation to the natural environment), whereas manaakitanga encompasses selflessness and generosity and is often used to express the type of responsibilities that a host has to his or her guest. When identifying the fundamental conceptual regulators that underpin tikanga, some scholars view manaakitanga as the primary value, while others view kaitiakitanga in this way instead. Though closely connected, the terms are not synonymous. Their distinct elements are particularly relevant to a consideration of tikanga in the twenty-first century.

Manaakitanga derives from the word *manaaki*, which itself is formed from mana and *aki*, a proto-Polynesian word which at one time conveyed the meaning of "reciprocal action," although it is no longer used this way in modern Māori. This suggests that "the giving and acceptance of kindness and hospitality bestows mana on both host and guest."[33]

Hirini Mead has explained how key principles of manaakitanga have remained relevant in contemporary Māori life.[34] Mead suggests that all Māori practices and protocols are based upon being careful about how others are treated and how relationships are nurtured. According to Mead, manaakitanga is always important, no matter what the circumstances might be.[35]

The importance of manaakitanga can also be seen in the Māui story cycle. In a number of narratives, Māui builds close relationships with various ancestors. Although he sometimes exhibits deceitfulness and a trickster's nature,[36] Māui initially builds these relationships on a basis of trust, respect, and manaakitanga. Reciprocal relationships are established, in which Māui provides care and support for his elders and, importantly, demonstrates his intelligence and ability. His ancestors in turn support Māui and, recognizing his ability, identify him as someone to whom they can pass on sacred knowledge and powerful and magical objects and tools. Māui is then able to achieve fantastic feats because of what he has gained from the reciprocal relationships that were built upon manaakitanga.[37]

The current meaning of "kaitiakitanga" has recent origins, even though the root word, *kaitiaki* (guardian), is clearly a traditional concept with a long history. Kaitiakitanga has become a key term in environmental law, used to express Māori interest in resource management decisions.

Early documented uses of the term suggest that a kaitiaki commonly took the form of an ancestor, an animal, or even a supernatural being rather than a living individual. A letter to the editor of a Māori newspaper at the turn of the twentieth century referred to the kaitiaki of the headland at Te Uruti. In this context, kaitiaki referred to the guardians of the headland, who took the form of tipua [supernatural beings]: "I still live on that headland now ... The *tipua* which live on the outskirts of Uruti are *kaitiaki* [guardians] that descend from crayfish, they are called Turuawahine, they are female and are ancestors of Ngai-Teao [the local people], I am their descedant."[38]

In 1903, writer and historian James Cowan recounted an earlier interview with the prominent Māori leader Te Heuheu, in which Te Heuheu describes an *atua* (god) as his kaitiaki.[39] Te Heuheu's personal identity is connected to this particular atua, named Rongomai. According to Te Heuheu, Rongomai appeared to him in the form of a star and acted as his kaitiaki, or guardian.

Māori Marsden, who later provided scholarship on the application of the concept of kaitiakitanga to resource management law, described the concept of a kaitiaki in terms of ancient spiritual beings who were directly descended from Ranginui (the sky father) and Papatuanuku (the earth mother).[40] These ancient ones were responsible for looking after various aspects of the natural world. Various rituals were, and to some extent still are, employed to access the resources over which these kaitiaki have oversight.

More recently, the term "kaitiakitanga" has taken on a specific statutory meaning through its use in the *Resource Management Act* (1991). The details of this legislation are not relevant to the present discussion, but it should be noted that the *Resource Management Act* was a major consolidation and, to some extent, a restructuring of environmental and planning law in New Zealand. The act requires that all those who exercise powers and functions under the legislation must have particular regard to a number of matters, one of which is kaitiakitanga. The statutory meaning of kaitiakitanga is "the exercise of guardianship by the tangata whenua [local people, literally "people of the land"] of an area in accordance with tikanga Māori ["Māori law and practice"] in relation to natural and physical resources; and includes the ethic of stewardship."[41]

The Waitangi Tribunal's recent report, *Ko Aotearoa Tēnei* (This Is Aotearoa/ New Zealand), uses the concept of kaitiakitanga to underpin its analysis of the range of law and policy affecting Māori culture and identity. The Tribunal suggests that kaitiakitanga is "an intergenerational obligation that arises by virtue of kin relationship."[42] This kin relationship may be between people or between people and natural resources; it supplements the idea of guardianship with "a core spiritual dimension that animates the concept."[43] The close connection between kaitiakitanga and concepts such as mana and rangatiratanga is illustrated in the Waitangi Tribunal's report. The tribunal notes that in the modern context, people who exercise mana must do so in accordance with the values of kaitiakitanga. The tribunal takes the view that mana and kaitiakitanga "go together as right and responsibility."[44]

Margaret Mutu also sees a strong connection between mana and kaitiakitanga. Her description of kaitiakitanga also reflects how this ethic of guardianship has its roots in the natural and spiritual world but, in a contemporary context at least, imposes obligations on present-day generations.[45] Mutu has identified that kaitiaki were traditionally spiritual beings. All aspects of the natural world would have such a spiritual assistant: "Each kaitiaki is imbued with mana ... There are many forms and aspects of mana, of which one is the power to sustain life."[46]

In specific terms, each whānau or hapū is kaitiaki for the area in which they hold mana whenua, that is, their ancestral lands and seas. Should they fail to carry out their kaitiakitanga duties adequately, not only will mana be removed but harm will come to the members of the whānau and hapū.

Tapu and Noa – Recognition of the Spiritual Dimension

Tapu and noa are complementary opposites, and both are central to the operation of Māori legal traditions. The concept of tapu recognizes the spiritual quality of all things and the associated restrictions and regulations that relate to the spiritual dimension. Noa suggests a freedom from such restrictions and regulations and is often used in the context of processes that normalize or make safe any interactions with elements that would otherwise be restricted. Settlers and anthropologists have often identified tapu as the key mechanism of Māori law, though tapu has religious and socio-political dimensions as well as strictly legal ones. Māori Marsden has described the concept as having both religious and legal aspects.[47] When tapu is invoked, it expresses the idea that a person or thing is dedicated to a particular deity. The person or thing is therefore set aside in the sense that it now occupies a sacred state. Marsden suggests that this could be seen as akin to the individual or thing having a contractual relationship with the *atua* (deity) in the sense of being set aside for the service of the atua in exchange for protection and the power to exercise rights and obligations in relation to specific aspects of the natural world.

The importance of the concept of noa in relation to tapu is explained by Hirini Moko Mead,[48] who notes that the concept of noa often refers to restoring balance or returning to a normal, everyday state. Mead cautions that noa should not be seen as the absence of tapu. For example, visitors to a *marae* (traditional community space) are highly tapu. Much of the purpose of the welcome ceremony is to manage the tapu of the visitors in the environment of the marae so that there can be normal, safe interactions. The inherent tapu of the person is not removed; however, potentially dangerous, high levels of tapu are managed. The same thinking applies to a person who is very ill or bleeding. While the symptoms exist, the person must be treated carefully because of a high level of tapu. When the symptoms have ceased, the person returns to a normal state, but still has a level of personal tapu.

Similarly, Ani Mikaere emphasises the role of noa,[49] contending that the ability to remove restrictions is just as important as the ability to impose them. In that sense, noa is as important a mechanism of social control as tapu. Mikaere notes that, for most people, everyday activities require the negotiation and management of situations and things that are either more tapu or more noa.

In *Economics of the New Zealand Māori,* Raymond Firth addresses the multi-dimensional nature of tapu.[50] He notes that it is unhelpful to try to distinguish or separate the conceptualisation of tapu as sacred from the idea that it is something "unclean." Both aspects are part of a single concept in the sense that both require the person or thing that is tapu to be set aside in some way, and for interactions with the tapu person or thing to be restricted and highly regulated. If the appropriate procedures are not undertaken to manage the tapu, or the restrictions are not observed, then some harm is believed to follow as a consequence.

Both the spiritual and more instrumental aspects of tapu are illustrated in the story of how Māui met his father. According to this story, Māui found his father by secretly following his mother, turning himself into a bird to disguise himself. When Māui identifies himself to his father, his father performs a blessing for Māui, but makes a mistake in the ceremony, which eventually has profound consequences for Māui.

There are two points of engagement with tapu and the spiritual dimension in the narrative. The first is when Māui uses a *karakia* (prayer or incantation) to turn himself into a bird. Although Māui is here clearly calling upon supernatural forces, he does so for quite a functional purpose. This reflects the fact that the existence and management of tapu is an ordinary and instrumental aspect of dealing with the spiritual dimension of all things in the natural world.

The second point of engagement with tapu illustrates the consequences of a breach of tapu. When one engages with spiritual matters, it is important to ensure that the proper rituals and processes are completed. In this instance, Māui's father does not complete the relevant ceremony correctly. This mistake has severe ramifications and costs Māui his immortality. As noted in *Hinatore ki te Ao Māori,* ceremonial processes and rituals must be conducted correctly and incantations recited accurately.[51] A mistake in such ceremonies would result in misfortune.

Tapu and noa still play a central role in the maintenance of Māori legal traditions. They provide a key motivation for obedience to laws; the perceived consequences of breaching tapu act as an enforcement mechanism.[52]

Utu – Reciprocity

Utu embodies the basic principle of reciprocity underlying the operation of all Māori legal traditions. It is perhaps most readily evident in cases of warfare, which has no doubt led to an emphasis on ideas of "revenge" when the term is translated into English. Yet the principle is also evident in economic transactions and the processes of gift-exchange, indicating that a definition that focuses on revenge is both "reductive and misleading."[53] The concept of utu relates more broadly to maintaining balance and, as Mead has pointed out, reflects the emphasis on whanaungatanga and the centrality of relationships within Māori legal traditions.[54] Mead suggests a basic three-stage framework that illustrates the motivating factors that underpin Māori legal traditions. This framework can be referred to as *take-utu-ea.* A *take* is the reason for action, something that has taken place and which, according to Māori legal traditions, requires a response. It can be thought of as a cause of action. *Utu,* the principle of balance and reciprocity, then determines what action is necessary to restore the balance and the relationships involved. Once the appropriate action has been completed, a state of resolution is reached and balance is restored. This state of resolution is called *ea.*

Other scholars have also noted the central importance of utu in the operation of Māori legal traditions. Joan Metge describes it as "one of the most important ordering principles in traditional Māori society."[55] Pākehā philosopher John Patterson has pointed to parallels between the concept of utu and Western concepts of punishment, but has suggested that the differences between the two concepts are significant.[56] Patterson notes that the key objective of utu is the restoration of balance, particularly a restoration of balance where mana has been lost. Where punishment is generally unpleasant or at least unwanted, utu need not be, and in some instances may be welcomed. Punishment can also be forgone, but utu cannot.

Utu is about restoring balance – not only by reciprocating the presentation of "good" gifts (food stuffs, items of clothing, tools, luxury items) but also by responding to "bad" gifts (insults, thefts, other offences).[57] Hirini Mead notes that there is not necessarily a single way of responding to a gift (good or bad) but that an assessment made according to Māori legal traditions will dictate the response in a given situation. The process of *muru* (ritualized confiscation) is one model for restoring balance. Historically, gifts of land were made by communities to their allies in order to acknowledge their services in war.[58] Mead suggests a number of questions that may be relevant to ask in order to determine an appropriate form of utu when a breach has occurred, including:[59]

- Who is implicated in the breach?
- What was the reason for the breach? Was harm intended? Or was the intention to benefit people?
- Did those responsible for the breach assess the likely effects on others before taking action?

The goal is to reach a state of resolution, where relationships are restored. Determining the course of action necessary to restore relationships will also include reference to the nature of the particular relationships at stake, the mana of those involved, the seriousness of any breach of tapu, and any precedent or past practice.[60] The appropriate response for a breach involving close kin will likely differ from a response for the same offence committed by a distant relative. One's own mana is affected by the mana of one's kin and, therefore, to impose severe penalties on close kin may also negatively affect the mana of the injured party, and consequently do little to restore balance. Historian Angela Ballara recounts an incident from the mid-nineteenth century involving several close relatives from the hapū of Ngāti Uru. In this incident, Te Puhi of

Whangaroa shot and killed a relative named Mahue. The nephew of both Te Puhi and Mahue, Young Te Puhi, took up a musket intending to kill the senior Te Puhi in retaliation for the murder but was persuaded by his relatives not to do so. Three days later, a party of 200–300 men came from a nearby settlement to punish the senior Te Puhi. They stripped the crops of Te Puhi's settlement, took two of Te Puhi's slaves, and killed another slave. Ballara notes that the killing of Mahue by a close kinsman was an aberration; if Mahue had not been a close relative of the senior Te Puhi, "matters would have been much more serious; war would have been inevitable."[61]

Māori Legal Traditions Today

Tikanga Māori has remained a dynamic mechanism of social regulation and has had a transformative impact on the regulation of New Zealand public life. It has done so in a number of important ways, chiefly through law, ritual, and dynamic Māori engagement with state processes.

While Māori legal traditions thus can be seen as part of the legal framework that regulates New Zealand society, their role is complex and has experienced ebbs and flows with changing social, environmental, and political circumstances. However, Māori legal systems are not simply passive recipients of these social changes. Like all legal cultures, Māori law both influences and is influenced by the society in which it operates. Competing pressures on the Māori legal order produce creative tensions, which in turn lead to change within that legal order. Such change is rarely straightforward. By considering the three broad tensions introduced earlier in this volume – adaptation (self-determined change versus reactive change); relationship with the Crown or treaty partner (engagement versus disengagement with the state legal system); and renewal (reinvigorating tikanga versus losing relevance) – we will achieve a more complete understanding of the contemporary state of Māori legal traditions and the role they play in New Zealand public life.

This section provides three brief examples to illustrate the range of situations in contemporary New Zealand society in which tikanga serves as an effective regulatory force. First, it can be effective in circumstances where the state legal system recognizes and enforces customary law. Second, it is the key mechanism of social regulation in Māori settings. For example, the traditional welcome ceremony, the *pōwhiri,* is a distinctly Māori process, usually carried out in a distinctly Māori space, and is governed by tikanga. Third, tikanga also guides Māori behaviour in some non-Māori settings.

Māori legal traditions have limited recognition in the New Zealand state legal system. There is also some statutory incorporation of aspects of Māori customary law, and customary law also has relevance to the modern application of the doctrine of Aboriginal or Native title.[62] There is a body of authority that indicates that the rules of Māori customary law form a part of the New Zealand common law.[63] Richard Boast has explained the process by which Māori customary law can be recognized, a process similar to the process by which foreign law can be recognized. The existence of the custom must be proved as a matter of fact (usually based on the evidence of appropriately qualified experts).[64] The New Zealand Law Commission has also produced a study paper that addresses the role of Māori customary law and values within the state legal system.[65] That report considers a range of ways in which Māori legal traditions contribute to the regulation of New Zealand public life. In particular, the study paper points to examples where Māori customary concepts and legal traditions are relevant to family law and matters relating to land and resource management.[66] Although Māori customary adoption is not legally recognized for the purpose of adoption law, the practice is still relatively common among Māori and can be recognized by the Māori Land Court for the purposes of determining a person's entitlement to succeed to Māori land interests.[67] Māori customary values have also been taken into account in custody disputes and family protection cases.[68] Māori customary values are also explicitly referred to in the *Resource Management Act* (1991). As noted above, anyone who exercises powers or functions under that act is required to "have particular regard to" kaitiakitanga.[69] Nevertheless, Māori legal traditions have a limited and constrained role within the state legal system, largely because the colonial relationship that has been established does not require that they be granted any more substantial recognition. The recent New Zealand Court of Appeal decision *Takamore v Clarke* illustrates both the willingness of the New Zealand courts to take account of Māori customary law and also the limitations of the recognition of tikanga in the courts.[70] In this case, James Takamore, a man of Māori descent, had died; a number of his Māori relatives had removed his body to be buried on his ancestral land, against the wishes of the executor. Two of the three judges in the Court of Appeal found that, although taking the body without the permission of the executor could not be recognized by the common law, the common law in New Zealand had developed to a point that Māori customs relating to burial, where relevant, must be taken into account by the executor. The New Zealand Supreme Court subsequently heard an appeal of the Court of Appeal decision.[71] The Supreme Court adopted slightly different reasoning, but did not directly overrule the lower court's reasoning or decision and upheld the result.

Māori legal traditions provide a more significant contribution to the regulation of New Zealand society through other mechanisms and in other contexts, however. The pōwhiri, or welcome ceremony, provides a useful insight into how "conceptual regulators" govern interactions within Māori legal systems. The pōwhiri is a common ceremony, primarily used to welcome guests.[72] Although important occasions may require that the ceremony take place on a grand scale, the key elements of the pōwhiri can be seen in a range of essentially everyday situations. A pōwhiri may be used to welcome delegates to a conference, or to welcome a new staff member to the workplace. A pōwhiri may also be used to welcome groups to public events such as graduation ceremonies, or to community events such as celebrations or funerals. In short, whenever a Māori community is required to greet and host visitors, a pōwhiri ceremony is likely to set the framework for the management of the relationships between hosts and guests. The ubiquitous nature of the pōwhiri is relevant to this discussion for two reasons. First, it indicates the relatively wide scope of the continuing influence of Māori legal traditions on the regulation of New Zealand society. Second, it reinforces the centrality of relationships within the Māori legal order. The widespread practice of the pōwhiri ceremony suggests that establishing an appropriate framework for interaction is of fundamental importance to Māori individuals and communities.[73]

The pōwhiri process reflects other important principles of the Māori legal order. The dual concepts of tapu and noa underlie many of the practices of the pōwhiri. The primary objective of the pōwhiri is to transition gradually from a state that is highly sacred and formal to one in which the interactions between hosts and visitors have been normalised.[74] Once the transition is complete, it can be said that a state of ea has been reached, where balance has been achieved because the correct protocols have been followed and all obligations fulfilled. This brings to mind the two key values of utu (relating to the imperative to seek balance and redress imbalance) and manaakitanga (relating to the obligations to care for others).

The final sections of this chapter focuses on two examples that illustrate the application of Māori legal traditions in non-Māori settings – the constitution of a political party and a "tikanga-based dispute resolution" process designed to facilitate the settlement of a significant group of Māori claims against the Crown.

Māori Party Constitution

The Māori Party was established in 2004; its establishment reflects the three tensions in Māori legal history identified above. The catalyst for the formation of the political party was the then government's determination to enact the *Foreshore and Seabed Act,* which many Māori saw as discriminatory and a confiscation of property rights in the foreshore area. This led to the resignation of a cabinet minister from both her government seat and the Labour Party. Eventually, she became the leader of the Māori Party in Parliament. The impetus for the party's formation can be seen as directly connected to a Māori assertion of self-determination. From its establishment, the party aimed to provide an independent and authentic Māori voice within the national Parliament, highlighting the carefully balanced relationship with the state legal system. The party founders have deliberately constructed a constitution that uses those aspects of tikanga that they determined to be relevant to the operation of a political party in the twenty-first century.

The Māori Party constitution recognizes that a distinctive Māori worldview is expressed through Māori songs, legends, prayers, proverbs, and other art forms that reproduce, transmit, and develop Māori culture. This worldview leads to a particular set of *kaupapa* ("principles, values, and philosophies"). These reflect the core values underlying the system of tikanga. In the context of the Māori Party's constitution, tikanga comprises the "processes and policies aligned to the kaupapa." The first kaupapa and associated set of tikanga in the constitution is manaakitanga.[75]

MANAAKITANGA

> Manaakitanga is behaviour that acknowledges the mana of others as having equal or greater importance than one's own, through the expression of aroha, hospitality, generosity and mutual respect. In doing so, all parties are elevated and our status is enhanced, building unity through humility and the act of giving. The Party must endeavour to express manaakitanga towards others, be they political allies or opponents, Māori and non-Māori organisations, taking care not to trample Mana, while clearly defining our own.

Tikanga of the Māori Party derived from Manaakitanga

1. to be recognized by Māori as a political organization that does manaaki the aspirations of Māori

2. to ensure that relationships between the Party and whānau, hapū, iwi and other Māori organisations are elevating and enhancing
3. to promote a fair and just society, to work for the elimination of poverty and injustice, and to create an environment where the care and welfare of one's neighbour is still important
4. to ensure that members agree to work together, treat each other with respect and act with integrity in their party work, and
5. to involve all peoples in the process of rebuilding our nation based on mutual respect and harmonious relationships.

The constitution goes on to list other core values and to describe the practices that derive from those values and which govern the actions of party members elected to the New Zealand House of Representatives. The tikanga derived from manaakitanga led to the party's MPs demonstrably avoiding personal attacks in Parliament. The constitution also includes tikanga based on the importance of the Māori language to Māori culture and identity. The Māori Party MPs make a deliberate effort to use the Māori language in the House. This has led to the development of much-improved processes for simultaneous translation of Parliamentary proceedings. The rules in the constitution apply only to the party's members, and yet they have an impact on the way the party engages with others. These values are evident in the way Māori Party MPs conduct themselves in the House, in the policies of the party, and in the content of legislation.[76] The position the party took in 2007 on the human tissue and organ donation legislation was determined by the tikanga relating to the integrity of the human body. At that time, the party was of the view that there had not been sufficient time for Māori to discuss the implications of the bill for tapu and noa as it relates to the human body. Furthermore, the party was concerned that the legislation privileged the choices of individuals in matters that are, in the Māori world, the concern of the collective. In relation to legislation regulating electoral campaign spending, the Māori Party's points of reference were the tikanga relating to the accountability of traditional leadership and the responsible and sustainable management of resources.[77]

Aspects of this tikanga-based constitution were tested and subjected to significant scrutiny when the party suspended one of its MPs from the parliamentary caucus in 2011. The constitution includes a mechanism for the "resolution of differences." All members of the party must "treat each other with respect and are expected to act ethically and with integrity in their party work."[78] Another rule sets out a procedure for disciplinary action against a member who refuses to comply with the constitution, improperly deals with party funds, or "in any other way wilfully brings the party or its members into public disrepute."[79] A disciplinary and disputes committee of the party's governing body, the National Council, can address serious complaints against a member.[80] The National Council aims to ensure that any such dispute "is resolved on the basis of the kaupapa of the Party,"[81] reinforcing those principles that derive from a Māori world-view.

In 2011, members of the Party's five-person caucus made a complaint against one of the party's Members of Parliament, Hone Harawira.[82] Following a series of controversial incidents involving Harawira,[83] an opinion piece written by Harawira and published in a national newspaper[84] provoked the complaint. Harawira's article criticised the Māori Party's cozy relationship with the governing National Party and reiterated his concerns about the Marine and Coastal Area Bill (now enacted), which the other Māori Party MPs supported and continue to promote as a major achievement. Harawira was suspended from the party's parliamentary caucus prior to the completion of the formal dispute resolution process.[85] According to the party's co-leaders, Harawira had breached the kaupapa and founding principles of the Māori Party:[86] "Having no regard for the constitution is one thing. It is quite another to have no regard for the kaupapa and tikanga of the party, and that is what has really brought us to this point."[87] Evidently, to the Māori Party leadership, the kaupapa and tikanga are not only reflected in the constitution but are also independent of the constitution; their independent status is seen by the Māori Party leaders to be more important, at least in terms of political justification and legitimacy.

The formal complaint reportedly stated that the other Māori Party MPs had "lost trust and confidence" in Harawira because he "acts unethically and without integrity" and "deliberately undermines" the party and the leaders.[88] Harawira criticised the complaint process in an interview with Radio New Zealand: "The process is not consistent with kaupapa Māori [Māori style of governance] ... I also think that it's very, very Pakeha the way that it's being run."[89] Harawira repeatedly stated that the issue ought to be resolved on the marae in accordance with Māori protocols and processes.[90] The party president, however, was adamant that the process was consistent with kaupapa Māori and emphasized that "[m]eeting face to face in a safe environment is Māori."[91] Again, the political legitimacy of the process seems to rest on whether it is consistent with kaupapa Māori rather than with the constitution of the party, which must of course be complied with as a legal requirement.

The disciplinary and disputes committee found that the differences between Harawira and his parliamentary colleagues could not be resolved and referred the matter back to the party's National Council, recommending that

Harawira be expelled from the party. Before this recommendation was considered by the National Council, Harawira resigned his membership of the party and announced he would seek re-election as an independent candidate. Re-elected in a by-election in June 2011, he formed a new party, the Mana Party. As the party's name suggests, it is intended to have a significant Māori focus. Interestingly, the Mana Party's interim constitution, approved in May 2011, makes no mention of kaupapa or tikanga.

Throughout this episode, the three tensions in Māori legal history are evident. The emphasis on the need for an authentically Māori process illustrates the desire to assert self-determination, even though the enforcement of the obligations in the constitution would ultimately have rested with the state legal system. The relationship between tikanga and the state legal system sits at the very foundation of this episode. The case highlights the different views as to how Māori voices might be most effectively heard within the state system; the catalyst for the dispute was the way that tikanga was expressed within state law (the *Marine and Coastal Area Act* [2011]). The application of the Māori Party constitution and the lack of explicit reference to tikanga in the Mana Party's interim constitution illustrate distinct and deliberate choices about the relevance of particular tikanga to the governance of Māori political parties within the New Zealand parliamentary system.

The Central North Island Forestry Settlement

The second example of contemporary application of Māori legal traditions relates to the settlement of Māori claims against the Crown. The Central North Island Forest Lands Collective Settlement is the result of negotiations between the Crown and various iwi and hapū groupings as part of the systematic program aimed at settling historic claims based on the 1840 Treaty of Waitangi.[92] Involving eight different iwi and hapū groupings representing more than 100,000 people, the settlement comprises 176,000 hectares of forestry land and is worth approximately $220 million NZ dollars.

In a treaty settlement dealing with forest land, the settling group receives not only land but also accumulated rental fees received by the Crown from third parties for forestry licenses over those lands. The proportion of the accumulated rentals that each tribal group within the Central North Island (CNI) collective will receive from the settlement was determined at the time the settlement package was agreed. However, the allocation of the land itself was to be determined by the iwi and hapū involved, in what is described as a "tikanga-based resolution process" that is set out in a schedule to the legislation and which implements aspects of this settlement. Core values that underpin Māori legal traditions are reflected in the principles of the resolution process:[93]

The iwi acknowledge their commitment to a resolution process that
- enhances and promotes the mana and integrity of all iwi
- is open and transparent
- promotes whanaungatanga, manaakitanga, and kotahitanga among the iwi and
- recognizes the desirability of post-settlement collaboration between them in the collective management of assets.

The maintenance of relationships is a central concern of the groups participating in this process. The principle of whanaungatanga is explicitly referred to in the CNI allocation/resolution process, and this is reinforced by the recognition of the desirability of future collaboration and other features of the resolution process, such as the references to mana enhancement, transparency, and the value of manaakitanga. As recorded in the legislation:[94] "The CNI Iwi Collective is committed to the iwi deciding upon the allocation of CNI forests land for themselves, on their own terms, answerable to one another." This statement also reflects an assertion of authority and responsibility on behalf of the participating iwi and thus links the concepts of mana and whanaungatanga.

The first stage of the process is the identification of the relative interests of the CNI iwi in CNI forests land, by reference to tikanga Māori.[95] The relevant interests are described as "mana whenua interests" (traditional authority and responsibility in relation to the land); evidence for the existence of such interests may be found in traditional Māori oral records such as songs, tribal histories, and genealogies, as well as in written sources.

The second stage of the process addresses overlapping interests, where two or more iwi have identified a mana whenua interest in a particular area of forest land.[96] Again, the key principles and practices of tikanga govern the procedure. In this stage, negotiations are *kanohi ki te kanohi* (face to face). The iwi involved in negotiation over particular interests will determine the tikanga that applies to those negotiations. These negotiations are intended to take place between representatives who have the authority to commit their iwi to agreements and who are themselves committed to engage in an open, principled, and trustworthy dialogue. The legislation refers to this as *kōrero rangatira* (chiefly discussion) drawing again on the basic principles that underlie Māori legal traditions. While iwi representatives may take expert advice, those advisers are not permitted to participate directly in the negotiations themselves.

If negotiations do not produce agreement about recognition of mana whenua interests and the allocation of CNI forest land, the unreconciled iwi may refer the matter to either mediation or adjudication.[97] The appointment of mediators or an adjudication panel also reflects Māori legal traditions. The legislation requires that mediators and adjudicators be fluent in *te reo* (the Māori language) and have knowledge of tikanga Māori, in particular tikanga-based dispute resolution and how mana whenua is held and exercised by iwi.

In June 2014, the CNI iwi collective announced the conclusion of this process and the ratification of a final allocation agreement. In the end, approximately half the settlement lands were referred to an adjudication panel and determinations on mana whenua were made by reference to Māori principles and in accordance with tikanga Māori. At the time of writing, the adjudication panel's determinations were the subject of ongoing litigation.

Māori Law Remains a Vibrant Force

A set of core principles or conceptual regulators underlie Māori legal traditions. The interlocking concepts of whanaungatanga (relationships, and the centrality of relationships to Māori life), mana (spiritually sanctioned authority, and the importance of this authority, as well as its limits on Māori leadership), tapu/noa (the spiritual character of all things, as well as the profane and everyday, and the importance of these), utu (the principle of balance and reciprocity), and manaakitanga (nurturing relationships) provide the basis of tikanga and the Māori legal order. The associated concepts of rangatiratanga (chiefly authority) and kaitiakitanga (guardianship or stewardship) are also particularly relevant to the treaty settlement context.

The three tensions in Māori legal history provide interpretive tools that help us analyse the dynamic application of tikanga in the twenty-first century. The adaptation of Māori legal traditions is a creative force in the Māori Party's explicit use of kaupapa and tikanga as the foundation of the constitution. The constitution asserts that the party's members want Māori values and principles to regulate the organization. Yet this is also a reaction to the operation of state processes. The Māori Party was formed to engage Māori in New Zealand's law-making processes and, in particular, to represent the Māori partner in the Treaty of Waitangi relationship.

The expression of Māori legal traditions within the Māori Party constitution was subjected to legal and political scrutiny when the party expelled Hone

Harawira. The way in which tikanga and kaupapa were interpreted and applied in that situation can be understood by reference to tensions in the adaptation and response of Māori legal systems. While all the protagonists emphasized the need for "a Māori process," the process was also determined by the party's need to remain within the discipline of a Westminster-style parliament.

While the CNI forestry settlement process is "tikanga-based," it is also an adaptation to the social and political circumstances of New Zealand today. It both expresses self-determination and recognizes the regulatory powers of the state. It reflects a desire to both engage with, and maintain distance from, the Crown. While emphasizing and reinvigorating relevant tikanga, the process does not mobilise traditions that many iwi deem to be unhelpful.

By analysing the role of Māori legal traditions in contemporary Māori institutions through three long-standing, historical tensions – adaptation, relationship to the Crown, and renewal – I argue that Māori law has survived and remains a vibrant force within New Zealand society, not by passively accepting change but by actively engaging with other legal traditions that regulate contemporary New Zealand society.

4

Treaty Settlements and Māori Law

TAPUWAE AND TE RAUHINA

"Pāpā, I heard someone today talking about Te ari a Te Maaha and Te ari a Tapuwae – what does that mean?"

"They will have been talking about the two sides of our river. Te Maaha and Tapuwae, two of your ancestors, were brothers, but they had a falling out when they were children and even when they grew up they did not get along. They were from a family of rangatira and would have been expected to take on leadership roles within the community. But their father became concerned that the hostility between them would create tensions in the community and even put the community in danger if they were to be attacked from outside forces."

"What does that have to do with the river?"

"Well, e Tama, when they were adults, their father decided that Te Maaha and Tapuwae ought to be separated. He sent Te Maaha to set up a community and to live on the eastern side of the river and Tapuwae to live on the western side. The different sides of the river thereafter became known as 'Te ari a Te Maaha' and 'Te ari a Tapuwae' and you sometimes hear the old people still use those names when talking about the banks of the river, like you heard today."

"That is sad that the two brothers didn't get along. Did they never have anything to do with each other after that? What about their families? They must have all been related, so did they talk to each other?"

"Ae, it is sad. For some time the two families remained quite separate, but eventually the two families did grow back together. The descendants of each of the brothers mixed and mingled and began to live together as a united community once again."

"Did the brothers forgive each other then?"

"It wasn't quite as simple as that. There was a lot of trust that needed to be rebuilt amongst the two families and the community as a whole. Fortunately, Tapuwae in particular was known for his great qualities as a leader and the courtesy with which he treated others won him respect from far and wide."

"What did Tapuwae do?"

"Well, it was not all down to Tapuwae of course. But he did a number of things which made it easier for the community to unite. One important aspect was his marriage to Te Rauhina. Te Rauhina was herself a woman of great mana. This marriage was important not only for the links this gave Tapuwae to other parts of the community, but the special leadership qualities that Te Rauhina herself embodied were vital."

"Why? What was Te Rauhina like?"

"Te Rauhina was a very compassionate and forgiving woman. She was sometimes called 'Te Wahine Korero Aio a Tapuwae,' which means 'the Peace-Talking Wife of Tapuwae.' She always spoke up in the interests of peace and unity. Her village became widely known as a place where people could always find sanctuary. People responded to the humanity of Te Rauhina and Tapuwae and we remember them now as two of the great leaders of the people of our region."

"So, is leadership as easy as that?"

"It is not always easy to forgive, to speak up for peace, or to show restraint and tact, but certainly a big part of their success comes back to those key values and principles. But also remember the story of Te Maaha and Tapuwae, because leaders can also damage relationships within a community if they are not careful. And sometimes the way in which the community is set up has a big effect – whether the community is built on the kind of linkages that were forged when Tapuwae and Te Rauhina came together, or whether it is defined by boundaries such as the river that separated the two brothers."

"I wouldn't want to live on a different side of the river from my brother."

"No, e Tama, I wouldn't want that for you either."

Peace-Talking and Treaty Settlements

Te Rauhina was renowned for her efforts at seeking peace and bringing people together. Seeking peace and bringing people together could also be used to describe the objectives of tino rangatiratanga and reconciliation in the treaty settlement process. As the story of Tapuwae and Te Rauhina illustrates, however, careful consideration needs to be given to the process by which those objectives are pursued in what are often complex situations. This chapter provides a description of the key components of the treaty settlement process and considers the implications of the process for Māori law-making at both practical and conceptual levels. I draw on some of the literature relating to the British Columbia treaty process, which has many parallels to the New Zealand process.

Overview of the Settlement Process

The treaty settlement process is now focused primarily on negotiations between Māori and the Crown. Court and Waitangi Tribunal hearings may have set the stage for the settlement process,[1] but they are no longer at its centre. For example, the Waitangi Tribunal's role in the settlement of treaty claims, though still important, is now slightly peripheral.[2] The tribunal is responsible for inquiring into and reporting on claims brought by Māori against the Crown, assessing these claims against the principles of the Treaty of Waitangi, and making findings and recommendations to the Crown for the practical application of treaty principles. Once the tribunal's work was underway and its recommendations for remedy and redress were regularly put before the government, it perhaps became inevitable that a systematic program for the settlement of these claims would develop.

The Office of Treaty Settlements (OTS), a unit within the Ministry of Justice, now engages with Māori groups and negotiates redress packages to settle their historical Treaty of Waitangi claims. The tribunal is not directly involved in the settlement of claims, but often a tribunal report will provide a starting point for settlement negotiations. The tribunal continues to provide some oversight of the settlement process when called upon to make specific recommendations as to remedy, or to assess issues of mandate and overlapping claims.[3]

In 1992, the New Zealand government agreed that officials should develop a set of principles to govern the settlement of historical claims based on the Treaty of Waitangi.[4] These principles were part of a set of proposals that were rejected by Māori but which became official Crown policy, in slightly amended form, in 1995.[5] These principles were largely developed in the wake of the pan-tribal settlement of all Māori claims to commercial fishing interests, which marks the beginning of the modern systematic settlement process. In 1994, the government established OTS within the Ministry of Justice. Settlements made between the Crown and the major tribal groupings Ngāi Tahu and Waikato-Tainui in the mid-1990s further established the framework for the current settlement process. The Crown had commenced negotiations with both Ngāi Tahu and Waikato-Tainui before the comprehensive settlement policy was formalised, though both settlements were concluded after the establishment of OTS. The *Waikato Raupatu Claims Settlement Act*[6] was the first implementation of the new policy, and both the Waikato and Ngāi Tahu settlements have provided key benchmarks for all subsequent settlement negotiations.

The Crown's settlement process is described in the OTS guide for claimants as having four phases:[7] preparing claims for negotiation; pre-negotiations; negotiations; and ratification and implementation. There are various important steps within each phase. The first step in preparing claims for negotiation is for the claimant to register a claim with the Waitangi Tribunal. This claim may be lodged on behalf of a wider community or on behalf of the individual claimant him- or herself. No new historical claims (that is, no new claims relating to Crown action committed prior to 1992) may now be registered with the Tribunal, though any registered claims may be amended. It is not necessary for the Waitangi Tribunal to report on the claim before negotiations with the Crown commence. There may well be significant research undertaken into the claim prior to registration and, whether the claim is the subject of a tribunal inquiry and report or not, further research will be undertaken subsequent to registration if the claim is to progress through the claims settlement process.

The next step in this first phase of the process is for the claimant community to give a mandate to representatives to advance the settlement of all historical claims of that community. Those representatives must be able to demonstrate to the Crown that they have been given such a mandate before the Crown will formally acknowledge that mandate.[8] There is no formal requirement to establish a mandate on behalf of a community in order to pursue claims through the Waitangi Tribunal, so this may be the first point at which questions of mandate are really tested. This may lead to significant tensions and conflict within the claimant community, as discussed in more detail below. The Crown will not enter into negotiations with groups that do not have a recognized mandate, nor will the Crown enter into negotiations with groups that do not have any well-founded claims or do not constitute a "large natural group."[9] The previous policy document referred to "large natural (customary) groupings."[10] The change is probably of only minor practical significance, but it does suggest a slight and further shift away from tikanga-based definitions of membership. There is no set number of members that a group must have for the Crown to deem it as a large natural group for the purposes of settlement negotiations; rather, the policy serves to protect the Crown's objective of organising settlement negotiations in the most administratively efficient way possible. Despite the fact that Waitangi Tribunal claims must be registered by individuals, the Crown will only engage in settlement negotiations with mandated representatives of large natural groups.

Once the minister for Treaty of Waitangi negotiations has recognized the mandate of a group to negotiate a settlement of its claims, the group can move into the next phase of the process: pre-negotiations. This phase comprises three key steps and begins to construct the framework of the negotiations in more detail.[11] In this phase, the Crown and the claimant community move towards agreeing to the terms of negotiation. The terms of negotiation effectively set the ground rules for the negotiation. The Crown will seek to ensure that the terms of negotiation clearly define the claimant group that will benefit from the settlement and also record that the settlement will be "full and final." Although the language of the *Healing the Past* booklet has moved away from "full and final" to "fair and durable," much of the rhetoric of finality and extinguishment remains in the settlement discourse, and the terms of negotiation record that the objective of the settlement is to finally settle all the historical claims of the settling community and to remove the jurisdiction of the courts and the Waitangi Tribunal in relation to those claims.[12] The Terms of Negotiation will also preclude parties from pursuing their claims through the Waitangi Tribunal or the courts while in negotiations with the Crown. The terms will provide for conduct of the negotiations themselves, stating that they will be undertaken in good faith, that they are private and confidential and without prejudice, and that any deed of settlement that results will remain conditional until the claimant group ratifies it and Parliament passes any necessary settlement legislation. Terms of negotiation also usually include reference to any treaty breaches that the Crown has already conceded and the claimant group's aspirations for the settlement.[13]

Two other steps in the pre-negotiations phase have an important effect on the negotiations process. In addition to the terms of negotiation, both the Crown and the mandated claimant body must establish their own parameters. At this stage, the mandated claimant body ought to identify specific breaches of the Treaty, areas of land that have been affected by the claims and/or are culturally important sites, and any Crown assets within the area covered by the claims and which it wishes to be considered as potential commercial redress. The Crown is already working within a number of established policy parameters, including fiscal constraints and the limitations effectively set by the precedents of previous settlement agreements. However, the Crown also has a responsibility to identify Crown properties that could be considered for potential redress, and also to consider any issues relating to overlapping claims. The

Crown's management of overlapping claims has been the subject of several Waitangi Tribunal reports, as discussed below.

The Crown will also make decisions about claimant funding in the pre-negotiations phase. The Crown will usually make a contribution towards the costs incurred by the claimant community in obtaining a mandate and agreeing to the terms of negotiation, as well as towards the costs of the negotiation and ratification of a deed of settlement.[14] The amount contributed towards claimant funding is separate from the money or other assets that comprise the redress for historical claims. However, many groups will also receive from the Crown advances of portions of their settlement redress in order to assist with costs in the later stages of the settlement process.

In the third phase of the settlement process,[15] negotiations take place between a Crown negotiating team and a claimant negotiating team. The Crown team is primarily composed of officials from OTS, though it may include officials from other government departments (such as Treasury or the Department of Conservation) as well as specialist advisors. The current Crown policy in most negotiations is to also deploy chief Crown negotiators, who, report directly to the minister. The mandated body will appoint the claimant negotiation team. In many instances, the claimant negotiators are appointed from among the mandated representatives, but that need not be so. In any case, the claimant negotiators are accountable to the mandated representatives, who are in turn accountable to the claimant community. As with the Crown negotiating team, the claimant negotiating team may also include specialist advisors.[16] During the negotiation phase, working groups might be set up to advance specific issues or areas of redress.[17]

The objective of the negotiation phase is to reach an agreement in principle and then agree upon a deed of settlement.[18] An agreement in principle records the basic outline of the proposed settlement and is often given effect by an exchange of letters between the minister and the mandated representatives. This basic outline may now also take the form of a letter of agreement[19] or simply a Crown offer.[20] Sometimes this outline is formally signed as the heads of agreement. The agreed and recorded outline of the settlement then forms the basis for working towards the more detailed deed of settlement. The deed of settlement is drafted by Crown officials, and OTS keeps tight control of the content of these documents. Once the deed of settlement is in a form that can be approved in principle, the mandated representatives and the minister will initial a draft deed of settlement.

The claimant community must then ratify the initialled draft deed of settlement before the finalised deed of settlement is signed and settlement legislation is introduced in the final phase of ratification and implementation. Ratification is a crucial step in the settlement process because it can provide a fairly rigorous check on whether the broader claimant community approves of the settlement package that has been negotiated.[21] Often, if communication between the mandated representatives and the wider community has been effective over the course of the negotiations, there will be clear support for the final agreement. However, ratification is by no means a formality; there have been settlements in which significant sections of the claimant community have been opposed to accepting the settlement package.[22] The Crown may then be faced with the difficult decision as to whether a sufficient level of support has been reached. This is not always a clear-cut decision; simply looking for a simple majority is unlikely to be appropriate in these circumstances, though the Crown has not set a specific threshold that must be met. This problem may be further exacerbated if there is a low voter turnout, which, in itself, undermines the robustness of any settlement. In terms of tikanga Māori, low participation is most likely to indicate a lack of support rather than disinterest.

Once the settlement package has been agreed upon and the deed of settlement finally approved, various actions must be taken to implement the settlement agreement. First, the claimant community, which can now be referred to as the "settling group," must establish a post-settlement governance entity (PSGE) to receive and administer settlement assets on behalf of the community.

The constitution of a settling community's PSGE must be ratified by the wider community and approved by the Crown. The establishment of a PSGE paves the way for the introduction of settlement legislation. Settlement legislation will be required to implement a number of aspects of the deed of settlement. This legislation goes through the normal parliamentary process, including scrutiny by a select committee and an associated call for public submissions. Settlement legislation is not necessarily the conclusion of the process: there may still be a number of actions to carry out in order to complete the implementation of the settlement agreement. For example, the Crown may have to raise title for property to be transferred, encumbrances affecting settlement properties may have to be executed, and affected third parties will need to be notified. For its part, the settling community's PSGE may need to choose representatives to be statutory advisers or members of a statutory board if those mechanisms are part of the settlement redress.[23]

There are three main components of a treaty settlement package: an historical account; cultural redress; and commercial redress. The historical account is a government-accepted statement that summarizes the past relationship between the Crown and the settling community. This provides the basis for the government to acknowledge breaches of the Treaty of Waitangi and apologize for injustices suffered by the settling group as a result of those breaches. It is usual for the historical account, acknowledgements, and apology to be set out in the deed of settlement in both English and Māori.

Commercial redress is provided in recognition of prejudice suffered by the settling group as a result of breaches of the Treaty of Waitangi. The commercial redress may include cash, the purchase of government properties within the claimant group's area of interest, rights of first refusal to purchase government properties in the future, or the purchase of Crown forestry land and the accumulated rentals from forestry licenses.

Cultural redress is "intended to meet the cultural rather than the economic interests of the claimant group."[24] A range of mechanisms is commonly used in settlements to provide cultural redress. This includes the vesting of lands that are of cultural significance to the settling group or instruments such as "statutory acknowledgements" and "deeds of recognition" that set out formal statements of the claimant group's association with a specific site. Any transfer of cultural redress properties is usually subject to restrictions such as the maintenance of public access and conservation values. These instruments create rights to be consulted in relation to the management of such sites. Cultural redress may also include arrangements for joint management of public land, place-name changes, or protocols that set out ways in which specific government departments ought to provide for input from the settling group into decisions that affect their recognized cultural interests.

Treaty Settlements and Māori Law-Making

The structure of the treaty settlement process creates significant pressures on Māori legal traditions related to law-making. Many of these pressures arise from the tendency of the settlement process to prioritize objectives of certainty over objectives of justice, an issue that sociologist Andrew Woolford has identified within the British Columbia treaty process as well. Clear parallels can be observed in the New Zealand settlement process.

Before considering Woolford's analysis and its application to the New Zealand context more fully, it is helpful to have a sense of the basic framework of the British Columbia treaty process and the context in which it developed. While the Treaty of Waitangi is used in New Zealand to frame the relationship between Māori and the Crown,[25] there is no comparable single treaty that performs the same function in Canada. However, across Canada there are several treaties that were made between First Nations and the Crown. In most parts of Canada, the transfer of Aboriginal land to the Crown was effected as part of these treaty agreements. But this was not the case in British Columbia. Almost all of mainland British Columbia sits outside of these treaties.[26] As a consequence, large parts of the province could potentially still be subject to Aboriginal or customary title. Since the 1970s, the Canadian courts, in particular the Supreme Court of Canada, have made findings that support the existence of Aboriginal title in the province. From *Calder v. Attorney-General of British Columbia* (1973) through *R. v. Sparrow* (1990) and *Delgamuukw v British Columbia* (1997), to *Tsilhqot'in Nation v British Columbia* (2014), the courts have issued judgments that required both the federal and provincial governments to develop and adjust policies to address First Nations' land claims. In 1990, against a backdrop of increasing direct action by First Nation communities, the federal and provincial governments and representative First Nations leadership agreed to establish the British Columbia Claims Task Force. The task force had three members appointed by First Nations, two members appointed by the Government of Canada, and two members appointed by the Government of British Columbia. Its terms of reference required the task force to "define the scope of negotiations, the organization and process of negotiations including the time frames for negotiations; the need for and value of interim measures and public education."[27] The task force's June 1991 report recommended that "[t]he First Nations, Canada, and British Columbia establish a new relationship based on mutual trust, respect and understanding – through political negotiations."[28] The task force made eighteen other recommendations for a just and effective negotiation process. This led to the establishment in 1992 of the British Columbia Treaty Commission, intended to be an independent keeper of the treaty negotiation process.

The British Columbia treaty process and the Treaty of Waitangi settlement process are very similar despite their different origins and the fact that the British Columbia process is one of treaty-making (as opposed to providing redress for breaches of an existing treaty). Like the New Zealand process, the British Columbia process is structured around progressive steps or phases. Much like in the New Zealand process, First Nations in British Columbia must move from initial claims and a demonstration that they are prepared and ready to negotiate through a framework agreement and agreement in principle to a final agreement, followed by the necessary implementation processes. The way the relevant government parties engage in these processes is also very similar across the two jurisdictions. Woolford's analysis of the British Columbia process is thus highly relevant to our investigation here.

The settlement of claims based on the Treaty of Waitangi takes place within a process structured around delivering certainty.[29] Primarily, this means certainty for the Crown and the wider New Zealand community that the Crown represents, although there are also some important aspects of certainty for Māori groups as well. Achieving certainty in relation to legal rights and obligations is a legitimate objective, one that can benefit both Māori and the Crown.[30] But certainty can become problematic if it is conceptualized as being primarily based on comprehensiveness, finality, and the extinguishment of Indigenous rights. Visions of certainty that are more consistent with justice in this context might aim for predictability in the treaty relationship between Māori and the Crown rather than a termination of that relationship.[31] This kind of approach would create more space for Māori law-making processes. A focus on certainty without sufficient consideration of justice is likely to limit the scope of Māori legal systems to maintain and develop law-making processes that are rooted in Māori autonomy and legal traditions. It also undermines the settlement process itself.[32]

The settlement framework established by the Crown circumscribes the parameters of the claims and the potential redress. First, the treaty settlement process deals only with "historical" claims.[33] These are defined as claims that relate to alleged breaches of the principles of the treaty that took place prior to September 21, 1992. This date is used as the boundary between historical and contemporary claims because it is the date on which the cabinet approved the development of general principles for the settlement of treaty claims.[34] The Crown continues to have obligations under the Treaty of Waitangi; contemporary claims relating to Crown actions or omissions post-1992 may be brought before the Waitangi Tribunal. However, OTS is not responsible for the settlement of contemporary claims. The government department responsible for the policy area at issue is also responsible for any Crown response to the contemporary claim. For example, the Crown's response to any contemporary claims relating to Crown minerals is managed by the Ministry for Business, Innovation, and Employment. This limitation is one of a number of indicators that suggest the Crown is primarily concerned with delivering a quite narrow vision of justice in relation to the treaty. More recently, the Waitangi Tribunal's governing legislation has been amended to prohibit the tribunal from accepting any new claims based on historical treaty breaches.[35] When this deadline was announced, thousands of claims were filed with the Tribunal. These claims, mostly pro forma, are intended to be broad enough to cover any specific issues that might be identified in the future, the details of which can be inserted by later amendments to the original statement of claim. This measure on the part of the Crown is clearly aimed to address the type of certainty desired by the Crown in treaty settlement matters. The Crown desires finality; it is not interested in delivering mechanisms for an ongoing articulation of Māori rights based on Māori legal traditions, or even based on a continuing interaction between Māori and state legal systems.

The Crown has also sought certainty by placing limits on the total amount of money available for the settlement of historical claims. Initially, the Crown's policy was that no more than a total of $1 billion (NZ) would be available for the settlement of all historical claims.[36] The original Crown proposals for the settlement of historical claims focused on the idea of a "settlement envelope."[37] This conceptual envelope was, in part, intended to address the scope of the claims that would be settled – that is, only historical claims would fit within the settlement envelope. However, most of the discussion related to the concept of the settlement envelope has focused on the fiscal cap that this envelope set for the settlement of all historical claims. The "settlement envelope"' quickly came to be understood as the "fiscal envelope." Circumscribing the scope of claims and setting a fiscal cap for settlements are not entirely unconnected measures. They are linked primarily by the Crown's vision of certainty, a very state-centric vision. The parameters set by the Crown are symptomatic of this state-centric vision, which constrains Māori law-making authority in the context of the settlement process and post-settlement governance. This model provides a process for identifying and defining discrete rights, but not for recognizing and managing overlapping powers of government and law-making authority in an ongoing relationship.[38]

In addition to fiscal constraints, the Crown has also set other limits on the redress available to settle historical claims. For example, the Crown has made clear that title to land in national parks or other designated conservation areas is generally not available for transfer as part of the settlement of claims.[39] Conservation land may be used in settlements where specific sites of particular cultural significance are identified; initially, however, it was rare for title to conservation land to be transferred as part of a settlement. Though this is now a more common occurrence, the existing conservation values for this land must be maintained post-settlement. The Crown's settlement offer to Ngai Tūhoe adds a significant gloss to this particular policy, though ultimately stops short of transferring title of national park land to the settling community. Te Urewera National Park was the subject of intense negotiation between Ngai Tūhoe and the Crown. The resulting offer, subsequently accepted by Ngai

Tūhoe, proposed that title to Te Urewera National Park be vested in a new legal entity that would be represented by a governance board with equal numbers of Crown and Ngai Tūhoe appointees.

In both the Te Urewera settlement and the recent Whanganui River settlement, novel legal arrangements deem a specified area of land or a river, as the case may be, to have its own legal personality. These innovative mechanisms have provided creative solutions to difficult issues within these settlement processes, and have rightly been heralded by some commentators as "groundbreaking."[40]

These settlements make significant advances in terms of establishing a framework that reflects a Māori perspective on human relationships with the natural environment and specific landscape features. However, this still falls far short of the type of recognition of Indigenous law that Tully suggests is a necessary part of reconciliation – fundamental to establishing just relationships between Indigenous peoples and settler populations and governments.

Although a key aspect of the Māori worldview in relation to the natural environment is that landscape features such as rivers have their own *mauri* (life force) and their own mana, this is not the equivalent of a legal personality. "Legal personality" is a Western legal concept. It comes close to expressing some fundamental ideas from within Māori legal traditions, and the people of Tūhoe and Whanganui should be congratulated for moving the Crown into this legal space. But it does not, in itself, recognize the value of Māori legal traditions. In fact, it confirms that Māori legal traditions will not be recognized on their own terms but instead only through the closest equivalent from the Western legal tradition. In effect, this mechanism enables law-makers to avoid trying to source laws for the regulation of rivers and other landscape features in Māori legal traditions, instead deploying a mechanism from the common law that is deemed by the Crown to be a close enough match.

Crown proposals for the settlement of Treaty of Waitangi claims make it clear that the Crown does not accept that Māori can claim any rights sourced in Māori law to regulate the management of natural resources.[41] Though some contemporary claims brought to the Waitangi Tribunal aim to address some of these issues, this serves to underscore the point that these issues are not being dealt with effectively through the OTS process. This severely limits the recognition of many elements of the injustices suffered by Māori groups and speaks to the Crown's view of both justice and certainty.[42] In one sense, this can be seen as another constraint upon the types of redress available within these settlements. But it also shows the Crown's view of the type of justice at stake in these negotiations. As in the British Columbia treaty process, non-Indigenous state parties tend not to take seriously any claims to difference (that is, cultural-symbolic justice as opposed to socioeconomic justice).[43] Without a genuine effort to recognize claims to difference and to address cultural-symbolic justice issues, treaty settlements will continue to encourage Māori legal systems to adopt law-making processes that are consistent with the Crown's vision of state authority, and to move away from tikanga-based law-making.

The move away from tikanga-based law-making is arguably evident in the way Māori commercial assets are managed in the settlement context. Linda Te Aho has suggested that directors responsible for Māori corporate governance entities, such as PSGEs, often appear to act in a manner that is contrary to tikanga. Given the central position that PSGEs tend to have within the community infrastructure of the iwi, the normalisation of "non-tikanga" behaviour has a very real impact on the legal traditions of the community and the reference points by which behaviour is judged and regulated. PSGEs have assumed a de facto law-making role in many communities; any shift away from tikanga-based governance in the rules and operation of the PSGE is likely to be reflected more generally in a shift away from tikanga-based law-making in the community.

Te Aho raises concerns about the environmental consequences of decisions that Māori 'corporate warriors' seem willing to take, notwithstanding tikanga to the contrary.[44] She notes that directors may take the view that commercial interests take precedence over tikanga concerns. The objective of the corporation becomes focused on creating wealth; how wealth is created and whether its creation is consistent with tikanga are not always considered.

Te Aho calls on the liberationist theories of Paulo Freire to explain why this might be the case.[45] Friere theorises that if there is no critical recognition of the causes of oppression, the oppressed will adapt to the structures of the oppressor and internalise the oppressor's vision of the world.[46] One factor likely to be at play in these instances is the internalisation of "exploitative colonial values."[47] I would argue, however, that such internalisation need not take place for directors of PSGEs to behave in a way that is at odds with tikanga. PSGEs are not tikanga-based structures; they are entities based on models of corporate governance primarily concerned with financial propriety, commercial accountability, and economic sustainability. While these are valuable aspects of corporate governance, they are not specifically derived from tikanga Māori. They may not be consistent with tikanga Māori and even may be quite contrary to tikanga. Quite simply, PSGEs can be constituted in a way that leads decision-makers to act in a way that is at odds with the principles of tikanga.

But that does not require such an approach to be internalised. Law-making within Māori legal systems need not shift away from a tikanga base. Neither is it necessary for PSGEs to move away from tikanga-based law-making if greater attention is given to the effect of the treaty settlement process on Māori legal traditions.

Clearly, PSGEs are established in the specific context of the settlement process and specific settlement agreements. The settlement documents (deeds of settlement and settlement legislation) address issues of decision-making, jurisdiction, and governance, and set the framework for the operation of Māori legal traditions within the settling community, at least in relation to matters connected with the PSGE and the settlement. It is thus helpful to consider the use of the key Māori legal concepts relating to law-making (mana, rangatiratanga, and kaitiakitanga) that are deployed in settlement documents.

As discussed earlier, mana is central to Māori leadership and authority and might be expected to be prominent in treaty settlements. The term "mana" is used in settlement documents to denote the following notions of autonomy:

- sovereignty
- autonomy
- authority
- power
- guardianship/custodianship
- control
- rights, and
- mandate.

Most of the Māori text in treaty settlement documents does not appear in the effective provisions of the deed of settlement but rather in preambles to the main document and in agreed-upon historical accounts, which include acknowledgements and apologies from the Crown as well as significant background to the settlement. There are many examples of the Crown acknowledging the detrimental effect that state law and policies have had on Māori authority and autonomy; "mana" is frequently used in the Māori text to convey these concepts. In this context, "mana" is variously used to mean "power," "authority," "autonomy" and "self-government."[48] The term is also often used in conjunction with other words. To give some examples, mana is used with *whenua* (land) *moana* (sea), *tangata* (person/people), "*ture*" (law) and "*whakahaere*" (management) to convey, respectively, the ideas of "protection and use of lands," "protection of the sea," "rights," "legal authority," and "control" (over lands and resources).

"Mana" is also used a few times in the substantive provisions of settlement instruments. These provisions generally relate to the cultural redress aspects of the settlement package. For example, the *Ngāti Awa Claims Settlement Act* refers to mana in the statutory acknowledgements in relation to the Ohope Reserve and the Whakatane River. In the case of the Ohope Reserve, the relevant part of the schedule states:[49]

> The traditional values of mana, mauri, whakapapa, and tapu are central to the relationship of Ngāti Awa with the Ohope Scenic Reserve. The mana of Ohope describes the power and importance of the reserve to Ngāti Awa. Mana also implies the responsibility of Ngāti Awa as tangata whenua and guardians of the area. The mauri of Ohope is the life force of Ohope. All forms of life have a mauri and all forms of life are related. One of the roles of Ngāti Awa as tangata whenua is to protect the mauri of the Ohope Scenic Reserve area. Whakapapa defines the genealogical relationship of Ngāti Awa to the Reserve. Tapu describes the sacred nature of the Reserve to Ngāti Awa. Mana, mauri, whakapapa, and tapu are all important spiritual elements of the relationship of Ngāti Awa with the Ohope Scenic Reserve area. All of these values remain important to the people of Ngāti Awa today.

The statutory acknowledgment in relation to the Whakatane River is similar, providing, among other things, "Mana also defines the custodian responsibility of Ngāti Awa as guardians of the river."[50]

The Ngai Tamanuhiri deed of settlement also contains reference to the concept of mana in relation to the cultural redress provided under that agreement:[51]

> 5.1 There are three main components of the cultural redress –
> 5.1.1 mana tangata (identity and heritage) redress, the objective of which is to assist Ngai Tamanuhiri to reclaim and promote their identity, tikanga and history; and
> 5.1.2 mana whenua/mana moana (protection and use of land and sea) redress; and
> 5.1.3 mana rangatira (enhancement of relationship) redress which contributes towards the protection and recognition of the right of Ngai

Tamanuhiri to exercise mana rangatira, mana tangata, mana tipuna, mana atua, mana whenua and mana moana.

The Rongowhakaata deed of settlement uses the term "mana whenua" to refer to the specific interests that a particular segment of the Rongowhakaata community has in an area of land to be returned under the settlement:[52]

6.15 Rongowhakaata –

6.15.1 wish to record their intention that, after the settlement date, the governance entity will transfer the fee simple estate in the London Street site to an entity approved by, and for the benefit of, Ngāti Oneone; and

6.15.2 acknowledge that –

(a) the transfer of the London Street site referred to in clause 6.15.1 is in recognition of Ngāti Oneone holding mana whenua in Kaiti; and

(b) after the transfer of the London Street site referred to in clause 6.15.1 has been completed, the property will be administered jointly by Ngāti Oneone, Ngai Tawhiri and Whanau a Iwi in recognition of the interests that the latter two hapu also have in the Kaiti area.

Perhaps mana is rarely used in the operational provisions because the operational provisions are mostly governed by English concepts, traditions, and laws, and mana is not needed to express such ideas. If that is the view taken by the drafters of these instruments, then it seems to suggest that while treaty documents are supposed to be a reflection of partnership between the New Zealand government and Māori communities, in effect, it is the laws, ideas, and philosophy of the New Zealand state that ultimately determine how treaty settlements are structured.

Notably, when the concept of sovereignty is used to describe the status and powers of the British monarch, "mana" is the term used to translate that concept into Māori.[53] Yet "mana" is not translated anywhere in the English version of the settlement documents as "Māori sovereignty."[54] Also notable is that although mana is a Māori concept, it is used in this example to express British notions of sovereignty for non-Māori people, rather than sovereignty for Māori themselves. The phrase *mana motuhake* (special or distinct spiritually sanctioned authority) is used as a key concept in the Crown's offer to Ngai Tūhoe to convey the idea of increased Tūhoe autonomy in relation to the delivery of social services. While this is an important aspect of the redress package, it is a more limited form of authority than would ordinarily be reflected in that concept.[55] The term "mana," then, is used to express various forms of autonomy, though it is rarely used in settlement instruments to express high levels of sovereignty and is instead used mostly to convey the concept of "authority."

"Rangatiratanga" is another Māori term that appears frequently throughout treaty settlement documents, to denote the following concepts:

- power
- authority
- autonomy
- sovereignty
- governance
- leadership
- control, and
- ownership.

"Rangatiratanga" has only infrequently been translated into English in these settlement documents. Rather, the precise meaning of the term has generally been left to the reader to ascertain. Where an English translation is provided, the term is most commonly rendered as "authority," "leadership," "control," and "ownership." These concepts are reflections of lower levels of autonomy. However, when used in conjunction with other Māori words, "rangatiratanga" is sometimes used to mean higher levels of autonomy. For example, *rangatira motuhake* is used to translate "Māori autonomy."[56]

In one instance, the term "rangatiratanga" is used in an English sentence. When this sentence is translated into Māori, the phrase *mana rangatira* is used as a translation.[57] This represents the drafters' slightly unusual choice to render a Māori concept differently in the Māori text. In any case, it is a slightly unusual use of the phrase "mana rangatira." The other occasion that "mana rangatira" is used in these settlement instruments is in the Ngai Tamanuhiri deed of settlement, in the section on cultural redress. Here it describes a component of the cultural redress and is translated into the English as "enhancement of relationships."

"Kaitiakitanga" appears throughout the treaty settlement documents (albeit less frequently than "mana" or "rangatiratanga") to convey the concepts of custodianship, guardianship, and stewardship. On two occasions "kaitiakitanga" is directly translated as "custodianship," and on two occasions the term is left untranslated. The very consistent and specific use of this term stands out from the wide range of meanings ascribed to "mana" and "rangatiratanga" in these settlement instruments. This is likely due to the fact that "kaitiakitanga" is used in the *Resource Management Act* of 1991 and its meaning through this act is becoming more entrenched for government authorities.

Custodianship is a lower level of authority/autonomy, indicating a reciprocal relationship between the custodian and the whenua to which the kaitiakitanga is linked, rather than governance over the land and the people in it.

The term "kaitiakitanga" is found solely within the more symbolic provisions of the settlement instruments, that is, within the preamble, background, or historical account. This again highlights the general paucity of Māori language within the operational provisions of these instruments. Given the centrality of the concept of kaitiakitanga to Māori rights and obligations, to Māori environmental law and policy, and even to New Zealand resource management law, it is perhaps surprising that the term does not appear more frequently in settlement instruments, particularly in provisions that give effect to forms of cultural redress that deal directly with these matters.

The use of "mana," "rangatiratanga," and "kaitiakitanga" in settlement instruments highlights four significant issues surrounding the instruments' use of Māori language and concepts. First, while all settlement instruments contain some Māori language, it is instructive to note that Māori language and concepts only rarely appear in the operative provisions of settlement instruments. Although the use of Māori language to record the background to these settlements and the history of the relationship between particular Māori communities and the New Zealand government ought to be applauded, there is clearly a division between these more symbolic provisions and the operative sections of the settlement instruments. If one of the intended effects of these settlements is to transfer authority to the settling communities, one might expect to see terms that express aspects of Māori authority regularly deployed in the delivery of settlement redress. Yet the use of such terms is the exception rather than the norm.

Second, there is a troubling co-option of Māori concepts within these settlement instruments. The starkest example of this is the translation of the term "mana" as "sovereignty" of the colonial government. The term is never translated as "sovereignty" when it describes the authority exercised by Māori.

Third, and related to the co-option of Māori concepts, is the ambiguity created when Māori concepts are used as part of New Zealand English within these documents. The term "rangatiratanga," for example, is frequently not translated from Māori. It may be argued that this allows the Māori concept to stand on its own terms without being overly constrained by the problems of translation and the definitions of English words. Yet, there are difficulties with this argument. In the case of "rangatiratanga," this approach tends to cloud the meaning and intent of the settlement agreement by allowing a Māori reader to ascribe a very high level of autonomy and self-determination to the term, while the government might argue otherwise, based on some of the lower levels of autonomy this term is used to express in several of the settlement instruments. As long as there is an asymmetrical and colonial relationship between Māori and the Crown, this language ambiguity in the settlement instruments creates difficulties for Māori. Despite initial appearances, problems of interpretation and definition remain.[58]

Finally, it is surprising that a term such as "kaitiakitanga," which has such a central role in expressing Māori interests in the management of the natural environment, is not used in the operative provisions of settlement instruments that directly address the role of Māori communities in environmental decision-making. The concept of kaitiakitanga, like mana and rangatiratanga, expresses fundamental aspects of the exercise of Māori jurisdiction and law-making. The fact that all three of these terms are used only rarely, if at all, in the practical and effective mechanisms of the settlement instruments raises serious questions about the ability of such instruments to give appropriate expression to Māori understandings of autonomy and self-determination.

Conceptual Issues for Māori Law-Making

The treaty settlement process also creates a number of conceptual difficulties for Māori legal traditions, and Māori law-making in particular. A key conceptual difficulty arises from the sovereignty claims asserted in the context of treaty settlements. Andrew Sharp, a political philosopher and the author of the pre-eminent text on justice and Māori claims,[59] has noted that the sovereignty claims made in relation to the treaty have affected the discussion of just settlements and reconciliation in that context.[60] Claims that the treaty provided for absolute Māori sovereignty – and that the treaty created "one people" with one official language, one culture, and "one law for all" under British sovereignty – are incompatible with the concept of justice and reconciliation between competing ethnic groups with different cultures. Such claims can be a basis for justice only in a homogenous society; in New Zealand, however, these claims argue for two separate and contradictory sovereignties.[61] Sharp does not argue that two distinct sovereignties cannot exist in New Zealand; rather, his point is that they cannot be the basis for justice and reconciliation between Māori and other New Zealanders because they are based on separateness, and mechanisms that address justice among different ethnic or cultural groups can have authority only if that authority is commonly accepted by those groups. The justice discourse within the Treaty of Waitangi settlement process is, therefore, coloured by the need to develop a framework for managing disagreement between Māori and the Crown that is rooted in the treaty's language of sovereignty and the Māori equivalent, tino rangatiratanga.

Jeremy Webber argues that the institutions of the liberal-democratic state can provide effective mechanisms for fairly managing disagreement between ethnic groups.[62] In other words, in any social order there must be mechanisms for resolving disputes, and the authority of state institutions can be justified if the institutions can be shown to manage disagreement fairly among members of society.[63] Sharp suggests that this has generally been the approach of the institutions of the New Zealand state in relation to managing justice between Māori and other New Zealanders. Crown sovereignty is seen to transcend and regulate "the differing conceptions of justice held by all its subjects."[64]

Sharp suggests that such an approach can be seen in the landmark decision in the *Lands* case,[65] which, arguably, aimed to reconcile competing claims for sovereignty in the context of the Treaty of Waitangi.[66] In the *Lands* case, the Court of Appeal spoke of Māori and the Crown as "partners" who should engage in constructive dialogue. The court required the partners to negotiate an agreed protection mechanism for potential Māori treaty interests before the Crown would proceed with the establishment of the state-owned enterprises. By focusing on partnership, the Court moved the discussion away from shared legal sovereignty. As McHugh notes, "the courts were not prepared to see Māori as a distinct legal sovereign sharing sovereignty with the Crown or legally limiting its power in Parliament, [but] they did recognize their political sovereignty as a tribal people."[67] This outcome sets the treaty partnership within a sovereignty frame by confirming "an asymmetrical relationship where the Crown's *legal* sovereignty could out-trump Māori's *political* version."[68] Although the *Lands* decision reflects a vision of justice in relation to the Treaty of Waitangi that is influenced by a sovereignty discourse, Sharp also notes that this case occurs in the context of both the Waitangi Tribunal's developing jurisprudence and Pākehā understandings of justice as formal equality.[69] This gives rise to a particular vision of justice in relation to the Treaty of Waitangi, a vision that is framed by sovereignty claims, but which is also historically focused and circumscribed by socioeconomic models of justice. That vision of justice is based on the requirement that Māori recognize the Crown's right to govern and that the Crown in turn make reparations for violation of Māori rights.[70]

The Crown sovereignty framework is in tension with a number of the New Zealand Law Commission's principles for Māori governance discussed in more detail in Chapter 5. In particular, this framework would appear to create some difficulties for the principles of autonomy, cultural match (that is, compatability between a community's culture and their governance structures), choice, and diversity. Māori communities that design governance entities in the context of the treaty settlement process are constrained by the Crown sovereignty framework in ways that limit their ability to control the constitutional-building process, limit their time to engage in a process of entity formation, and generally limit their choices, including choices about the role of Māori legal traditions within the new entity.

The broad framework of the process established by the Crown for the settlement of claims circumscribes the parameters of those claims and potential redress. The financial limits on redress effectively construct a treaty settlement discourse that is centred on symbolic reparation, which also affects principles of Māori governance.

Both Māori and Crown views on the just settlement of claims and on what might be required to enable reconciliation are framed by the treaty relationship. After all, Māori and the Crown have a relationship that is based on an agreement that set out certain standards of justice. The treaty settlement process is based on the premise that these standards of justice have not been met, that is, that the terms of the agreement have been breached; therefore, a just settlement must specifically address the particular breaches of the agreement. Although this provides a helpful focus on injustices of the past, it also, perhaps, results in a narrow view of the requirements of justice and reconciliation.

Sharp suggests that the treaty-based framework in New Zealand infuses the settlement discourse with a focus on past injustices and, therefore, ideas of reparative justice.[71] The basic idea of reparative justice is that, if a wrong is committed, measures are to be taken to repair that wrong and to restore the wronged party to the position it would have been in had the wrong not occurred.[72]

While this might suggest the actions necessary to achieve justice in simple situations, there are a number of subjective matters contained within this definition.[73] For instance, there may not be agreement between the parties as to what constitutes a wrong action, what benefit has accrued to one party, and what prejudice has been visited on the other. Without agreement on those matters, it is difficult to find agreement on what would constitute a just outcome. Furthermore, the situation becomes more complicated when the bona fide rights of third parties are involved, or when it is no longer possible to return exactly what was taken or to restore the situation to precisely what it would have been had no wrong occurred. Sharp notes, therefore, that reparations can be conceptualized as either restitution or compensation.[74] Restitution results in the situation being restored to what it was before the wrong occurred. Compensation, on the other hand, is reparation made when parties cannot be restored to their original positions; reparation aims to achieve as close a restoration to the original position as possible through other means, such as the payment of money or other goods as a substitute.[75]

Interestingly, the New Zealand treaty settlement process aims at neither restitution nor compensation in a strict sense. Because of the complex and often countervailing interests of third parties, true restitution of Māori groups is acknowledged as unrealistic. However, the Crown also makes clear that it will not provide compensation for the full value of the prejudice suffered by Māori. It will offer only Crown-defined "redress."

The Crown's approach to the total value of each settlement is described in official publications as follows:[76]

> The task for the Crown in developing the current settlement policy was to devise an approach to financial and commercial redress that, within a negotiated settlement as a whole:
>
> - enables the claimant group's sense of grievance to be resolved
> - contributes to the economic and social development of the claimant group
> - is fair between claimant groups, and
> - takes account of New Zealand's ability to pay, considering all the other demands on public spending such as health, education, social welfare, transport and defence.

Crown policy in this area was modified in 2000, so now also includes the following:[77]

- redress should relate fundamentally to the nature of the breaches suffered
- different claimant groups should be treated consistently, so similar claims receive similar redress, and

- while maintaining a fiscally prudent approach, each claim is treated on its merits and does not have to be fitted under a pre-determined fiscal cap.

As there is no longer a formal fiscal cap in place, there is now at least theoretical flexibility in relation to the value of settlement assets that may be available.[78] Notably, however, the original cap continues to cast a shadow over settlement negotiations. Both Ngāi Tahu and Waikato-Tainui, two large groupings whose negotiations and settlements essentially set the framework for the new-style settlement process, each included a relativity clause within their settlement agreements.[79] These provisions acknowledge that these groups settled their claims on the assumption that the total value of assets available for the settlement of historical claims was $1 billion. The agreements, therefore, allow for their settlements to be "topped up" if necessary to maintain relativity with other settling groups. Even without these clauses, the Crown sees it as a matter of fairness to maintain relativity between the different settling groups.[80] This also has implications for the kind of justice the Crown perceives should be delivered through this process. That is, it places a premium on relativity between groups rather than on the provision of just redress according to the injustice suffered by any particular group.[81] The subject of treaty settlement negotiations becomes, therefore, the nature of appropriate symbolic reparation.

Governance entities that are constituted for the narrow purpose of receiving reparations are unlikely to meet the Law Commission's identified principles of community empowerment, recognition, or early entity development. PSGEs manage a range of redress on behalf of the settling community. For example, alongside the commercial redress, which could take the form of cash and/or assets worth tens of millions of dollars, the PSGE will also be responsible for participating in joint-management arrangements with the Department of Conservation or local councils and a range of relationship agreements with government agencies that might provide advisory roles for the settling group. The limits on settlement redress, both financial and conceptual, also limit the roles and functions of PSGEs, and this ultimately affects the role of Māori legal traditions within PSGEs.

The choice of entity to act as a PSGE represents a significant decision for the settling community. It is also a significant matter for the Crown because decisions about governance and representation of an iwi or hapū unavoidably address key aspects of self-determination and tino rangatiratanga. Given this, it is ultimately the Crown that determines whether or not it will accept an entity as a PSGE. The Crown's position is that it is a matter for the settling community to determine what type of legal entity will best serve that community's needs, but that the Crown also has obligations to members of the settling community, as well as to all tax-payers, to ensure that certain fundamental governance standards are met.[82] The Crown describes these standards as reflected in principles of representation, accountability, and transparency.

The Crown must be satisfied that the PSGE is genuinely representative of the settling community and that all adult members of the community have an opportunity to participate in the affairs of the PSGE. When assessing the suitability of a proposed PSGE, the Crown will want to be confident that all beneficiaries of the settlement (that is, all those people whose claims are to be settled) will be entitled to register as members of the PSGE. The PSGE must therefore have provisions in its constituting instrument (which may be a constitution, charter, trust deed, or other instrument, depending on the form the entity takes) setting out the process for registration, the criteria for registration, who makes decisions about registration, and whether those decisions can be appealed or disputed.[83]

All adult registered members ought to have a say in who the representatives of the governance entity will be. The Crown considers matters such as how many representatives of the PSGE there will be and who is eligible to be appointed or elected as a representative. Though elections can be structured in various ways, the Crown will take note of whether representatives are chosen from an "at large" vote or whether there are specific selections of representatives on the basis of iwi, marae, hapū, or other groups. There ought to be clear rules about the voting process itself, and the Crown will seek to ensure that the term of office of the representatives is reasonable and allows for stable governance, and that, if there are circumstances in which a representative can be removed from office, these are clearly set out.[84]

The Crown requirements in relation to representation (highlighted by the issues of mandate and overlapping claims, discussed below) may create difficulties in terms of the principle of cultural match, especially when it comes to questions of membership. Kirsty Gover has undertaken a comprehensive examination of the membership rules used by different Indigenous governance entities in New Zealand, Australia, Canada, and the United States.[85] Membership is an important aspect of the way these governance entities operate and the way Indigenous communities define themselves. Gover's work on membership helps to provide a platform for the analysis of the effects of the establishment of PSGEs on Māori law.

All the iwi within Gover's study base their membership on whakapapa or kinship connections and descent. Gover identifies four basic conceptions of descent that are used by iwi in the context of their governance entities:

- descent from a person named in a historic document or base roll[86]
- descent from a named ancestor[87]
- descent from a named (eponymous) ancestor,[88] and
- descent from a collective (usually an iwi).[89]

Iwi that have been through the treaty settlement process tend to use the claimant definition used in the deed of settlement when they define membership in the constitution of their PSGE.[90] The Crown insists upon direct incorporation of the deed of settlement definition because it is anxious to ensure that the beneficiaries of the PSGE are exactly the same group of people whose claims are being settled. The claimant definition used in the deed of settlement must be negotiated and agreed between the Crown and the claimant community. The usual form of the claimant definition is to define membership of the claimant community by descent from one or more ancestors,[91] consistent with the conceptions of descent identified by Gover.

Gover also notes that often there is very little guidance from the constitution of a PSGE as to what kind of evidence would prove membership, though membership application forms indicate the type of information required.[92] This is usually the names of immediate ancestors (back to great-grandparents is not uncommon). Often other social divisions or identity markers are sought, such as a primary hapū or marae to which the applicant affiliates. Sometimes this information needs to be certified or endorsed by an elder or someone in a position to confirm the applicant's whakapapa.

Mandate and Overlapping Claims

Two other issues relating to representation within the settlement process and a number of the identified principles of Māori governance have been repeatedly brought before the Waitangi Tribunal: challenges to the mandate of settling groups; and issues relating to the way that overlapping interests are managed within the settlement process. Although these can be characterised as two distinct issues, there are important connections between them. Both speak to the way Māori groups interact and relate to each other, addressing significant matters of tikanga and the application of concepts such as mana and rangatiratanga, whanaungatanga, and manaakitanga.

The Crown's policy and practice in relation to the management of overlapping claims has been found wanting by the Waitangi Tribunal on a number of occasions.[93] In the *Ngāti Tuwharetoa ki Kawerau Settlement Cross-Claim Report,* the Waitangi Tribunal summarised the expectations of the Crown in relation to managing overlapping claims issues.[94] The tribunal noted that managing relationships through the process for dealing with overlapping claims requires a sophisticated understanding of Māori communities:[95]

> It is a hard job, and a demanding one, because the honour of the Crown is on the line, and the durability of these settlements, and the quality of the relationships that spring from them, will depend in large measure on how well these officials perform. It is, as they say, a big ask. But it is one underpinned by Treaty principles and the imperative of fairness. We should not hesitate to insist on high standards when lower ones can have such serious, and long-lasting, consequences.

The tribunal here draws a connection between the quality of the settlements and the settlement process in terms of reconciliation, a measure applied in this book to consider the effects of the settlement process on Māori law.

The *East Coast Settlement Report* is one of a series of reports that address aspects of the treaty settlement process itself. In fact, this report provides a helpful summary of previous Waitangi Tribunal comment on Crown settlement policy. The *East Coast Settlement Report* considers the settlement negotiations between the Crown and Te Rūnanga o Ngāti Porou. A number of claimants who submitted claims for the Waitangi Tribunal's East Coast district inquiry did not wish to enter direct negotiations with the Crown without first going through a full district inquiry. Some of these claimants, who claimed to represent the kin groups Ruawaipu, Uepohatu, and Te Aitanga-a-Hauiti, sought recommendations from the tribunal that the settlement between the Crown and Te Rūnanga o Ngāti Porou be delayed. They contended that the Rūnanga had no mandate to negotiate the settlement of their claims and that the Crown's recognition of the Rūnanga's mandate was contrary to the principles of the treaty. The tribunal held an urgent hearing of these claims in December 2009 and reported its findings and recommendations in the *East Coast Settlement Report.*[96]

The report identifies a number of aspects of the mandating process that could be improved, although the tribunal determined that any flaws in the process were not substantial enough to warrant delaying the settlement. The tribunal was mindful that such a delay would significantly prejudice those who support Te Rūnanga's mandate. Furthermore, the tribunal noted that a full inquiry was unlikely to address many of the issues at the heart of the claimants' concerns, which were really issues between Māori groups, upon which the Waitangi Tribunal has historically been reluctant to comment.

However, the tribunal did find a number of flaws in the Crown's treaty settlement policy and recommended a number of changes to that policy to ensure that the settlement process is fair and that settlement agreements are durable.[97] This included the recommendation that the Crown take a more proactive role in monitoring the mandating process. The tribunal also recommended that the body seeking the mandate be required to provide more specific information about the claims to be settled and that the Office of Treaty Settlements seek submissions on the mandate early in the process as well as after a deed of mandate is received.

In August 2012, the Waitangi Tribunal again addressed issues relating to the Crown's treaty settlement policy and practice in the *Port Nicholson Block Urgency Report*.[98] The tribunal was critical of the "silo approach" to negotiations within the Office of Treaty Settlement, which had contributed to a lack of awareness of the overlapping interests between two neighbouring Māori groups. The tribunal noted that the same issues in relation to managing relationships in the settlement context had been raised in the *Tāmaki Makaurau Settlement Process Report* in 2007; the tribunal expressed disappointment at the need to raise these matters again.[99] (It should be noted, however, that some more recent tribunal reports relating to remedies have been criticised for being too deferential towards the Crown's settlement policy parameters.[100])

The Importance of Process

The issues of mandate and overlapping claims are significant in the context of PSGEs because they speak directly to questions of identity, authority, and relationships. The Crown sees accountability to the settling community as crucial to the ongoing legitimacy of the settlement. Consequently, bodies such as Māori trust boards that have been used as governance entities in the past may not be appropriate for use as a PSGE.[101] For similar reasons, the Crown does not consider that a charitable trust is an appropriate vehicle for a PSGE (despite having accepted some exceptions to this policy). The Attorney-General (who, coincidentally, for most of the time since the establishment of OTS, has been the minister in charge of Treaty of Waitangi negotiations) maintains a supervisory role in relation to charitable trusts. There are also additional complications that would occur if the trust were to wind up. In that circumstance, it would not be possible for the trust's assets to simply be allocated among the settling community. Despite these concerns and the Crown's general preference that Māori trust boards not be used as PSGEs, however, the recent partial settlement with Ngāti Maniapoto used Te Maniapoto Māori Trust Board as the PSGE.

The Crown is concerned to ensure that the PSGE is accountable to the settling community, and to nobody else. The Crown therefore makes inquiries as to how decisions by the PSGE will be made, who will determine what benefits are available to beneficiaries and how that will be determined, and what kind of obligations the PSGE will have to report to its members.[102] The Crown also takes note of how the rules of the PSGE may be changed and whether there are processes for planning, monitoring, or reviewing decisions of the PSGE, and what members can do if they disagree with a decision made by the governance entity.[103]

The Crown must also be satisfied that the operations of an entity are transparent before it will recognize the PSGE. Essentially this means the entity must meet basic requirements, such as preparing audited accounts and financial reports, ensuring copies of the rules of the PSGE and financial and other reports are available to members, and providing members with appropriate minutes of meetings and resolutions.[104]

Conclusion

The various stages of the treaty settlement process outlined in this chapter are not simply neutral procedural steps: they are designed to give effect to particular Crown objectives. Consequently, the treaty settlement discourse becomes coloured by both the idea of Crown sovereignty and the concept of symbolic reparation. These characteristics and the Crown's specific requirements of representation, accountability, and transparency for PSGEs create friction, if not actual conflict, with Māori legal traditions. This gives rise to issues of mandate, membership, and dispute resolution and highlights tensions in Māori legal traditions.

5

Post-Settlement Governance and Māori Law

MOEWHARE

"Pāpā, tonight, let's have a story about a great battle."
"Do you like to hear about your warrior ancestors, e Tama?"
"Ae. Well, sometimes – so long as the ending isn't too sad."
"Well, there is usually sadness present whenever our people are divided by warfare."
"I know, but so long as it isn't *too* sad. That will be alright."
"Okay, then. How about the story of Tāne-te-Kohurangi?"
"Who?"
"You might have heard of him by another name – Moewhare."
"Who?"
"Well, let me tell you a story about a battle that he was involved in. This was a battle in which loyalties amongst the community were divided and Moewhare had to make some principled decisions about whether or not to get involved and, if he did, how to proceed."
"What happened, Pāpā?"
"First of all, you should know some of the key people who were caught up in this conflict. Moewhare was a rangatira from Wairoa, and all the other important people in this story were in some way connected to him. His two sisters were involved – Patupuku and Te Whewhera – as well as his younger brother, Te Huki. Patupuku was married to a man called Te-O-Tāne, with whom Moewhare had quarrelled in the past."

"Was the battle between Moewhare and Te-O-Tāne, then?"

"No, interestingly, Moewhare sided with Te-O-Tāne in this instance. It seems there were more important things at stake than their past arguments."

"Like what?"

"People's lives! Moewhare was drawn into this battle, on the side of Te-O-Tāne, because he was concerned to protect his sister Patupuku. The community within which Te-O-Tāne and Patupuku lived was under attack, and Moewhare went to their aid."

"But of course he would. That would have been an easy decision."

"Not exactly. You see, the leaders of the raiding party were also closely related to Moewhare – they were the children of his other sister, Te Whewhera. So Moewhare had to make a difficult decision about what he should do."

"How did he make that decision?"

"Well, he looked to our tikanga and the principles that underlie it. He considered the responsibilities that came from his whakapapa and his relationships with the other people involved. He considered the history of the peoples in the Wairoa area and past disputes over resources. He thought about what was right and fair and just according to our tikanga and what the consequences would be of following one path or another."

"But he chose to help Patupuku and Te-O-Tāne and everything turned out okay, right?

"He certainly helped to ensure that Patupuku was safe, but his nephews never forgave him."

"Why not?"

"He had taken sides against them. And perhaps they did not see that tikanga justified Moewhare's actions."

"That seems a bit unfair to me."

"Maybe. But relationships can be fragile things, especially if everyone has different views about what is fair."

The Settlement Process and Māori Governance Principles

When establishing a post-settlement governance entity, Māori communities will usually try to give expression to the responsibilities that come from whakapapa and relationships with others. But the establishment of post-settlement governance entities shows, in stark relief, the challenges faced by Māori legal traditions. As discussed in this chapter, these challenges arise in the context of dispute resolution and areas of substantive law, such as membership rules. These matters, and others, need to be given careful consideration as Māori work through governance issues.

Waikato-Tainui and Ngāi Tahu: Setting the Framework for Post-Settlement Governance Entities

It has been noted above that the major settlements with Waikato-Tainui and Ngāi Tahu in the mid-1990s provided a foundation for the systematic settlement of historical claims. Similarly, the post-settlement governance arrangements established for the purpose of receiving and managing redress from these two settlements have provided a framework for post-settlement governance in subsequent settlements and Crown policy in this area. The Waikato-Tainui and Ngāi Tahu PSGEs have not been used as templates for PSGEs in later settlements, and, as with the substantive settlements, the Crown has been reluctant to approve some arrangements that were agreed to as part of these two early settlements. However, a brief description of the Waikato-Tainui and Ngāi Tahu PSGEs illustrates the way in which settling groups seek to put in place mechanisms that address the particular issues of Māori governance in the settlement context. In particular, we can see from the post-settlement governance arrangements for these two communities that, while there is the potential to include elements of Māori legal traditions, these entities are primarily designed for commercial activity – that is, economic, but not necessarily political, self-determination.

Waikato-Tainui

The post-settlement governance arrangements for Waikato-Tainui cannot be fully understood without reference to the Kīngitanga, or Māori King Movement. Established in 1858 in response to the activities of the colonial government, the Kīngitanga sought to bring together iwi from across the country in order to provide an effective bulwark against further land alienation and to be a single point of authority that could engage with the British Crown on equal terms. Not all iwi supported the Kīngitanga, and even those that did maintained their own autonomy to greater or lesser degrees. The Kīngitanga continues to this day and, as has been the case since its establishment, finds its strongest adherents among the iwi and hapū of Waikato-Tainui. Any governance arrangements for Waikato-Tainui must be viewed against the backdrop of the Kīngitanga.

It is unsurprising then, that Waikato-Tainui's PSGE draws on some of the institutions of the Kīngitanga and also includes a role for the King or Queen (as the case may be). The central governing body of the PSGE is known as Waikato Tainui Te Kauhanganui Incorporated (Te Kauhanganui). This uses the same nomenclature as was used to describe the council of the Kīngitanga when it was first established. Te Kauhanganui includes representatives elected from each marae (a marae in this case effectively stands in for an electorate or community) covered by the settlement. There are two representatives per marae in accordance with governance reforms that were implemented in 2015. Each of the sixty-eight marae represented in Te Kauhanganui has one vote. Members of Te Kauhanganui are also responsible for electing ten of their number to an executive body, known as Te Arataua. One further member is appointed to Te Arataua by the Māori king.

The rules of Te Kauhanganui state:

1. The objects for which Te Kauhanganui is established are as follows:
   (a) to uphold, support, strengthen and protect the Kiingitanga (which incorporates the principles of unity, the retention of the tribal base in collective ownership and co-operation among peoples)
   (b) to protect, advance, develop and unify the interests of Waikato
   (c) to foster among the members of Waikato the principles of whakaiti, rangimaarie and kia tuupato
   (d) to achieve a settlement of outstanding claims to the Waikato River, the West Coast Harbours and Wairoa and Maioro Land Blocks
   (e) to act as Trustee of the Waikato Raupatu Lands Trust established by the Deed creating the Waikato Raupatu Lands Trust, and
   (f) to do or cause to be done all such other things as the Members of Te Kauhanganui shall consider necessary or desirable for the attainment of all or any of the objects of Te Kauhanganui which are consistent with the spirit and intent of the 1995 Deed of Settlement between Waikato Tainui and the Crown and the Trust Deeds.

There are only two references to tikanga in the rules of Te Kauhanganui, and these are both in relation to the dispute resolution process. Where a dispute is referred to mediation, tikanga will be taken into account in terms of both the skills required of a person appointed as a mediator and the venue of mediation meetings. As with Te Rūnanga o Ngāi Tahu, this also conforms with the pattern, played out in PSGEs of other iwi established subsequently, of some reference to tikanga in relation to disputes, and some attempt to reflect traditional communities within the election process, but otherwise very little reference to anything distinctly Māori and very little reference to anything directed at strengthening Māori law-making and enhancing the recognition of Māori legal traditions as part of a reconciliation process.

Te Rūnanga o Ngāi Tahu

Ngāi Tahu's PSGE was established by private legislation. This is an approach that the Crown has subsequently been reluctant to adopt, largely because the process of preparing bills and getting them on to the legislative program is time-consuming, but also because neither the government nor the settling iwi has complete control over the passage of legislation through the House. However, private legislation was also used to establish the PSGE for Ngāti Awa some years later. In both cases, one motivating factor for the iwi insisting that legislation be used to establish the PSGE was that each iwi had, prior to settlement, been operating under a statutory Māori trust board. Māori trust boards had been established to receive and administer previous settlements; the iwi were interested in retaining the authority that a legislative foundation is seen to provide. Some aspects of a standard trust model are not well suited to the objectives of PSGEs, however; a legislative provision is required to adjust the standard trust. For example, settling groups that use a trust for their PSGE will include in their settlement legislation a provision that exempts the PSGE from the rule against perpetuities, which would otherwise require that the trust be wound up after 80 years.

Ngāi Tahu's PSGE is Te Rūnanga o Ngāi Tahu (TRONT), established by the *Te Runanga o Ngai Tahu Act* of 1996. The act defines the membership of Ngāi Tahu, establishes TRONT as a body corporate, and provides for the dissolution of two previous bodies, the Ngaitahu Māori Trust Board and Te Runanganui o Tahu Incorporated. The act sets up an electoral college system whereby members of Ngāi Tahu elect eighteen district councils, called Papatipu Runanga. Members are entitled to participate in Papatipu Runanga in each district with which they can demonstrate their affiliation. Each Papatipu Runanga then appoints representatives to Te Rūnanga o Ngāi Tahu. This basic framework is provided for in the act, but the details of the governance arrangements are set out in the charter of TRONT.[1] The charter requires that each Papatipu Runanga have a democratic election process to elect a committee to appoint representatives to Te Rūnanga o Ngāi Tahu. There is little mention of tikanga in the charter. The Papatipu Runanga are intended to reflect traditional leadership bodies within Ngāi Tahu and, where disputes about membership arise, those appointed to make an assessment on the membership question must have "knowledge of Tikanga Ngāi Tahu sufficient to enable that person to interpret and make informed judgments on matters relating to or governed by Tikanga Ngāi Tahu."[2] The over-arching principles set out as "Te Kawenata o Ngāi Tahu" (the covenant of Ngāi Tahu) illustrate the focus of the PSGE on the maintenance of an economic base for its beneficiaries.[3] This is entirely consistent with the structure of the settlement process in general and underlines the need to change the substance and process of settlement if there is to be a change in the way that Māori legal traditions are valued within a process of reconciliation.

Principles of Māori Governance and Treaty Settlements

The New Zealand Law Commission[4] has produced several important publications that address Māori legal traditions and treaty settlement issues and provides useful guidance on principles of Māori governance. Eddie Durie, a former chairperson of the Waitangi Tribunal and a justice of the High Court of New Zealand, was one of two commissioners responsible for the report on Māori governance entities, known as the *Waka Umanga* report. The key role of Eddie Durie in the production of this report lends significant weight to its authority.

In the *Waka Umanga* report, the law commission sets out the key principles that it considered to be important in the development of an appropriate governance entity for Māori tribal (and other) organisations. These principles are as follows:[5]

- the principle of autonomy
- the principles of cultural match and mandated vision
- the principles of community empowerment and participatory democracy
- the principles of consensus and assisted dispute resolution
- the principles of fair process, protection of minorities, and access to law
- the principle of choice
- the principle of diversity
- the principle of maintaining economies of scale
- the principle of rationalization
- the principle of early entity development
- the principle of recognition, and
- the principle of ensuring good governance.

These principles provide an important framework for assessing Māori governance arrangements. They are particularly relevant to our subject as they were articulated in a report that specifically focused on Māori governance in the context of treaty settlements and the post-settlement era.

The law commission notes that the principle of autonomy has been recognized in some of the leading projects relating to the governance of Indigenous peoples in North America.[6] To those listed by the commission, we can now also add the provisions in the United Nations Declaration on the Rights of Indigenous Peoples. The commission also notes that in the New Zealand context the principle of recognizing the rights of Indigenous peoples is supported by the Treaty of Waitangi with its guarantee of tino rangatiratanga.[7] The law commission suggests that the key points of this principle are that communities themselves must control the process of designing a governance entity and developing a constitution.[8] This requires a transparent process that provides opportunities for genuine engagement from the community. Traditional processes that rely on consensus and community participation should be used where possible.

An important dimension of this principle is to give effect to Indigenous peoples' right to self-determination. In the New Zealand context, we can also see this principle as the Crown fulfilling its obligations under the Treaty of Waitangi. But this is not simply about meeting human rights standards and maintaining the honour of the Crown. There is also a very practical aspect of this principle. That is, the international literature suggests that governance entities are likely to be more effective representative institutions and more responsive to the needs of the community if the community drives the development of the governance entity. An important part of this and other principles is the idea that community involvement, control, and ownership encourages the community to "buy into" the operation of the governance entity, to support that entity, enhancing its ability to fulfil its role effectively.[9]

"Cultural match" is a term coined by the Harvard Project on American Indian Economic Development; the New Zealand Law Commission draws heavily on the approach advocated by that project.[10] The basic idea underlying the term (and the principle referenced by the term in the commission's list) is that the governance entity, its structure, and its processes ought to align closely with the community's cultural worldview, particularly with respect to matters such as how authority operates, how decisions are made, and other aspects of the exercise of leadership.

The law commission notes that the principle of cultural match reflects community understandings of how people see themselves, especially in relation to wider descent groups, and expresses the community's preferences in the development of a constitution.[11]

The commission also suggests that this principle must reflect the past, present, and future of the community.[12] That is, cultural match should not be seen to limit the community to historical social structures or concepts, but the history of the community is an important element to consider in determining the character of governance structures. Also important is the way the community conceptualises itself today as a people how it sees itself in the future as a people.

The concept of cultural match is now widely used in Indigenous governance discourse. However, some commentators have suggested that the way the concept is used by the Harvard Project researchers is more limiting than many Indigenous communities might wish. Patrick Sullivan, a prominent Australian critic of the Harvard Project's conclusions, has argued that cultural match is less about developing governance models that are consistent with Indigenous values and more about legitimising Western ideas of good governance.[13] Sullivan's critique suggests that Indigenous communities ought to take care when deploying the principle of cultural match in the development of governance entities.

The principle of community empowerment and participatory democracy is about recognizing and engaging the constituent groups that comprise the wider community. In the case of PSGEs, these include the individuals, hapū, or whānau that comprise the settling community. The law commission notes that in the case of treaty settlements, engagement with particular sections of the community will be crucial to the success and durability of settlements.[14] Within any given settlement, there are likely to be issues or sites that relate to specific sub-groups within the broader settling community. PSGEs must include mechanisms that ensure sub-group interests are recognized, while at the same time attending to the collective needs of the entire settling community in a fair and equitable manner.

The commission draws on Māori and non-Māori sources for this principle.[15] The commission found that concepts such as community empowerment and participatory democracy can be observed in traditional Māori leadership structures and values. It also noted that the *New Zealand Bill of Rights Act* of 1990 recognizes similar values. And though the commission does not state so explicitly, arguably the form of the treaty itself also supports this principle. The treaty was not signed on behalf of all Māori but, rather, by the rangatira of individual hapū; this suggests that this was the primary level of leadership responsibility and accountability, though this did not preclude a group from entering jointly into an agreement such as the Treaty of Waitangi.

The principles of consensus and assisted dispute resolution also have direct antecedents within Māori culture and traditional forms of decision-making. Consensus decision-making is consistent with the way that leadership and authority operate in accordance with the values and principles associated with the concept of mana. However, the law commission notes that a number of factors have "undermined the traditional value of consensus in modern Māori society."[16] The governance entities with which many Māori are familiar often operate according to majority votes. For example, the rules and regulations that govern entities such as Māori trust boards, Māori incorporations, and trusts that manage Māori land under Te Ture Whenua Māori/*The Māori Land Act* (1993) all require that decisions be made by voting. Government policy and action have also played a role in undermining traditional leadership structures, often contributing to tensions within communities by encouraging dissension.

Many of these factors are at play in the treaty settlement dynamic. For example, the overlapping claims policy employed by the Crown has been found by the Waitangi Tribunal to foster exactly the kind of dissension and "patch disputes" that the law commission refers to.[17] The tribunal has expressed concern that the Crown's approach, which has tended to shut out communities with overlapping interests until too late in the settlement process, undermines the objective of achieving stable and durable settlements.[18] This is merely one of the more recent examples in a long history of colonial interaction that has encouraged Māori communities to exaggerate their own claims at the expense of other Māori communities.[19]

The basis of the principles of fair process, protection of minorities, and access to law is that, in order to maintain its legitimacy, the governance entity must be demonstrably established in a way that is fair and transparent. According to the law commission, a central feature of the establishment process must be to ensure that there exists "a faithful record of proceedings that provides conclusive evidence that the entity structure and charter has the free and informed approval of most members in each constituency."[20]

Furthermore, the constitution of the governance entity ought to also embody the concept of fair process by ensuring that appropriate dispute resolution procedures are available to its members, including the ability for members to access the protections provided by state law as a last resort. The constitution should also protect the rights of minorities or particular constituencies among the general membership.[21] These measures not only provide for fairness (at least procedural fairness) to all members of the community but, in doing so, they also legitimize the governance entity's claims to represent the interests of its members. The law commission also contends that decisions relating to community governance should, as far as possible, be left to the community itself to determine.[22]

The Waitangi Tribunal has similarly found that the principles of the Treaty of Waitangi include the principle of options.[23] There is of course a balance to be struck between choice and ensuring fair process. This balance involves careful and, inevitably, value-laden judgments as to what constitutes fair process. If "fair process" is simply an imposition of Western liberal democratic values, then the nod towards autonomy and choice might well be questioned. In any case, in order to assess how this principle of choice is implemented (or not), it is instructive to consider the treaty settlement process and the "fair process"-based limitations that the Crown imposes on PSGEs.

The principle of diversity aims to reflect the diversity of Māori communities. The commission is clear that a "one size fits all" approach is not appropriate in the context of Māori governance entity design and implementation.[24] Different iwi and hapū will have been affected differently by colonization. They will have distinctive social, cultural, and economic histories that result in distinctive governance needs today. Different groups may also hold very different views about the optimal way to structure their relationships with each other and externally.[25] The principle of diversity is also a necessary corollary of the principle of choice described above. The requirements imposed by the Crown on PSGE structure create difficulties for the application of the principle of diversity in the settlement context. As Māori legal academic Robert Joseph has noted, nineteen of the "20 Questions" that the OTS considers when determining whether proposed governance structures are acceptable for use as a PSGE refer to "Western standards of corporate governance and do not seek to reflect practices and traditions of the Māori community involved."[26] As a consequence, there is little diversity among Crown-approved PSGEs.

One of the key motivations behind the *Waka Umanga* report was the concern that the ad hoc development of Māori governance entities in response to immediate and specific needs (as opposed to being based on wider strategic objectives) was leading to a proliferation of governance bodies, creating duplication and inefficiencies. The commission, therefore, recognizes the importance of developing a system of Māori governance that encourages efficient use of limited tribal resources and takes advantage of economies of scale. As noted earlier, patterns of ramification and aggregation can be seen as aspects of Māori political and constitutional history. That is to say, that there is no tikanga-based objection to the principle of maintaining economies of scale. Māori groups have historically come together for large-scale projects and continue to do so today. It is important to note that the commission is not advocating the aggregation of Māori communities without regard to other factors.

The commission suggests that for such aggregation to be successful, the resulting governance entity ought to:[27]

- represent the largest group that is consistent with the people's perception of their history and identity and that is acceptable to them for the purpose given, and
- expressly support the traditional autonomy of each constituency.

These factors are particularly important in the context of the settlement of historical treaty claims. OTS policy is to negotiate with "large, natural groups." This policy reflects the objective of achieving economies of scale, and as long as proper regard is given to the "natural" criterion, then it will be consistent with the approach advanced by the commission.

In its reference to the problem of multiple entities, the law commission notes particularly the various requirements of the *Māori Fisheries Act* and the requirements imposed by the Crown through their confirmation of PSGEs: "To achieve a reasonable alignment in forming new entities, Māori must have time to debate the option of combining with others already existing. Where the constituencies are not the same, provision may be considered for a common administration that manages separate accounts."[28] As the commission points out, Crown settlement policies have worked against rationalisation of governance entities. This is not only a result of the different sets of requirements that must be met for the settlement of commercial fishing claims and other historical treaty claims. The structure of the negotiations process leaves little space for the consideration of joint-governance arrangements where there have not been joint negotiations or a joint settlement (though this may now, belatedly, be changing).

A central concern of the commission is that the development of Māori governance entities has been ad hoc and reactive rather than strategic and proactive. The principle of early entity development is intended to address this particular issue.[29] Though sensible, however, few communities have the infrastructure and resources necessary to work through a principled and participatory process for the establishment of a representative entity without the funding and incentives created by participation in the settlement process. There are few recent examples of iwi and hapū that have been able to establish, outside of the settlement process in a carefully managed and deliberate fashion, the representative entities designed to be used for PSGEs in treaty settlements, among other things.

The principle of recognition is that an entity with a proven mandate to represent an iwi, hapū, or other community should be recognized as the legitimate representative of that community, as legally and exclusively entitled to represent the community to third parties and in legal proceedings on all matters relating to the community's affairs, save to the extent that it is constrained in doing so by its charter.[30] If this principle is to be effective and legitimate, then it must be put to the community expressly at the point of formation of the PSGE. At present, this is not the case. That is, currently PSGEs are expressly established for the management and implementation of the settlement. They are not required to seek a mandate for any wider purposes or general representation. This principle also further conflates the iwi, hapū, or community with the governance entity. Admittedly, many of the cultural redress mechanisms also have the effect of putting the PSGE in the place of the iwi or hapū and/or traditional community leaders.

The principle of good governance is aimed at ensuring that the governance entity operates according to recognized standards of good governance and management. It is hard to argue against such a principle. It should, after all, be the overriding objective of the governance entity to deliver good governance for the community. A PSGE should aim to operate in a way that demonstrates good governance practices; in doing so, it maintains the mandate of the community and the confidence of third parties with whom it may have contractual or other relationships.[31] However, the general principle does raise a number of specific questions, such as whose standards are being recognized and deployed as standards of good governance? Does the community itself determine the standards of "good governance"? Or are these standards externally imposed? Depending on the answers to these questions, one might also ask whether this principle is about securing the interests of Indigenous peoples or ensuring that Indigenous peoples are tied into the systems of global capital. Arguably, while the *Waka Umanga Report* identifies a number of issues relating to Māori governance in the context of the treaty settlement process, and proposes several governance principles as a way to avoid exerting undue external pressure on Māori legal traditions, a number of aspects of the current settlement process make it difficult to apply these governance principles.

Post-Settlement Governance and Māori Dispute Resolution

There are three important points that can be made about Māori legal traditions in relation to dispute resolution and how the treaty settlement process affects these traditions. First, the maintenance of relationships can be characterised as an exercise of authority and tino rangatiratanga. Dispute resolution can be viewed, essentially, as a process of structuring relationships at points of conflict or disagreement. Choices about models of dispute resolution in the treaty settlement context, with its overlay of tino rangatiratanga discourse, are therefore of particular significance.[32] Second, the claims and settlement process inevitably places the Crown at the centre of the dispute. Dispute resolution models in this context tend to be models that are favoured by the Crown and/or that have the greatest likelihood of engaging the Crown. Third, even in situations where Māori are able to construct dispute resolution processes within the settlement context that aim to give effect to Māori legal traditions, these processes nevertheless play out in the shadow of the state legal system and the threat of judicial review; inevitably, they implement Māori legal traditions only up to a certain point.[33]

The Waitangi Tribunal's *Tamaki Makaurau Settlement Process Report* describes the importance of relationships within Māori society and frames the maintenance of relationships and the resolution of disputes as functions of tino rangatiratanga.[34] In the report, the Waitangi Tribunal strongly criticized the Crown's approach to managing intersecting Māori interests in the context of settlement negotiations. This was neither the first nor the last time that the tribunal had leveled such criticisms at the Crown. At the heart of the tribunal's analysis was its view on the adverse effect of the Crown's policy on whanaungatanga and the relationships between Māori groups. As emphasised earlier, whanaungatanga is a key principle underlying Māori legal systems. It is crucial for determining rights and obligations and fundamental to Māori dispute resolution processes. If the settlement process damages relationships between and among Māori communities, then it also damages the ability of those communities to apply Māori legal traditions relating to dispute resolution. This leads to a reliance on the Crown, as illustrated by the two examples that follow: the Ngāti Tama/Ngāti Maniapoto mediation and the CNI forestry settlement.

There can be no real argument with the statement that the treaty claims and settlement process focuses dispute resolution processes on the Crown. Perhaps the clearest illustration of this is the nature of the Waitangi Tribunal process and the type of claims that may be registered with the tribunal. All claims must be made by Māori against the Crown. While this is often exactly as it should be, from time to time, the tribunal is asked to intervene in disputes that are really Māori–Māori disputes. For the tribunal to inquire into such disputes, they must be framed as being directed at Crown actions.

In 2000, a boundary dispute arose between two neighbouring iwi – Ngāti Tama and Ngāti Maniapoto. The urgent need to resolve the dispute was created by the then imminent settlement of Ngāti Tama's historical claims against the Crown. The dispute, therefore, arose in the context of the treaty settlement process; in order to engage the Waitangi Tribunal, it was framed not as a dispute between Ngāti Tama and Ngāti Maniapoto but as a claim against the Crown and its processes.

The tribunal directed the parties to undertake a process of mediation. Two co-mediators were appointed – one with skills and knowledge relating to tikanga, Māori law, and dispute resolution; and one mediator trained in Western forms of alternative dispute resolution. I have written elsewhere of this process as a good example of the ways that Māori traditions can be deployed in the context of Treaty of Waitangi claims and settlement.[35] Here, I consider a different aspect of using such an approach – that is, the way the settlement process affected the nature of the engagement between the two iwi.

An important factor in determining the structure and mechanisms of dispute resolution processes is the particular vision of justice that a community collectively pursues. Dispute resolution processes formed in the context of, or, in the case of PSGEs, as an outcome of, the settlement process, are in part shaped by the vision of justice that underlies the settlement process itself. This is evident in the Ngāti Tama/Ngāti Maniapoto mediation.[36] While it appears that Ngāti Maniapoto approached the mediation as a Māori dispute resolution process, concentrating on tikanga rights and obligations, Ngāti Tama, understandably, were focused on concluding their settlement. This led Ngāti Tama to pursue the type of justice that the settlement process itself gives priority. As the following discussion illustrates, this can be quite different from tikanga-based visions of justice. This has implications not only for the settlement process but also, more specifically, for dispute resolution processes that develop from the settlement process. Similar issues have been noted among First Nations in Canada;[37] analysis of the British Columbia treaty process again provides a useful platform from which to consider these issues in the New Zealand context.

Woolford has pointed to the strong focus within the British Columbia treaty process on procedural justice that is consistent with non-Indigenous conceptualizations, rather than visions of substantive justice that might align with Indigenous expectations of the process.[38] Within the British Columbia treaty process, Woolford notes that "one can observe the reliance on the dialogical rationality of opposing parties to forge just arguments through fair and equal negotiations."[39] But, as Tully has argued, such reliance is premised on the parties entering into the process as equals and developing a process that incorporates the different cultural understandings of justice and proper procedure that each might hold.[40] Unfortunately, that has not been the experience of First

Nations groups who have engaged in the treaty process,[41] nor has it been the experience of Māori claimant groups that have negotiated Treaty of Waitangi settlements.[42]

The theoretical capacity of a fair process to deliver just outcomes is "confronted by the obstacles standing in the way of what Habermas refers to as the 'ideal speech situations.'"[43] In order for an ideal speech situation to be achieved, the parties must be genuinely engaged in a communicative interaction aimed at developing mutual understanding. The parties must not be guided by instrumental objectives in this scenario. Woolford points out that these conditions are not present in the British Columbia treaty process, largely because the constraints on the non-Indigenous government parties "prevent them from participating in the open, interest-based negotiations necessary for communicative interaction."[44] Woolford also notes that, although the non-Indigenous governments see themselves as participating in interest-based negotiation, this does not match up with the reality.[45] The non-Indigenous governments, in fact, enter into negotiations with a whole range of issues on which they will not compromise. It is difficult to describe issues on which there will be no compromise as "interests" and not "positions."

In Treaty of Waitangi settlement negotiations, the New Zealand Crown adopts a similar approach. The Crown comes to the negotiating table with a range of positions from which it will not shift. There is, in reality, very little to negotiate in these "negotiations." The discussions become focused on relatively peripheral matters – which properties will be transferred as part of the commercial redress, for example, rather than how the value of the commercial assets ought to be calculated; how many statutory acknowledgements (or other cultural redress instruments) will be appropriate, rather than the most appropriate way to reflect the treaty relationship between the settling group and the Crown and its agents; what matters should be included in the historical account, rather than considering which interests are being met (and those being overlooked) in constructing a negotiated history. One of the central concerns that claimant representatives have expressed about the settlement process is that, although the process is labeled a "negotiation," it really does not resemble negotiation in any accurate sense of the word.[46]

Furthermore, as noted above, Indigenous peoples make justice claims that are based on difference as well as sameness (that is, claims to both cultural-symbolic justice and socioeconomic justice).[47] In the New Zealand context, political philosopher Andrew Sharp has also identified the tension between distinctiveness and equality within the justice claims made by Māori in relation to the Treaty of Waitangi. While the concept of justice between parties requires two (or more) identifiably distinct groups (or individuals), Sharp argues that a condition of justice is that there must exist to some degree a sense of unity between the parties – otherwise the space between disputing parties is simply conflict based on force and power and cannot be properly called justice.[48] Much the same point is made by Jeremy Webber, though from a legal pluralist perspective rather than from within the framework of political philosophy.[49] Sharp suggests that this tension between sameness and distinctiveness can be seen in Māori social organization, which could be characterized as traditionally structured around "opposition within unity."[50]

The Crown's vision of justice does not yet appear to acknowledge the need to address issues of distinctiveness and equality.[51] The Crown proposals for the settlement of Treaty of Waitangi claims give some indication of the Crown's perception of justice within these settlements. The detailed proposals circulated by the Crown for consultation note that in redressing claims the Crown will take into account:[52]

- the requirements of justice and equity
- the best interests of all New Zealanders
- what is affordable, and
- relativities between claims (i.e., the relative severity of the grievance in relation to other claims).

Only the first bullet point actually refers to the justice required to redress a particular treaty breach. This suggests the narrow role that the Crown sees for the concept of justice in the settlement of historical treaty breaches. The result is that the justice delivered by the treaty settlement process is constrained by both the concentration on certainty and the imposition of non-Indigenous governments' visions of justice. In the Ngāti Tama/Ngāti Maniapoto mediation, the narrow role of "justice" within the settlement process consequently narrowed the role of substantive justice in a dispute resolution process between two iwi – a process that had the potential to be based more on tikanga principles and Māori visions of justice.

The Ngāti Tama/Ngāti Maniapoto mediation was constrained by the parameters of the Waitangi Tribunal process. But even in cases where iwi have more freedom to set their own dispute resolution processes, the ultimate supervision of the state courts ensures that these processes always take place under the shadow of the state legal system. Although there is greater potential in such situations for the incorporation of tikanga-based processes, there is also greater potential for Māori legal traditions to be transformed through engagement with the state system if the dispute resolution process is perceived to reflect and implement tikanga (even when, in reality, it is regulated by the state court system).

The Central North Island forestry settlement provides an illustration of this type of transformation. The process for resolving any disagreements in relation to the allocation of lands included in the Central North Island forestry settlement was designed by the iwi who made up the collective, and was intended explicitly to be a tikanga-based dispute resolution process. However, the operation of that tikanga-based process is affected by the participants having the ability to remove the dispute to the state court system.[53]

Though the tikanga-based process has now taken place, the CNI allocation of land was earlier the subject of litigation. The judge who heard the case, former Waitangi Tribunal Chairperson Justice Joe Williams, counseled the parties on this very issue, cautioning them about the effect on their own self-determination of seeking adjudication from the state legal system on a tikanga-based process.[54]

In a 2015 decision, dealing with a dispute arising out of a treaty settlement with an iwi from Taranaki, Justice Williams expressed his concern about the lack of engagement with tikanga issues (and, consequently, the lack of tikanga evidence presented to the original decision-maker in that case). Justice Williams noted that this "has the effect of reframing what is primarily a question of ancestral right (at least in the first instance) as a modern mandate question."[55] While the experience in both New Zealand and British Columbia suggests that it is difficult to remove settlements and associated disputes from the supervision of the state courts,[56] it is essential for the durability of those settlements to revitalize the autonomy of Māori legal traditions.

Post-Settlement Governance and Substantive Māori Law: Membership Rules

There have also been changes to the substance of Māori laws and legal principles identifiable within the context of the Treaty settlement process. This section considers the issue of membership and membership rules. As Kirsty Gover's work has demonstrated, the ways in which Māori communities identify and confirm membership, and the rights and obligations that go along with membership, are subject to significant pressures in the context of the settlement process and the establishment of PSGEs.[57] The tensions in Māori legal history are reflected in the constitutions of these purpose-built PSGEs and the rules they adopt in relation to membership.

Membership rules can also be seen as an aspect of the particular form of "certainty" that is sought by the Crown and which permeates the entire settlement process. Non-Indigenous governments' focus on certainty also imposes a range of particular constraints on justice in treaty negotiations. These constraints are often explained in terms of what is "practical," "reasonable," "politically acceptable," or "pragmatic." For example, in Treaty of Waitangi settlements, parties explicitly confirm that the settlement package is "fair *in the circumstances*".[58] The British Columbia treaty process has also been motivated in large part by the non-Indigenous governments' desire to achieve certainty.[59] Woolford has outlined the importance, to non-Indigenous governments' visions of certainty, of finally and comprehensively settling land claims issues.[60] Māori legal academic Ani Mikaere has also described the type of thinking that appears to be central to non-Indigenous governments' visions of certainty in the context of treaty negotiations. In a 1997 article on the processes aimed at settling Indigenous claims, Mikaere points to comments made by one of the key architects of the Treaty of Waitangi settlement process, then New Zealand Minister of Justice, Doug Graham, who had rejected the possibility of Māori receiving anything close to full compensation – the estimates of early settlements suggested that they represented approximately 2 percent of the total value of the land lost – but was definite in his position that settlements would be final.[61]

The language in official policy documents has since shifted from "full and final" to "fair and durable," though the Treaty settlement discourse remains firmly rooted in "finality."[62] The dominant discourse reflects a particular vision of certainty, but also the way in which this vision of certainty constrains visions of justice. In using the certainty language of "realism" and "finality," non-Indigenous governments assert their own social and economic logic, values, and norms in an attempt to create a "universal" common-sense vision of justice.

There is an important link between the aims of comprehensiveness and finality, which appear to be the key pillars of non-Indigenous parties' conceptualization of certainty in treaty settlement negotiations, and the pressures exerted on substantive Māori legal traditions, such as those relating to membership. Ravi de Costa has addressed the issue of the comprehensiveness of the scope of Indigenous rights dealt with in the context of the British Columbia treaty process[63] and notes that the non-Indigenous governments' aims of comprehensiveness and finality can also be seen in the treaty process.[64] Furthermore, he suggests that this process is, rather ambitiously, premised on the idea that Aboriginal and non-Indigenous leaders will be able, at this particular point in time, to "comprehensively and conclusively set out the needs and desires of their communities."[65]

De Costa also notes, however, that it is not necessary for the British Columbia treaty process to proceed on that basis. *The Report of the British Columbia Claims Task Force* envisaged that the treaty-making process would take some time for each First Nation to complete and that demanding that agreements only be confirmed as comprehensive treaties could be problematic. Therefore, the task force proposed that a range of interim measures be employed to ensure that First Nations interests in lands and resources would be protected throughout the treaty negotiation process. These included:[66]

- notification of potential impacts on issues that may be discussed at treaty tables, particularly unilateral action on lands and resources
- consultation over that action
- consent for such initiatives
- joint management processes requiring consensus, and
- restrictions or moratoria on land and resource use.

De Costa also points out, however, that interim measures have not been used in the way that First Nations leaders had hoped.[67] The province has generally been unwilling to implement interim measures before an agreement in principle is reached.[68] Essentially, this approach applies the same sort of requirement of comprehensiveness that is central to the Treaty of Waitangi settlement process in New Zealand. As in the New Zealand case, the primary objective in the British Columbia treaty process appears to be to achieve certainty for the non-Indigenous government parties. This effectively shapes the requirements of membership rules imposed on PSGEs by the settlement process.

As noted above, non-Indigenous governments' objectives of certainty include finality as well as comprehensiveness. This conceptualization of certainty requires not only that all "outstanding" justice claims be addressed in one agreement but also that the agreement should deal with those claims finally. This finality is most often manifested as an extinguishment of rights. In her 1997 article on Indigenous claims processes, Ani Mikaere notes the problem of basing settlements on the extinguishment of Indigenous peoples' rights. She concludes that structuring treaty settlement policy in this way actually puts in place significant barriers to Māori having their treaty rights properly recognized.[69]

Mikaere points to recommendations made by the Canadian Federal Government's 1985 Task Force to Review Comprehensive Claims Policy and the 1996 Royal Commission on Aboriginal Peoples that the objective of settlements ought not to be the extinguishment of Aboriginal peoples' rights.[70] She also notes examples of settlements that have invoked the claim of finality by aiming to extinguish the rights of Indigenous communities, which resulted in perpetuating disputes, undermining not only the delivery of justice but also the non-Indigenous parties' objectives of certainty.[71]

A recent example from New Zealand of the development of settlement-related policy initiatives demonstrates the way certainty is often conceptualized by non-Indigenous governments. In July 2009, the New Zealand government produced a list of seven ideas to improve the settlement process. This list makes it clear that the Crown views the difficulties with the settlement process to be primarily – if not exclusively – about the efficiency of the process. The seven ideas are directed at streamlining the process and improving certainty, not justice. The list envisages implementing the following measures, each of which can be characterized as directed at improving certainty:[72]

- using more mediation to resolve mandating issues prior to settlement [certainty of claimant group]
- providing information to claimant groups early in the process about the type of redress that is available [certainty of forms of redress]
- encourage claimant groups joining together for settlement negotiations purposes [certainty of the number of negotiations that need to be completed]
- increased transparency from the Crown on who it intends to negotiate with and potential settlement quantum [certainty of claimant group and value of redress]
- greater use of senior Crown negotiators and facilitators [certainty of decision-making authority]
- less Crown involvement in settlement decisions [certainty of Crown responsibility], and
- streamlining the legislative process [certainty of legislative content and timetable].

These measures are not necessarily contrary to Māori groups' objectives. Most settling groups would share the Crown's desire for a speedy and efficient settlement process. It should also be noted that these measures are not wholly in conflict with the concept of justice. For example, the proposals to support mediation of mandate issues as early as possible and to allow settling groups to work through some matters without the Crown's interference may lead to more just resolutions. However, as a whole the list indicates the characteristics that non-Indigenous governments often see as important in these processes and the way such governments tend to conceptualize and emphasize certainty. The objectives of finality, comprehensiveness, and rights-extinguishment that contribute to the Crown's vision of certainty are inter-connected and influence not only the Crown's conceptualization of the treaty settlement process but also the way the settlement process contributes to the tensions in Māori legal history, particularly in areas of substantive law, such as membership rules.

Kirsty Gover's comprehensive study of membership in tribal constitutions illustrates how the rules of a PSGE might affect the Indigenous legal traditions relating to membership. Issues of membership comprise a significant area of substantive change to Māori legal traditions, demonstrating how Māori legal systems are responding to the settlement process.

Gover describes how substantive rules or laws relating to membership in modern settlement processes have tended to focus primarily on descent, despite the fact that this may distort or misrepresent Indigenous legal traditions relating to membership. As Gover notes, this approach to membership provides certainty for non-Indigenous governments but severely limits the autonomy of Indigenous communities.[73]

Gover's work provides an analysis of corporate membership within Indigenous communities that places Indigenous agency at the centre of the discussion. The question of Māori agency is a central part of what animates the adaptation tension considered in this book. The focus on Indigenous agency also moves Gover away from the assumption that formality and institutionalization are incommensurable with custom, an assumption that has obscured other issues, such as those of agency, in some pluralist accounts.

Gover identifies two key concerns raised in the literature relating to the juridification of Indigenous nations. The first is a concern that formal rules cannot accurately reflect the customary law relating to membership, that the customary system has an inherent flexibility that cannot be matched by a formalized constitution that inevitably fails to capture the nuances of cultural practice. The second concern is that juridification actually distorts the customary membership rules.[74]

Gover rejects this strictly oppositional approach, arguing instead that formality per se need not be seen as necessarily inconsistent with Indigenous legal traditions.[75] Culture must be understood as a dynamic process rather than a "static attribute of a community."[76] Members of the community are actively engaged in a process of cultural production. In the field of legal pluralism, this might be described as legal subjects participating in the construction of the legal orders by which they are regulated.

There is no reason that the type of formalization seen in membership rules of Māori communities as a result of the establishment of PSGEs cannot be a part of this dynamic process of Indigenous law-making as cultural production. John Borrows has described a number of sources of Indigenous law, illustrating the fact that custom is only one source and that Indigenous legal systems can have space for formalization and institutionalization of laws.[77] That being the case, the real issue is not whether the treaty settlement process results in the formalization of membership rules but, rather, to what extent Māori have determined that membership rules ought to be formalized: Gover's key question of Indigenous agency.[78]

Gover notes that descent tends to be the key criterion for membership of an Indigenous community within the common law jurisdictions that her study encompasses. She views this as allowing plenty of scope for Indigenous agency.[79] However, the emphasis on descent has proved quite limiting for Māori. Descent is a vitally important aspect of community membership according to Māori legal traditions, but it is not the only relevant criterion. For example, the rights and privileges of membership are also dependent on one's participation in community life and one's maintenance of a connection with ancestral lands. The recent application of descent rules to PSGEs is not dissimilar to the approach taken by the Native Land Court with regard to the identification of customary interests in land. In both instances, particular criteria appear to be given priority in order to facilitate administration by the state legal system. In the Native Land Court, rights that came through conquest and the appropriation of land became predominant, regardless of the Māori legal systems' concern with other matters, such as ancestral connection to the land.[80]

This all reflects the Crown's particular vision of certainty in the settlement process, which is further illustrated by a range of procedural requirements imposed on groups wishing to enter settlement negotiations.[81] These requirements are primarily aimed at achieving the kind of certainty sought by the Crown; they have been widely criticized by Māori for overlooking requirements of substantive justice, thereby hindering the settlement process.[82]

In particular, the Crown seeks to achieve its vision of certainty by requiring that all negotiations be comprehensive and by entering into negotiations only with "large, natural groups." The negotiations and the resulting settlement agreements are intended to be comprehensive in the sense that they aim to settle all the historical claims of the settling group.[83] The scope of each settlement is usually defined by listing the specific claims registered with the Waitangi Tribunal, identifying all members of the settling group by reference to tribal ancestors, and delineating the geographical boundaries of the settlement area.[84] There have been some notable exceptions to the Crown's policy of comprehensiveness, but these are anomalies.[85] The Crown has attempted to frame the requirement of comprehensiveness as being necessary to deliver justice.[86] But it is difficult to read the primary objective of comprehensiveness as anything other than the Crown's desire for a particular kind of certainty.

On the other hand, the Crown is entirely open about its desire for certainty being the driving force behind its preference for negotiating with large, natural groups.[87] The Crown's guide to claims and negotiations argues that, in addition to certainty, this policy also delivers just settlements, by both enabling the use of a wider range of redress instruments and addressing all overlapping interests at the same time. The Crown also sets the framework within which any group wishing to enter settlement negotiations must achieve and demonstrate a mandate to negotiate on behalf of the claimant group. It is, of course, important that those who claim to represent a claimant group really do have the authority to speak for that group on these issues. This demonstrates again that there are important connections between justice and certainty discourses. Yet the Crown's overriding concern in this area still appears to be the objective of certainty. This demand for certainty places clear pressure on Māori legal traditions that relate to matters such as membership.

Conclusion

I have argued here that the treaty settlement process places pressure on Māori legal traditions, affecting dispute resolution and substantive law. Without any detailed case studies based on empirical research covering changes over time and across Māori communities, it is not possible to assert that particular aspects of the settlement process have led directly to specific changes to Māori legal traditions. It is possible, however, to comment on the nature of the pressures created by the settlement process and how these pressures might contribute to tensions in Māori legal history. That analysis, in turn, enables some assessment about whether the treaty settlement process is fulfilling its claims to provide self-determination and reconciliation.

In relation to the tension of adaptation, the settlement process appears to limit the way in which Māori legal traditions can change and adapt. Key Māori principles that underpin law-making processes are constrained, and the Crown's reluctance to address cultural-symbolic justice issues further limits the scope for tikanga-based law-making processes to flourish within PSGEs. The philosophical underpinnings of the settlement process can also shape the way that Māori design and enter into dispute resolution processes. As illustrated by the Ngāti Tama/Ngāti Maniapoto mediation, the settlement process conditions participants to embrace a particular vision of justice, a vision that makes it difficult for settling groups to be anything other than reactive. Central to the tension of adaptation is the question of Indigenous agency, which Kirsty Gover addresses in her work on tribal membership. It is difficult to see a great deal of Indigenous agency in the parameters set by the Crown in its pursuit of its objectives of "certainty."

The examples in this book also suggest how the treaty settlement process affects the contribution of the Treaty second key tension, the relationship to the treaty partner. The settlement process places pressure on Māori legal systems to become more connected to and focused on the state and state legal institutions. This tends to direct the development of Māori legal traditions towards more engagement with the state and towards a more state-centred operation. This feeds into a vision of only weak legal pluralism, and does not reflect the stronger concepts of legal pluralism that assist with de-centring the state and which are more consistent with Indigenous self-determination projects. The limited use and interpretation of Māori legal principles relating to law-making and the content of the settlements themselves frame Māori as very much a junior partner in the treaty relationship. PSGEs that come out of the settlement process are, to some extent, predicated on that framework. The Ngāti Tama/Ngāti Maniapoto mediation exemplifies how the Crown is very much the focus of disputes relating to the treaty, and the Central North Island forestry settlement shows how difficult it can be for groups coming through the settlement process to engage with each other without resort to the state legal system. In the case of membership rules of PSGEs, it seems clear that these rules are, first and foremost, established for the benefit of the Crown, to make engagement with PSGEs administratively simple for officials and to secure the Crown's objectives of certainty.

This analysis also indicates that, in terms of the third tension, renewal, the settlement process encourages and in many cases requires that Māori communities move away from tikanga-based law making, dispute resolution, and substantive legal practices. The basic structures of PSGEs are founded on Western law and values, with only a limited recognition of Māori legal traditions in some instances. In the area of law-making, the treaty settlement process appears to encourage the discarding of Māori law rather than the re-invigoration of applicable tikanga. The Crown imposes a range of requirements on the rules and structures of PSGEs, and yet none of these rules addresses standards that derive from Māori legal traditions or Māori conceptions of leadership and accountability. The result is that PSGEs are based on Western ideas of governance. Both the Ngāti Tama/Ngāti Maniapoto mediation and the Central North Island forestry settlement litigation reflect the way that participants may move away from tikanga-based processes, even in instances where the parties have gone to some effort to incorporate Māori legal traditions. Similarly, in the case of membership rules, many settling groups will go to considerable effort to ensure that the membership of the PSGE reflects the traditional membership of the community; however, the requirements imposed by the Crown are effectively prioritised in order to enable the implementation of the settlement agreement.

These examples suggest that the pressures created by the treaty settlement process have a significant role in animating the key tensions in Māori legal history. This has significant implications for the stated aims of the settlement process of reconciliation and self-determination.

6

New Stories and Old Stories Re-Told

TIMI KARA

"Look at that cloak, e Tama. That belonged to one of your ancestors, Ta Timi Kara."
"Is that the same person that they call Sir James Carroll?"
"Ae, that's right. My great-grandmother – your great-great-grandmother – was a Carroll."
"Why is his cloak in this museum?"
"I suppose it is because it is very beautiful."
"But why isn't it back in Wairoa?"
"That's a very good question! There are many taonga that museums have now that they look after. There are long arguments about some of the rights and wrongs of that. But do you remember that we did take one cloak that belonged to Timi Kara back to Wairoa?"
"Oh, yeah. We brought it back from that museum in Canada."
"That's right."
"And Aunty and Uncle had organised a big celebration to welcome it home."
"Yes. Because Timi Kara was such an important person, it was an important event when his cloak came back to Wairoa."
"Why was Timi Kara important?"
"Well, he was another leader of our people."
"Like Tamatea and Kahungunu and Rongomaiwahine and Tapuwae and Te Rauhina and all that lot."
"In some ways, very much like those great leaders. But he lived in a different time and so he necessarily had to provide leadership in a different kind of way."

"What do you mean?"
"Well, Tamatea and Kahungunu and Rongomaiwahine didn't need to deal with Pākehā laws and government. There were no Pākehā in Aotearoa in their time. But that had all changed by the time that Timi Kara was born. So, Timi Kara sought ways of helping his people by engaging with Pākehā law and government."
"What do you mean by 'government'? Do you mean like the Prime Minister and stuff?"
"Yes, that's basically it. In fact, Timi Kara got to be Acting Prime Minister a couple of times."
"Really!?"
"Yes. He was widely respected in the Pākehā world as well as in the Māori world. He often helped to broker agreements between the Pākehā government and Māori – whether that was with the Māori Parliament, the Māori King, or iwi such as Tūhoe. Things didn't always lead to the outcome he envisaged, but he did his best to find mechanisms of Pākehā law that would protect our lands and also create space for the exercise of Māori authority."
"Was he a warrior then?"
"Maybe you could say that he was a word warrior. He was famous for his oratory, being an eloquent speaker in both Māori and English. Some people still talk about a time when he had defended his administration of Native affairs with such skillful rhetoric, imagery, and passion that even his main detractor walked across the floor of Parliament to congratulate him."
"No way!"
"That's what they say."
"And do people sometimes call him Jimmy Taihoa?"
"They do! You know how 'taihoa' means to slow down, right? Well, Timi Kara always counseled the need for patience, delay, and reflection when making decisions. Many of his ideas around the buying and selling of Māori land seem to have been based on this kind of idea."
"And doesn't he have something to do with the meeting house at our marae?"
"You seem to know a lot about him!"
"I remember Nanny saying something about that when we were driving up to Wairoa one day."
"Yes, you're right. Or at least your kuia is. She was probably telling you that the meeting house was dedicated as a memorial to Timi Kara. You see that beautifully carved house that stands on our marae now was not the original meeting house. In fact, at one point there were two meeting houses on this site, but both burned down. Shortly before Timi Kara's death, people had started talking about re-building our meeting house. Ta Timi Kara was really taken with the idea and encouraged our people to take on the challenge of reviving the marae, upholding our traditions and customs,

and moving into the future with a unity of purpose. Our people took this to heart, and that is why the dining hall is named as it is."

"'Tātau, tātau'?"

"That's right – 'all of us together.'"

Reconciliation and Self-Determination in the Treaty Settlement Process

Reconciliation and self-determination are two key objectives of the treaty settlement process. In fact, these two concepts underlie much of the post-contact history of Māori legal traditions. The influence of these concepts can be traced back through Māori legal history until at least the Treaty of Waitangi. These ideas can be seen in the story of Timi Kara. The treaty itself might be seen as having these two concepts at its very heart – Māori self-determination is arguably reflected in the guarantee of tino rangatiratanga in Article 2, while the recognition of kāwanatanga in Article 1 arguably reconciles the presence of the settler population and its institutions of government in Aotearoa with the continuing tino rangatiratanga of Māori.

But is the treaty settlement process supporting reconciliation and tino rangatiratanga when it comes to Māori legal traditions? The three tensions in Māori legal history (adaptation, the relationship to the treaty partner, and renewal) provide a framework to address this issue. When the dynamics of these tensions are measured against the objectives of reconciliation and tino rangatiratanga, it becomes apparent that the settlement process, at least in regard to Māori legal traditions, is currently failing to meet the objectives upon which the entire claims and settlement system is founded.

The Treaty of Waitangi settlement process is often described as being about reconciliation. That is, one of the key objectives, if not the primary objective of the process, is reconciliation. There is little precise or explicit definition of the "reconciliation" envisaged, but one is able to discern some sense of this by examining the way in which the key players engage in and describe the process.

The OTS publication *Healing the Past, Building a Future* reflects something of reconciliation in its title but contains surprisingly little clear guidance on the objective of settling claims. In describing the settlement process, however, the text does provide some clues to the state party's understanding of reconciliation in this context. For example, for settlements to be fair and durable, they must remove a sense of grievance held by Māori against the Crown and its past action.[1] *Healing the Past* also emphasizes the restoration of the relationship between Māori and the Crown: "The strengthening of the relationship between the Crown and Māori is an integral part of the settlement process and will be reflected in any settlement. The settlement of historical grievances also needs to be understood within the context of wider government policies that are aimed at restoring and developing the Treaty relationship."[2]

According to *Healing the Past,* an important part of the restoration of the relationship between the Treaty partners will be an acknowledgment by the Crown of historical wrongs it has committed in breach of the principles of the Treaty of Waitangi:[3]

> The Crown's acknowledgement of and apology for well-founded breaches of the Treaty and its principles is vital to rebuilding the relationship between the Crown and claimant groups. It is also important for the claimant groups to record their agreement that their historical grievances have been finally settled, so that both parties can move on to a more positive future.

Apologies have important symbolic value and the potential to contribute to transformative healing.[4] However, if apologies appear to distance the apologizer from responsibility or are otherwise seen to be tokenistic, then they are likely to hinder rather than assist reconciliation. Regan notes that "ethical reconciliation requires more than words of regret. Such words must be spoken in conjunction with monetary and cultural reparations."[5] The Crown's acknowledgment and apology are formally recorded in the deeds of settlement. A brief survey of the forms this apology has taken in early-twenty-first-century settlements suggests the role the apology is seen to play in reconciliation.

In the Ngāti Raukawa deed of settlement, the apology is linked not only to reconciliation but also to self-determination through its reference to mana and rangatiratanga:[6]

> The Crown apologises for its past failures to acknowledge the mana and rangatiratanga of Raukawa and looks forward to building an enduring relationship of mutual trust and cooperation with Raukawa that is based on respect for the Treaty of Waitangi and its principles.

This short statement also incorporates some of the important aspects of negotiating reconciliation through the type of treaty relationship advocated by Tully. Mutual trust, cooperation, and respect are identified as central factors in building a new relationship between Ngāti Raukawa and the Crown.

The apology in the Te Rarawa deed of settlement also refers to a new relationship between the Crown and the settling group that is enabled by the settlement, and the apology contained within it, but also adds the concept of atonement:[7]

> Through this apology the Crown seeks to atone for these wrongs and relieve the burden of historical grievance so the process of healing can begin. The Crown looks forward to building a new relationship with Te Rarawa based on Te Tiriti o Waitangi/the Treaty of Waitangi and its principles.

The ideas of apology, atonement, and the removal of a sense of grievance are thereby built into the reconciliation framework in this settlement. The use of the concept of atonement suggests that the Crown is not trying to back away from its responsibility for the wrongs to which the statement refers.

These themes are also clearly evident in the Taranaki Whānui deed of settlement, which adds the dimension of forgiveness on behalf of the settling community:[8]

> Through this settlement the Crown is seeking to atone for its past wrongs towards you, restore its honour which has been tarnished by its actions, and to begin the process of healing. It is the Crown's hope that this apology will mark a pivotal point in the rebuilding and enhancement of our relationship with you. We look forward to building a relationship of mutual trust and cooperation that can flourish in the future . . .
>
> . . . E kite nei mātou i te kaha hiahia o te Karauna kia ea ai tērā i hē i a ia, kia tika ai tōna tū, otirā kia ara ake i tēnei mate nui. Ka pono mātou ki te kupu a te Karauna, kia tutuki marire tēnei hiahia nui ōna, ā, ko tō mātou, kia rite tētehi huarahi kia mahi tahi, kia aronui ki te tika i ngā tau kei te heke mai.
>
> We acknowledge that the Crown seeks to atone for its past wrongs and to restore its honour and begin the process of healing. We accept the Crown's commitment to act in good faith and we look to building a relationship of mutual trust and cooperation in the future.

The Waitangi Tribunal has also articulated its own view of the treaty claims and settlement process in general, and its own role in particular. The tribunal has referred to the need to resolve grievances, restore the wellbeing of Māori communities, and "reconcile Māori communities with the state and other parts of society."[9] Here one can see how the objective of resolving grievances is explicitly linked by the tribunal to the language of restoration and reconciliation. The tribunal understands that its role in this process is to:[10]

- investigate to find the truth of the past
- listen to claimant communities, and to the Crown
- affirm claims where they are proven, and
- explain where they fall short.

These functions might be seen as part of the truth-telling that Waziyatawin speaks of, and potentially even the re-storying that many Indigenous scholars see as a vital aspect of reconciliation processes.

Government ministers responsible for treaty settlement negotiations have also spoken of the particular characteristics of reconciliation in the contexts of the settlement of claims based on the Treaty of Waitangi. At a forum on the progress of the treaty settlement process, the current Minister of Treaty of Waitangi Negotiations stated:[11]

> achieving settlements is about a number of very[,] very positive things. First it is about our shared history, trying to achieve a measure of justice for the negative impact [that] elements of that history have had on iwi and hapū. Secondly, achieving settlements can generate relationships with the Crown that are much more productive than in even the relatively recent past. We all acknowledge that they retain frustrating elements, but post-settlement relationships are largely positive rather than negative, and finally effective cultural and economic redress gives settling groups a platform for further development based on their own choices about what they want to do and where they want to go[,] and too few have had this autonomy in the past.

Within this statement are the ideas of resolving grievance and building new relationships between Māori and the Crown which have been features of official policy in this area since the establishment of the modern treaty settlement process. The minister's statement also includes an important reference to building a platform for the autonomy of Māori communities, bringing in an element of the self-determination discourse. In an address at the same forum, the associate minister of treaty negotiations placed even greater emphasis on the practical aspects of restoring the capacity of Māori communities, and also suggests a re-storying of the history and future of Māori-Crown relations:[12]

> We talk of addressing longstanding relationship mamae [injury] of greater economic capacity and the restoration of tribal estates. We talk about redirecting, redirection of our energy on both sides of the relationship from

> negotiations to developmental modes. Of parallel importance is that completing settlements will be a significant milestone for the Crown – it will indicate the restoration of Crown relationships with iwi, and progressing into the future. The Crown will have more confidence that these relationships are no longer based on negative equity.

At an earlier forum, also convened by the government to discuss issues in the treaty settlement process, the prime minister touched on the key themes of acknowledging the wrongs of the past, contributing to the restoration of Māori communities, resolving grievances, and building a new relationship between the Crown and more independent Māori communities:[13]

> Breaches of the Treaty by actions of the Crown have caused great harm to Maori. It is time those breaches were dealt with and the wounds they have caused were healed.
>
> Both Maori and the Crown benefit from settlements. Maori gain a settlement package that provides redress for those breaches. While the Crown, in negotiating that settlement and providing redress, has its honour restored. And all New Zealanders benefit from the resulting improvement in the Crown-Maori relationship.
>
> In short, settlements address our past and they invest in our shared future.
>
> I am impatient to see all Maori standing strong, economically independent and fulfilling their true potential. I see the completion of historical Treaty Settlements as an essential part of achieving that. Because only when the wrongs of the past have been addressed, will we all truly move our sights to the promise of the future.

As noted above, the type of tino rangatiratanga reflected in the treaty settlement process may be a legal construct that is distinct from the fuller self-determination implied by the concept within Māori legal traditions. Although there may not be agreement as to the precise level of self-determination that the settlement process is intended to deliver to Māori, it is clear, from statements made by key actors within the process, that some degree of sharing of public power is intended (as in the relationship described in the treaty itself), even if the terms of that power-sharing are not precisely defined. In any case, the philosophical foundations of reconciliation require the mutual recognition of the authority of both state and Indigenous forms of law and government. Self-determination and reconciliation are therefore interdependent concepts in the context of the relationships between Indigenous peoples and states.

Key Tensions and the Settlement Process

The treaty settlement process makes claims about delivering, or at least contributing to, reconciliation and self-determination. It is possible to use the three major tensions in Māori legal history to assess whether such claims are credible when applied to Māori legal traditions.

Adaptation

The tension of adaptation directs Māori legal traditions towards either more self-determined change or more reactive change. The settlement process pulls Māori legal traditions towards more reactive change, largely as a result of the visions of justice and certainty imposed on the settlement process by the Crown.

The virtual absence from the substantive provisions of settlement instruments of concepts such as kaitiakitanga, mana, and rangatiratanga raises serious questions about the ability of those instruments to provide for the appropriate expression of Māori understandings of self-determination. This in turn suggests that the settlement process places considerable constraints on the deployment of tikanga-based law-making within that process.

Corntassel's approach to sustainable self-determination is based on the idea of moving beyond rights-based discourses to an articulation of self-determination that is constructed on an Indigenous framework. The treaty settlement process appears to be pushing Māori legal traditions in the opposite direction. Treaty settlement agreements are couched in the language of rights and purport to regulate not only rights as between the settling community and the state but also rights as between the collective and the individual community member. The mediation involving Ngāti Maniapoto and Ngāti Tama illustrates the way that engagement in the settlement process encourages Māori communities to articulate their issues within a rights discourse and to move away from tikanga-based approaches to understanding and expressing the relationships between and within Māori communities, not to mention relationships between Māori communities and the state. Many of the Waitangi Tribunal reports that have dealt with the Crown's policy and practice relating to the settlement process have pointed to the deleterious effects of the settlement process on relationships and whanaungatanga.[14]

When one considers the treaty settlement process in terms of adaptation, it becomes clear that self-determination / tino rangatiratanga in relation to Māori legal traditions is not being advanced through the settlement process. In fact, it is probable that self-determined changes to Māori legal traditions will become less likely as settling communities are required to adopt governance structures and law-making processes based on the rights discourse that currently permeates the settlement process.

According to Tully, genuine reconciliation between Indigenous peoples and states requires a treaty relationship that is based in part on mutual recognition. Mutual recognition implies recognition that different forms of self-government and legal-political institutions should co-exist on equal terms. The tension of adaptation illustrates that the Crown has difficulty with some aspects of Tully's mutual recognition, notwithstanding the fact that the settlement process makes claims of reconciliation.

The Crown's visions of justice and certainty rest on the concept of Crown sovereignty, which frames the entire settlement process. The Crown sovereignty framework poses particular problems for reconciliation in relation to adaptation. The Crown sovereignty framework appears to be in conflict with some of the principles of Māori governance. Māori governance entities that are constructed upon constitutions designed in the context of the settlement process are constrained by the parameters of this Crown sovereignty framework, which entrenches systems of law-making that are reactive as opposed to self-determining.

It need not be this way. It is quite possible to develop a treaty relationship that respects Indigenous and state forms of political authority. Furthermore, genuine reconciliation cannot take place if the new relationship is not established on the basis of mutual recognition and the coexistence of the political authority of both the state and Indigenous peoples. A settlement process that advanced reconciliation would create space for more tikanga-based law making, more self-determining change in respect of Māori legal traditions. The present process closes down that space by reinforcing a vision of exclusive Crown sovereignty.

Relationship to the Treaty Partner

The treaty settlement process feeds into the second key tension in Māori legal history, pushing Māori legal traditions towards reinforcing a particular relationship with the Crown. When this is considered in the context of reconciliation and tino rangatiratanga, it appears that the treaty settlement process does not support these objectives, and may even undermine them, at least in so far as Māori legal traditions are concerned.

The relationship to the treaty partner is central to the discussion of tino rangatiratanga in the context of the Treaty of Waitangi. When the courts and the Waitangi Tribunal have applied the principles of the treaty, they have tended to describe tino rangatiratanga in relation to the Crown's exercise of kāwanatanga, with each form of political authority being qualified by the other. When we consider tino rangatiratanga outside of the strict legal definitions elaborated in the application of Treaty principles, the nature of the relationship between the treaty partners takes on a slightly different shape, with even greater scope for the coexistence of independent polities.

That type of relationship would support quite strong forms of legal pluralism, which would assist with the de-centring of state law. However, the current settlement process encourages Māori legal systems not only to engage with state law but to focus on the state legal system. The examples of the Ngāti Tama/Ngāti Maniapoto mediation (where questions about the relative authority and the relationships between the two groups became a simple boundary dispute) and the disputes relating to the Central North Island forestry settlement both illustrate the tendency of settling groups to focus on the state legal system and to develop their own legal traditions in ways that also engage state law. This relationship of Māori legal traditions to state legal traditions tends to be one of subordination rather than one that enhances tino rangatiratanga/self-determination.

Ideas of reconciliation are described by key actors within the treaty settlement process as being based on restoring a healthy relationship between the treaty partners, or even establishing a new and better relationship. However, the very limited use within settlement instruments of Māori law-making principles casts the settling Māori community in the role of junior partner in the treaty relationship. This is inconsistent with the approach to reconciliation that James Tully describes. Tully's concept of reconciliation is based on an equality of cultures and legal-political institutions; effective reconciliation cannot take place if the state party requires the Indigenous community to engage purely on the state's terms, by reference only to state legal traditions.[15] Instead, there ought to be a process of intercultural negotiation and dialogue that would create space for the operation of distinct legal systems – those of both Indigenous peoples and the state. The relationship between legal systems would then be based on interaction and not subordination or assimilation.

Renewal

Issues relating to the design of post-settlement governance entities and the constitutionalisation of iwi bring the tension of renewal to the fore. This third and final major tension in Māori legal history operates along an axis between models of legal change that encourage the reinvigoration of tikanga and models that facilitate the perception that specific Māori legal traditions are losing relevance within the public life of the community.

Very little self-determination/tino rangatiratanga is being cultivated by the treaty settlement process in relation to renewal. Earlier, I suggested that the Ngāti Tama/Ngāti Maniapoto mediation and the Central North Island forestry settlement litigation show that the settlement process can encourage participants to see the state legal system as more relevant than Māori legal systems, even in those cases where the settling communities have gone to significant lengths to try to incorporate and/or reflect Māori legal traditions. The central strand of Corntassel's concept of sustainable self-determination is that the standards and benchmarks for that self-determination must be constructed by Indigenous communities themselves. By encouraging Māori communities to see the legal traditions of the state as more relevant to their own law-making, dispute resolution, or substantive laws on matters such as membership, the treaty settlement process effectively undermines self-determination/tino rangatiratanga in relation to Māori legal traditions.

There are also shortcomings in the Treaty settlement process when assessed against the objective of reconciliation in the context of the tension of renewal. There are a number of aspects of Tully's reconciliation that are overlooked in the Treaty settlement process. Tully asserts that reconciliation between Indigenous peoples and states must be based on intercultural dialogue and negotiation that takes place in a philosophical and cultural middle ground. That approach would value Māori legal traditions and reinforce their relevance to New Zealand society in the 21st century. Yet the Treaty settlement process has basic structural characteristics that prevent that type of dialogue and, consequently, that type of reconciliation. The Crown sets the parameters of the settlement process unilaterally and dictates both financial and conceptual limits on settlement redress, which ultimately constrains the role of Māori legal traditions within the settlement process. The settlement process cannot then be described as a process of intercultural dialogue that is based on mutual respect and the equality of Indigenous and state forms of legal-political institutions.

The post-settlement governance phase is founded on Western ideas of governance, virtually without reference to Māori legal traditions relating to leadership and accountability. The basic structures of PSGEs are based on Western law and values with only a very limited recognition of Māori legal traditions. Far from being an intercultural dialogue, there is a structural bias within the settlement process that encourages the discarding of Māori legal traditions rather than their re-invigoration. The requirements imposed by the Crown on PSGEs relating to representation, accountability, and transparency ensure that the Crown's concerns are prioritized and as a consequence the settlement process tends to encourage Māori communities to move away from their own legal traditions.

TAMA

"Pāpā?"
"Yes, e Tama?"
"Are all these stories about my tīpuna true? Did these things really happen?"
"That's what the stories say."
"Yes, but are they the truth?"
"They tell us truths."
"What kind of truths?"
"All kinds – qualities we ought to value, ways we ought to behave, principles that are important, consequences of our actions, who we are, how to live together and fulfill our aspirations."
"All of that?!"
"Yes, e Tama, all of that and more. As a Cherokee man once said, the truth about stories is that's all we are."
"So, am I just the stories of my tīpuna?"
"Not only those stories – you have your own stories too."
"What kind of stories? Ones with pirates and dinosaurs?"
"Probably not. But there might be warriors and a Leviathan."
"Levia-what?"
"Never mind – that's not important. The important thing is that we keep telling the stories of our tīpuna."
"Why?"
"Because that's who we are as Māori, as Ngāti Kahungunu, as Ngai Te Apatu. If we stop telling those stories, we start to lose control of our own stories."
"If I get to control my own story, I'm definitely having pirates and dinosaurs in it."

The Treaty of Waitangi Settlement Process in Māori Legal History

The story of Tamatea that begins this book reflects ideas of change within Māori legal traditions. The focus of the book is the way that Māori legal traditions have changed over time – in particular the pressures exerted by the

Treaty of Waitangi claims settlement process and how Māori legal traditions have responded to those pressures. The analysis of the treaty settlement process suggests that a number of important stories need to be heard: the story of the Treaty settlement process; the story of Māori legal history; and new stories that are yet to be told.

Re-Storying the Settlement Process

If the treaty settlement process is to achieve its objectives of increased Māori self-determination and reconciliation between Māori and the New Zealand state, there must be significant change in the way the settlement process is executed, even in the settlement framework itself. The settlement process needs to tell a different story.

The story of treaty settlements cannot be written only by the Crown. It must instead be co-authored by the Treaty partners, iwi Māori and the Crown. This is the only approach that can end the colonial relationship and move towards the type of treaty relationship described by Tully.[16] This approach would imply a shift away from the narrow conceptions of justice and certainty that currently constrain the settlement process.[17] Self-determination and reconciliation in this context require that Māori legal traditions be recognized as part of a legitimate social and political culture that existed in Aotearoa prior to the establishment of the New Zealand state.[18]

If Māori legal traditions are recognized as the first law of Aotearoa,[19] treaty settlements would proceed along very different lines. Processes and structures that subordinate Māori legal traditions to those of the state would not be acceptable.[20] The treaty settlement process would not be based on asserting Crown sovereignty. Crown visions of justice and certainty would need to be considered alongside Māori visions of justice and certainty.[21] Settlements would not be understood as a process of the Crown acknowledging Māori claims but, rather, as a process in which iwi Māori acknowledge the presence of the institutions of the New Zealand state. That is, it is the state that is actually making a claim on the pre-existing authority of iwi Māori.[22] The processes, structures, and objectives of the settlement process would be set through intercultural negotiation, and the outcomes of the settlement process, the settlement agreements themselves, and the new relationships for which they establish a platform would reflect both Māori and state legal traditions. Principles of whanaungatanga, mana, utu, manaakitanga, and tapu and noa would contribute to the shape of the negotiation process and any settlement agreements that came out of that process.

If the treaty settlement process is to achieve self-determination and reconciliation, greater attention will need to be given to the effects of this process on Māori legal traditions. I do not argue here that the settlement process ought to have no effect on Māori legal traditions; indeed, it seems unlikely that any effective settlement process could (or should) avoid doing so. A process that delivers on the goals of self-determination and reconciliation is almost certain to demand that Māori legal systems respond in some way. This is where the major tensions in Māori legal history can provide a useful framework. By examining the settlement process in light of these tensions, one is able to ascertain whether or not the process is animating those tensions in a way that supports the mutual recognition of Māori and state legal traditions and institutions of law and government.[23] These tensions help us to identify when the process is skewing Māori legal traditions towards more reactive, more state-centric, less tikanga-based forms of law-making, dispute resolution, and substantive law.

It is not as though we do not possess the conceptual tools to construct a settlement process that tells this different story. The theoretical framework set out in this book illustrates that creating an intercultural, pluralistic legal space is possible.[24] What is more, the Treaty of Waitangi itself gives expression to a vision of two distinct polities co-existing in Aotearoa. The treaty tells its own story of reconciliation and self-determination. It is the product of intercultural negotiation, and its terms speak of a mutual recognition of legal and political traditions. The language and form of the treaty also reflect mutual respect and sharing. It suggests all the qualities of a genuine treaty relationship necessary for reconciliation.[25] It guarantees the tino rangatiratanga of Māori, confirming the self-determination of iwi Māori. The beginning of the story is, therefore, already in place. A better understanding of the changes to Māori legal traditions over time and the tensions in Māori legal history that drive those changes enables us to re-write the current treaty settlement story in a way that removes the colonial relationship and honours the treaty partnership.

Re-Storying Māori Legal History

Rejecting the colonial relationship will also require telling a different story about Māori legal traditions and the changes to those traditions over time. This book has focused specifically on changes to Māori legal traditions in the context of the treaty settlement process, but it also illustrates issues that are relevant to the study of Māori legal history more generally.

First, it is vital to develop appropriate conceptual tools for the study of Māori legal history. Here I have drawn on Kaupapa Māori research, Indigenous legal theory, and legal pluralism to construct a theoretical framework for the analysis of Māori legal traditions. Kaupapa Māori research places Māori concepts, principles, and processes at the centre of Māori legal history.[26] This approach expands the scope of Māori legal history beyond the confines of state law that affects Māori to include Māori legal systems and the interaction between state law and Māori legal traditions. Indigenous legal theory reinforces these ideas by using the cultural and experiential groundings of Indigenous communities, in this case Māori communities, to develop the conceptual tools necessary to examine Māori legal traditions and changes to those traditions over time.[27] Re-storying Māori legal history is also assisted by recent scholarship in the field of legal pluralism. Understanding the Māori legal order on its own terms is an important part of re-storying Māori legal history; this requires a de-centring of state law. The modified form of critical legal pluralism suggested by the work of Webber[28] and Tamanaha[29] provides a theoretical model for de-centring state law by recognizing the role of legal subjects in the operation of law. It also assists in re-centring Indigenous legal orders by acknowledging the role of legal institutions and the fundamentally social nature of processes by which legal orders are created.

These conceptual tools also help to reveal the legal dimensions of tikanga without requiring that they be decoupled from other aspects of tikanga. To establish an analytical framework that suggests the broad shape of changes to Māori legal traditions, but also captures the complexity and diversity of those changes, I have used three major tensions in Māori legal history. These tensions help to identify pressures on Māori legal systems and the general nature of the legal system's responses to those pressures. Viewing the tensions in Māori legal history can be useful in re-storying that history: while the tensions reflect creativity and dynamic change, they also allow for the co-existence of multiple perspectives, strategies, and approaches.

New Stories

The task of re-storying the treaty settlement process and re-storying Māori legal history would be supported by further research in a number of areas. I have provided a general conceptual framework for the analysis of changes to Māori legal traditions, but further empirical research would reveal finer detail. Kirsty Gover's work in relation to membership and "tribal constitutionalism" is an example of the kind of empirical work that assists to flesh out those details.[30] A number of other discrete areas could be studied in this way. The constitutions of PSGEs (and similar entities), which formed the basis of

Gover's study, also contain dispute resolution mechanisms and provisions for the election or appointment of a governing body, as well as setting the powers of the governing or executive body. Empirical research that focused specifically on provisions that relate to any one of these areas would provide a valuable foundation for examining the operation of PSGEs within the framework of Māori legal traditions.

The objectives of reconciliation and self-determination, insofar as they apply to Māori legal traditions, would also be supported by further research aimed at identifying specific Māori legal principles and developing scholarship that supports the practical application of these principles today. The New Zealand state legal system has always had the ability to recognize Māori customary law; recent years have seen an increasing recognition that Māori legal traditions exist as part of a distinct Māori legal system, regardless of what the state legal system will enforce as customary law. This is an important element of mutual recognition and reconciliation and suggests a need to explore ways to move from a philosophical and conceptual framework to the practical operation of dynamic and healthy Māori legal systems.[31]

This work would help to shift the discussion about Māori legal traditions away from the general and towards specific legal principles and examples of legal practice. Prominent Māori jurists such as Sir Edward Taihakurei Durie[32] and Justice Joe Williams[33] have helped to articulate the structures and principles underlying Māori legal systems, as have researchers at the Te Mātāhauariki Research Institute.[34] The New Zealand Law Commission built on some of this scholarship in its 2001 study paper, *Māori Custom and Values in New Zealand Law,*[35] and the Ministry of Justice has sought to explore the philosophical underpinnings of Māori perspectives of justice in *He Hinatore ki te Ao Māori – A Glimpse into the Māori World.*[36] The next step would be to provide an internal perspective of Māori legal systems,[37] with a view to understanding Māori legal traditions on their own terms rather than through the lens of the state legal system.

This approach would build on not only the theoretical and methodological basis of this book but also the important work undertaken by Val Napoleon, Hadley Friedland, and others involved in the major collaborative research project relating to Indigenous peoples and governance. Napoleon and Friedland contend that Indigenous legal traditions ought to be treated "substantively as law – to be debated, applied, interpreted, argued, analyzed, criticized, and changed."[38] To do this in Aotearoa, in a way that is both robust and respectful of Māori legal traditions, would require significant engagement between legal scholars and Māori communities. If undertaken carefully and thoughtfully, such engagement ought to give rise to many new stories of Māori legal traditions and Māori legal history, which could assist Māori communities to fulfill their self-determinationaspirations.

A New Beginning for Stories of Māori Law

This book has aimed to analyse broad changes to Māori legal traditions in the context of the Treaty of Waitangi using a framework that can be applied to Māori legal traditions in other contexts. Many more stories of Māori legal traditions remain to be told. There are also different types of stories to be told about Māori legal traditions, even in the context of the treaty settlement process – stories that detail specific legal traditions and suggest a bridge between an appropriate philosophical framework and the practical operation of vibrant Māori legal systems. Those stories will be vital if we are to move towards the objectives of reconciliation and Māori self-determination. The story that runs through this book is that of a settlement process that undermines these objectives because of the pressures it places on Māori legal traditions. But if parties to the treaty settlement process take the objectives of self-determination and reconciliation seriously, and pay careful attention to changes to Māori legal traditions that take place in the context of that process, a different story can be told – a story in which treaty settlements signify not the end of a treaty relationship but, rather, a new beginning.

Epilogue: Māui and the People of the North

"Pāpā, can we have a story about Māui tonight?"
"Of course. There are lots of stories about Māui. Which one do you want to hear? The one about him fishing up this island we live on?"
"Nah, I know how that one goes."
"How about the one where he slows down the sun?"
"I know that one, too."
"What about the one where he gets the secret of fire from his great ancestress, Māhuika?"
"You tell me that one all the time! Aren't there any new stories about Māui?"
"You want a new story about Māui?"
"Yeah."
"A new story … let's see now … Okay, how about this. This is a new story about Māui, one where we find Māui many, many years after his most famous adventures. But at a time when Māui was becoming restless again. Māui always craved excitement, adventure, and change. Not for him a quiet life, whiling away the hours, fishing, weaving, or playing golf. In his day he had tamed the mighty sun itself! Even challenged the very mortality of human beings! Admittedly, that hadn't worked out as well as he had hoped, but it had been worth a try. Anyway, that was all a long time ago. He knew it was not his day anymore. Though surely he still had a few tricks up his sleeve, a few more adventures yet to be had. And there was still plenty that needed to be done. He saw many communities suffering great hardships. But where would he be of most use? Where could he use his powers to make real change in people's lives?"
"Then he remembered a place he'd heard people speak of – 'The Law,' it was called. Some people said that The Law was the only place you could find justice. Others

said that it was a site of oppression. Māui had heard many different things about The Law – that it was the location of a proud and ancient civilization, that it was an empty, crumbling ruin, that it was a vibrant, dynamic, and cosmopolitan place. So many different and contrasting views! But all the stories suggested that, for good or ill, The Law had a huge effect on the lives of people who had been there. Māui was intrigued. He decided he wanted to see The Law for himself."

"So, Māui set off for The Law. But it was not an easy journey. For a start, Māui wasn't exactly sure where The Law was. It wasn't clearly marked on any maps, though if he looked hard he could make out some smudged markings that gave him a general sense of where to look for The Law, but no more than that. Travellers he met along the way weren't much help either. Their directions were not especially precise, and often Māui felt as though they were talking about completely different places."

"Just when he was on the verge of abandoning his journey, Māui caught a glimpse of a settlement off in the distance. Could this be The Law? As he came closer, he began to appreciate the elaborate construction of this settlement. Some of the structures mirrored the natural environment – the contours of the land, the progress of the waterways, the life-cycles of plant and animal life, the balance and inter-dependence of the natural world. Some buildings had a spiritual quality to them that he could not quite put his finger on. They were not like churches exactly, but he could sense they were imbued with the powers of the gods and the spirit world, like awe-inspiring cathedrals or the intricacy of the carvings on the meeting-house in his own village. Other buildings had obviously been carefully and deliberately built by people for particular purposes – fortress-like structures to protect what was kept within, bridges that reached out to forge new relationships, high walls to set boundaries and prevent encroachment. And the wide streets and tree-lined avenues had obviously been designed to facilitate and encourage movement in some directions and to discourage or prevent movement in other directions. Māui marveled at the complexity of it all. Sure, there were some parts of town that looked as though they had developed in a slightly haphazard and chaotic fashion, but Māui felt that all added to the charm of the place."

"As Māui rounded a corner in what seemed to be a slightly neglected area of town, he came across a large group of people huddled around a map and deep in conversation. They exchanged greetings, and Māui discovered the group had come from the North. Like him, they were interested in finding out as much as they could about The Law. They told him they had been here before. In fact, they were once very familiar with this place, but things had changed. Others had built over the top of the landmarks they had used to navigate. When Māui looked at their map, he saw that it did not show the roads and streets of the settlement they were within, but there were clearly other paths, tracks, alleyways, promenades laid out, which one could use to travel through

The Law. Māui could see that following these pathways would show you very different aspects of The Law from what you would see from the streets."

"Yet the group still seemed uncertain about how best to proceed. The issue seemed to be that not all members of the group wanted to use the map. It wasn't as though anyone wanted to use the official roads and streets, but there was some concern that the map provided a very incomplete picture of the vast network of paths and tracks that crisscrossed The Law. Some of the guides amongst the group said that their methods of navigation cannot be represented by lines or icons on a map. Others felt that it was unwise to follow a path on the map when the map could not show all of the connecting paths that link to places outside the boundaries of the map. Then, an elder rose to speak. The elder acknowledged the expertise of the guides and the importance of taking account of their concerns. But, the elder noted, the guides were not the only ones who ought to have a say in this matter. The map contained some useful information. And using the map might in fact help the community to re-connect with some of those matters the guides spoke of. Travelling the pathways on the map might encourage people to re-discover the connecting paths that were not represented on the map. Getting used to travelling through The Law once again might build the confidence of the group to more widely use the other navigational tools available to them."

"The group seemed persuaded by these arguments put forward by the elder and readied themselves to set off again. Māui bade farewell to the people from the north and continued on his own journey. After a short while, he reached the top of a rise from where he overlooked the entire settlement. He could see the people from the north making their progress through The Law and, as they did so, Māui noticed something quite unexpected. As the group travelled through the settlement, they actually appeared to be changing the very landscape of the city itself. The shapes of the buildings were modified. The layout of the streets began to bend before his eyes to align more closely with the group's journey. Or was that just his eyes playing tricks on him? If it was, it was a good trick. He blinked, shook his head and started the long journey home."

"Is that the end?"

"Well, it is the end of one story, but also the beginning of others."

"Like the story of Māui's journey home?"

"Yes."

"And the story of the people of the North?"

"Yes."

"And the story of The Law?"

"Maybe, yes."

"Will you tell me those stories one day?"

"I can tell you some of them, but you might have to help me figure out more endings and beginnings."

"I'll help you, Pāpā."

"Ka pai, e Tama. Then they really will become your own stories."

"Our own stories, Pāpā."

"Ae, e Tama, our own stories."

"Pinepine te Kura"

Pinepine te kura, hau te kura
Whanake te kura i raro i Awa-rua
Ko te kura nui, ko te kura roa
Ko te kura o tawhiti nā Tu-hae-po
Tenei te tira hou, tēnei haramai nei
Ko te umu-rangi, nā te Whatu-i-apiti
Nau mai e tama, ki te taiao nei
Ki' whakangungua koe ki te kahikatoa
Ki te tūmatakuru, ki te tara ongaonga
Ngā tairo rā e nāhau, e Kupe
I waiho i te ao nei.
Pike ake, kake ake I te toi huarewa
Te ara o Tawhaki i piki ai ki runga
I rokohina atu rā Maikuku-Mākākā
Hāpai o Māui, he waha i pā mai
"Taku wahine purotu, Taku tāne purotu"
Kōrua ko te tau e.

Little tiny treasure, treasure of renown,
The treasure that came from below Awarua;
The noble treasure, the famous treasure,
The treasure from afar off, the treasure of Tuhaepo!

A strange visitor is he, lately arrived here:
He is Te Umurangi, descended from Te Whatuiapiti.
Welcome, O son, welcome to this world of life.
You are to be ritually strengthened with the kahikatoa [tea tree],
With the tūmatakuru [thorny shrub native to Aotearoa] and the taraongaonga [tree nettle];
These were the thorny obstructions that you, O Kupe,
Bequeathed unto this world.
Climb up, ascend by the suspended way,
The pathway of Tawhaki when he ascended on high,
And there found Maikuku-Mākākā,
Attended by Hāpai [advance guard] of Māui,
and greetings were uttered:
"My beautiful lady!" "My handsome man!"
A tribute for you two, O loved ones.

Notes

Preface

1. Cover, "Foreword."
2. See McLaren and Foster, "Hard Choices and Sharp Edges," 4–5. See, e.g., Foster, Berger, and Buck, eds., *The Grand Experiment.*
3. See R. Williams, *Linking Arms Together,* 83–97; Borrows, *Canada's Indigenous Constitution,* 59–106.
4. Borrows, *Recovering Canada,* 13.
5. See, e.g., Borrows, *Drawing Out Law.*
6. Borrows, *Recovering Canada,* 13.
7. R. Williams, *Linking Arms Together,* 83–97.
8. Ibid., 85.
9. Ibid.
10. Ibid., 84.
11. Ibid.
12. Bell, *And We Are Not Saved.*
13. Cain, "Feminist Jurisprudence."
14. Delgado, "Storytelling for Oppositionists and Others."
15. Turner, *This Is Not a Peace Pipe,* 50–51.
16. Pihama, *Tihei Mauri Ora – Honouring Our Voices,* 131.
17. Lee "Māori Cultural Regeneration," 8.
18. Ibid., 12.
19. Archibald, *Indigenous Storywork.*
20. Borrows, *Drawing Out Law.*
21. This need is identified in Chapter 6.
22. Lee, "Māori Cultural Regeneration," 10.
23. Ibid., 11.
24. T. King, *The Truth about Stories,* 153.
25. Ibid., 2.

Chapter 1: Tino Rangatiratanga and Māori Legal History

1. Mitira, *Takitimu*, 32.
2. Throughout the book, the term "culture" refers variously to legal culture and to the general culture of a community. The use of "culture" and "cultural" to denote various types of culture does not suggest uniformity or homogeneity. Part of the reason I have used the concept of tensions within Māori legal history is to provide scope for the possibility of diverse thought and action across Māori society at any one time. My use of the term "culture" is intended to suggest that there are some shared values within a community, and some shared understandings about ways of acting and communicating in a social context. Importantly, this does not imply that everyone within a given community will behave uniformly, or even predictably.
3. Reeves, *Long White Cloud*, 131.
4. Waitangi Tribunal, *He Whakaputanga me te Tiriti.*
5. Cooke, "Introduction."
6. Palmer, *The Treaty of Waitangi.*
7. Although there are significant content differences between the two texts (which, in relation to at least some key matters, may be irreconcilable), I generally use "the Treaty" and "te Tiriti" interchangeably to refer to both texts and to reflect the meanings ascribed to the agreement over time. I do not intend to obscure the important differences between the two texts or to suggest that the two versions signify a uniformity of understanding or can be reconciled to express a unitary meaning. As Margaret Mutu, and others have pointed out (see Mutu "Constitutional Intentions: The Treaty of Waitangi Texts"; Mikaere "The Treaty of Waitangi and Recognition of Tikanga Māori"; Waitangi Tribunal, *He Whakaputanga me Te Tiriti*, 521-22) there are good reasons (both in terms of logic and in terms of international law) to prefer the Māori text, and I subscribe to that perspective. Thus, in this book, "the Treaty" and "te Tiriti" are used to capture the discourse relating to the agreement and include a range of meanings ascribed to the treaty itself by different communities over time.
8. *New Zealand Māori Council v Attorney-General* [1987] 1 NZL.R. 641 at 663 (C.A.) [*Lands case*].
9. See, e.g., ibid.
10. Brookfield, *Waitangi and Indigenous Rights*, 85–107.
11. Ibid., 17–18.
12. Ibid., 181–84.
13. Brookfield suggests that these legitimating factors include the passing of time and the benefits Māori have received from the constitutional arrangements of the New Zealand state. Scholars such as Moana Jackson and Ani Mikaere have raised serious questions as to whether there is a sound constitutional or theoretical basis to assert that those matters can be seen as legitimating factors See, for example, Mikaere, "The Treaty of Waitangi and Recognition of Tikanga Māori"; and Jackson, "The Treaty and the Word."
14. Palmer, *The Treaty of Waitangi.*
15. See, for example, Mikaere, "The Treaty of Waitangi and Recognition of Tikanga Māori," 330; and Jackson, "The Treaty and the Word," 1.
16. Mikaere, "The Treaty of Waitangi and Recognition of Tikanga Māori," 332–34.
17. Mikaere, *He Rukuruku Whakaaro*, 111–15. Margaret Mutu makes a similar argument based on her analysis of the texts of the 1835 Declaration of Independence and the

Treaty of Waitangi (in both Māori and English). See Mutu, "Constitutional Intentions," 13.

18. Jackson, "Comment."
19. Mikaere, "The Treaty of Waitangi and Recognition of Tikanga Māori."
20. Jackson, "The Treaty and the Word," 6–7.
21. Waitangi Tribunal, *Muriwhenua Land Report,* 117.
22. Waitangi Tribunal, *He Whakaputanga me te Tiriti,* 430.
23. Ibid., 474.
24. Ibid.
25. Ibid., 525.
26. Ibid., 526–27.
27. See, e.g., *Mabo v Queensland (No 2)* (1992) 175 C.L.R. 1; and *Calder v. Attorney-General of British Columbia* [1973] SCR 313.
28. *Māori Representation Act* (New Zealand) 1867.
29. *R. v. Symonds* (1847) NZPCC 387.
30. *Wi Parata v Bishop of Wellington* (1877) 3 NZ Jur. (NS) 72 (S.C.), 78.
31. Ibid.
32. *Hoani Te Heuheu Tukino v Aotea District Maori Land Board* [1941] AC 308.
33. Palmer, *The Treaty of Waitangi,* 231.
34. *Huakina Development Trust v Waikato Valley Authority* [1987] 2 NZL.R. 188 (H.C.) [*Huakina Development Trust*].
35. Ibid.
36. *State Owned Enterprises Act* (New Zealand) 1986, s 9.
37. *New Zealand Māori Council v Attorney-General* [1989] 2 NZL.R. 142 (CA).
38. *New Zealand Māori Council v Attorney General* [1991] 2 NZL.R. 129 (CA) [*Radio Frequencies*].
39. *New Zealand Māori Council v Attorney-General* [1994] 1 NZL.R. 513 [*Broadcasting Assets*].
40. See *Radio Frequencies,* and *Broadcasting Assets.*
41. *Ngai Tahu Māori Trust Board v Director-General of Conservation* [1995] 3 NZL. R. 534.
42. *Barton-Prescott v Director-General of Social Welfare* [1997] 3 NZL.R. 179 (H.C.).
43. Ibid.
44. See, e.g., *Haronga v Waitangi Tribunal* [2011] NZSC 53.
45. Ibid.
46. See, e.g., Waitangi Tribunal, *Tāmaki Makaurau Settlement Process Report.*
47. P. Joseph, *Constitutional and Administrative Law in New Zealand,* 83–91.
48. See Maaka, "A Relationship, Not a Problem," 201.
49. See J. Williams, "Quality Relations," 260.
50. See Wilson, "A Path to Constitutional Change," 247.
51. Though there is some variation in the terminology used, there appears to be agreement on the basic substantive content of these concepts. See, e.g., Mead, *Tikanga Māori,* 28–32; Joe Williams, *He Aha te Tikanga Māori?,* 8; New Zealand Law Commission, *Māori Custom and Values in New Zealand Law* 28–40.
52. Berman, *Law and Revolution,* 49–51.
53. Ibid., 10.
54. Glenn, *Legal Traditions of the World,* 24.

55. Te Mātāhauariki is based at the University of Waikato. It was established to explore ways in which the legal system of Aotearoa/New Zealand can evolve so as to accommodate aspects of both Māori and non-Māori legal traditions.
56. See, e.g., Frame, "Te Heuheu's Case in London 1940-41."
57. Bargh, ed., *Māori and Parliament.*
58. Fox, "Change, Past and Present," 41.
59. McHugh, *Aboriginal Societies and the Common Law.*
60. For a detailed discussion of the concept of tino rangatiratanga, see M. Durie, "Tino Rangatiratanga," 3.
61. Alfred, "Warrior Scholarship," 88.
62. Ibid., 95–96.
63. Turner, *This is Not a Peace Pipe,* 95.
64. Ibid., 95–96.
65. Marsden, *The Woven Universe,* 110–11.
66. "Self-location," an explicit reflection on the situation and position of the researcher or author, particularly in relation to the subject matter of the research, is an important part of various critical methodologies, including other Indigenous approaches and many feminist methodologies. See Kovach, *Indigenous Methodologies,* 110–11.
67. Denzin and Lincoln, "Introduction" 9.
68. Tau, "Matauranga Māori as an Epistemology," 66.
69. Awatere, *Māori Sovereignty,* 54.
70. Borrows, *Canada's Indigenous Constitution,* 61.

Chapter 2: Reconciling Legal Systems

1. Christie, "Indigenous Legal Theory," 197.
2. Ibid., 201; See also Christie, "Law, Theory and Aboriginal Peoples."
3. See Anaya, "Indigenous Law and Its Contribution to Global Pluralism."
4. Christie, "Indigenous Legal Theory," 203. This also appears to be consistent with the literature relating to the study, and theorizing of legal traditions more generally. See, e.g., Glenn, *Legal Traditions of the World.*
5. See, e.g., Nelken, "Towards a Sociology of Legal Adaption," 7; and, in the New Zealand context, Frame, *Grey and Iwikau,* 25–33.
6. Christie, "Indigenous Legal Theory," 206.
7. Monture-Angus, *Journeying Forward,* 40.
8. Ibid., 56.
9. Ibid., 135–57.
10. Ibid.,135–47.
11. *R. v. Sparrow* [1990] 1 S.C.R. 1075.
12. Monture-Angus, *Journeying Forward,* 88–115.
13. Ibid., 92 and 106.
14. Ibid., 60.
15. Christie, "Indigenous Legal Theory," 228.
16. Henderson, *First Nations Jurisprudence and Aboriginal Rights,* 122.
17. In referring to an "implicate order," Henderson draws on the terminology used by physicist David Bohm in *Wholeness and the Implicate Order,* 149: "There is the germ of a new notion of order here. This order is not to be understood solely in terms of a regular arrangement of objects (e.g., in rows) or as a regular arrangement of events

(e.g., in a series). Rather, a total order is contained, in some implicit sense, in each region of space and time. Now, the word 'implicit' is based on the verb 'to implicate.' This means 'to fold inward' ... so we may be led to explore the notion that in some sense each region contains a total structure 'enfolded' within it."

18. Henderson, *First Nations Jurisprudence and Aboriginal Rights,* 128–29.
19. Ibid., 129–63.
20. Ibid., 178–227.
21. Ibid., 163.
22. The procedures and functions of the potlatch ceremony, common among Indigenous peoples of the Pacific Northwest region, are an example of the type of performative jurisprudence Henderson describes. See Borrows, *Canada's Indigenous Constitution,* 40–41.
23. Henderson, *First Nations Jurisprudence and Aboriginal Rights,* 168.
24. Ibid., 169.
25. Ibid.
26. Ibid., 168.
27. Ibid., 192.
28. Borrows, *Canada's Indigenous Constitution,* 24.
29. Ibid., 23–58.
30. Ibid., 24.
31. Ibid., 59–106.
32. Ibid., 61.
33. Ibid., 137–76, 138.
34. Christie, "Indigenous Legal Theory," 213.
35. Ibid., 215–18.
36. Ibid., 217.
37. Ibid., 221.
38. Borrows, *Canada's Indigenous Constitution,* 8.
39. Ibid., 239–70.
40. Ibid., 6–7.
41. Ibid., 9–11.
42. Ibid., 10.
43. Ibid.
44. Ibid., 270.
45. Napoleon, *Ayook.*
46. Ibid., 245–63.
47. Ibid., 254.
48. Ibid., 255.
49. Ibid., 258–60.
50. Ibid., 244.
51. Ibid., 261–81.
52. Ibid.
53. Ibid., 244.
54. Christie, "Indigenous Legal Theory," 215–18.
55. See, e.g., R. Williams, "Vampires Anonymous and Critical Race Practice" and "Documents of Barbarism."

56. See, e.g., Kovach, *Indigenous Methodologies*, 59-60, where she describes the role of language in knowledge transmission as not being rigidly fixed but rather contingent on the communication between speaker and listener.
57. Ibid.
58. Ibid.
59. Christie, "Indigenous Legal Theory," 222.
60. See Mikaere, "Māori Women." Though in a slightly different context, see also Marsden, *The Woven Universe*, 22–23.
61. It should be noted that tikanga is not equivalent to customary law, though the two concepts share many characteristics. Tikanga is not a definite set of rules that apply to discrete areas of social life; rather, tikanga operates in all aspects of Māori life and incorporates spiritual, cultural, and practical aspects that are beyond a strictly legal domain. See Jackson, *The Māori and the Criminal Justice System*, 43.
62. See e.g., Hirini M. Mead, *Tikanga Māori: Living by Māori Values* (Wellington, NZ: Huia, 2003), 28-32; Joe Williams, *He Aha te Tikanga Māori?*, (Paper presented to the Mai i Te Ata Häpara Hui, Te Wānanga o Raukawa, Otaki, New Zealand, 2000) [unpublished], 8; New Zealand Law Commission, *Māori Custom and Values in New Zealand Law*, (Wellington, New Zealand: New Zealand Law Commission, 2001), 28-40.
63. J. Williams, *He Aha te Tikanga Māori?*, 8.
64. Mead, *Tikanga Māori*, 29.
65. J. Williams, *He Aha te Tikanga Māori?*, 8.
66. Ibid
67. Ibid.
68. Mikaere, "The Treaty of Waitangi and Recognition of Tikanga Māori," 332.
69. Mead, *Tikanga Māori*, 336.
70. D. Williams, "He Aha Te Tikanga Māori," 16.
71. New Zealand Law Commission, *Māori Custom and Values*, 17.
72. Jackson, *The Māori and the Criminal Justice System*.
73. Twining, *Globalisation and Legal Theory*, 242.
74. Mead, *Tikanga Māori*, 337–38. See also Patterson, *Exploring Māori Values*, 17–45.
75. A Taranaki Veteran, "The Great Muru.".
76. Jackson, "Criminality and the Exclusion of Māori." See also Patterson, *People of the Land*, 13–24.
77. Jackson, "The Treaty and the Word."
78. See, e.g., Mikaere, "Cultural Invasion Continued."
79. For further discussion on Māori concepts of leadership and authority, see Mahuika, "Leadership," 42.
80. Jackson, "Tipuna Title."http://www.converge.org.nz/pma/mjtipuna.htm.
81. For example, the common law concept of "fee tail" or "entail" has some characteristics similar to Jackson's "tipuna title" in that it is inalienable and maintains the kin group's land holding; however, the common law concept is based on the values and imperatives of English feudal society, and must be understood in that context.
82. Jackson, "Tipuna Title."
83. Ibid.
84. Ibid.
85. For historical background relating to the signing of the Treaty of Waitangi, see Orange, *The Treaty of Waitangi*.

86. For a flavour of the scholarly discourse relating to the Treaty of Waitangi, see Belgrave, Kawharu, and Williams, eds., *Waitangi Revisited.* The Waitangi Tribunal and the ordinary courts have also given judgments on the appropriate interpretation of the treaty and its "principles." See, e.g., *Lands case*; and Waitangi Tribunal, *Report of the Waitangi Tribunal on the Manukau Claim.*
87. Belgrave, Kawharu, and Williams, eds., *Waitangi Revisited*, 391–92.
88. Mikaere, "The Treaty of Waitangi and Recognition of Tikanga Māori," 330. Though I would contend that it is specifically the legal dimensions of tikanga that comprise "the first law of Aotearoa," this contention does not detract from Mikaere's basic argument.
89. Ibid.
90. Jackson, "The Treaty and the Word," 7.
91. Borrows, "Ground-Rules."
92. Griffiths, "What Is Legal Pluralism."
93. Ibid.
94. Ibid.
95. Woodman, "Ideological Combat and Social Observation," 34.
96. Merry, "Legal Pluralism," 879.
97. Santos, *Toward a New Common Sense*, 95.
98. Havemann, "Perspectives on Māori Rights and Pākehā Duties," 61.
99. Ibid.
100. Jackson, "Justice and Political Power," 243.
101. Ibid.
102. Jeremy Webber, "Legal Pluralism and Human Agency."
103. Kleinhans and Macdonald, "What is a *Critical* Legal Pluralism?," 34
104. Melissaris, "The More the Merrier?," 71.
105. Kleinhans and Macdonald, "What is a *Critical* Legal Pluralism?," 38.
106. Ibid.
107. Melissaris, "The More the Merrier?," 74.
108. Cover, "Foreword."
109. Melissaris, "The More the Merrier?," 74.
110. Ibid.
111. Webber, "Legal Pluralism and Human Agency," 181–82.
112. Ibid.
113. Ibid.,182.
114. Ibid., 189.
115. Ibid., 190. See also Tully, *Strange Multiplicity*, 99–139.
116. Webber, "Legal Pluralism and Human Agency," 189–90.
117. Schneiderman, "Pluralism, Disagreement, and Globalization."
118. Ibid, 203.
119. Moore, *Law as Process*, 210.
120. Schneiderman, "Pluralism, Disagreement, and Globalization," 203–4.
121. Webber, "Legal Pluralism and Human Agency," 189–90.
122. Roughan, "The Association of State and Indigenous Law."
123. Tamanaha, "Understanding Legal Pluralism," 402–3.
124. Ibid., 406–7.
125. Kleinhans and MacDonald, "What is a *Critical* Legal Pluralism?," 46.
126. Tamanaha, "Understanding Legal Pluralism," 406–7.

127. Ibid., 406.
128. Ibid., 407.
129. See, for example, Daes, "Some Considerations."
130. See, for example, Kymlicka, *Multicultural Citizenship*.
131. Corntassel, "Toward Sustainable Self-Determination."
132. Ibid., 105.
133. Ibid., 107.
134. Ibid.
135. In a statement endorsing the declaration, Minister of Māori Affairs Pita Sharples noted these qualifications, among others: "In moving to support the Declaration, New Zealand both affirms those rights and reaffirms the legal and constitutional frameworks that underpin New Zealand's legal system. Those existing frameworks, while they will continue to evolve in accordance with New Zealand's domestic circumstances, define the bounds of New Zealand's engagement with the aspirational elements of the Declaration ... In particular, where the Declaration sets out aspirations for rights to and restitution of traditionally held land and resources, New Zealand has, through its well-established processes for resolving Treaty claims, developed its own distinct approach." Press release, 20 April 2010, available at www.beehive.govt.nz.
136. Waitangi Tribunal, *Tāmaki Makaurau Settlement Process Report*.
137. Ibid., 13–14.
138. Ibid., 102.
139. Ibid.
140. Corntassel, "Toward Sustainable Self-Determination," 116.
141. Ibid., 119.
142. Ibid.
143. Ibid.
144. See also Mikaere, *He Rukuruku Whakaaro*, 179–86.
145. M. Durie, "Tino Rangatiratanga," 4–6.
146. Ibid., 6.
147. During this period, the Crown Congress Joint Working Party (CCJWP) was set up by an agreement between National Maori Congress and the Crown. Its purpose was to establish whether a prima facie (i.e., first appearance) case of treaty breach could be demonstrated for iwi with an interest in particular Railcorp properties, and to negotiate settlements clearing those properties for sale to the public. The work of the CCJWP was also an important part of the background of the modern treaty settlement process.
148. M. Durie, "Tino Rangatiratanga," 6–8.
149. Mutu, "Constitutional Intentions," 26.
150. *Taiaroa and Others v Attorney-General* [1994] (H.C.) 4 October, unreported, CP No 99/94 at 69.
151. Waitangi Tribunal, *Māori Electoral Option Report*, 3–4.
152. Jackson, "The Treaty and the Word."
153. Waitangi Tribunal, *Ngāi Tahu Sea Fisheries Report*, 269.
154. Waitangi Tribunal, *Ngāwhā Geothermal Resources Report*, 101.
155. Waitangi Tribunal, *Te Arawa Representatives Geothermal Resources Report*, 32.
156. Waitangi Tribunal, *Te Whānau o Waipareira Report*, 26.

157. Waitangi Tribunal, *Report of the Waitangi Tribunal on the Muriwhenua Fishing Claim*, 181.
158. Waitangi Tribunal, *Report of the Waitangi Tribunal on the Orakei Claim*, 149.
159. Waitangi Tribunal, *The Taranaki Report: Kaupapa Tuatahi*, 5, 20.
160. Dwyer, "Reconciliation for Realists," 96. See also Lederach and Lederach, *When Blood and Bones Cry Out*.
161. Dwyer, "Reconciliation for Realists," 106.
162. Ibid., 108.
163. Corntassel, Chaw-win-is, and T'lakwadzi, "Indigenous Storytelling, Truth-telling, and Community Approaches to Reconciliation," 145.
164. Ibid.
165. Waziyatawin, *What Does Justice Look Like?*
166. Ibid., 71–96.
167. Regan, *Unsettling the Settler Within*, 62–82.
168. Waziyatawin, *What Does Justice Look Like?* 97–118.
169. Ibid., 119–66.
170. Ibid., 167–76.
171. Tully, *Public Philosophy in a New Key*, 225–28.
172. See also Nadasdy, "The Antithesis of Restitution?"
173. Tully, *Public Philosophy in a New Key*, 229.
174. Ibid., 229–32.
175. Ibid., 231.
176. Ibid., 231–32.
177. Ibid., 232.
178. Ibid., 233.
179. Ibid., 234.
180. Ibid., 226–28.
181. Ibid., 234.
182. Ibid., 239–40.
183. Nadasdy, "The Antithesis of Restitution?"
184. Ibid., 95.
185. Tully, *Public Philosophy in a New Key*, 241.
186. Ibid.
187. Ibid., 243.
188. Ibid., 244.
189. Ibid., 244–50.
190. Ibid., 244–46.
191. Ibid., 247.
192. Ibid.
193. Ibid., 248.
194. Ibid., 250.
195. *Lands case*, 664.
196. *Te Rūnanga o Wharekauri Rekohu v Attorney-General* [1993] 2 NZL.R. 301 (C.A.) at 304.
197. Waitangi Tribunal, *Te Whānau o Waipareira Report*, xxvi.

Chapter 3: Māori Law Today

1. See Waitangi Tribunal, *Ko Aotearoa Tēnei*. Relying on evidence presented by Māori in the course of this inquiry and other research, the tribunal identifies whanaungatanga as the defining principle that frames Māori knowledge systems and the rights and obligations that were relevant to the inquiry. See, for example, *Ko Aotearoa Tēnei*, 16–17, 35–38, 81–84, 115–18, 237.
2. Patterson, *Exploring Māori Values*, 75.
3. As it did, for example, in the ground-breaking Australian Native title case *Mabo v Queensland (No. 2)* (1992) 175 C.L.R. 1.
4. Turcotte, "Why Legal Flexibility Is Not a Threat," 191–92.
5. Mead, *Tikanga Māori*, 18–19.
6. Ibid., 18–19.
7. Ibid.
8. See Tomas and Quince, "Māori Disputes and Their Resolution," 207–8.
9. Ibid., 212–15.
10. Matiu and Mutu, *Te Whānau Moana*, 162.
11. Ibid., 163.
12. Māui is a central figure in Māori mythology. He is not a god, but many of his relations are gods, and Māui himself exhibits some god-like qualities. Among other great achievements, he is said to have fished up the North Island of New Zealand and slowed down the sun. The stories of Māui are well known and provide important guidelines for appropriate behaviour.
13. Ministry of Justice, *He Hinatore ki te Ao Māori*, 22.
14. Metge, *New Growth from Old*, 291.
15. Note that the effective application of tikanga and key conceptual regulators, such as whanaungatanga, to issues of concern to contemporary Māori communities is challenged by the ongoing effects of colonisation, which have eroded Māori social structures and actively suprressed tikanga over a long period of time. However, there is an increasing recognition of the value of cultural reconnection and the recovery of Māori knowledge and tikanga and the resources that this heritage provides to construct a platform from which Māori can confidently face the future. See Mead, *Tikanga Māori*, 21–23, 233–35.
16. Ibid.
17. Waitangi Tribunal, *Te Whanganui-a-Orotu Report (Wai 55)*, para 2.5.6.
18. Waitangi Tribunal, *Te Whānau o Waipareira Report (Wai 414)*, 42.
19. Marsden, *The Woven Universe*, 4.
20. Benton, Frame, and Meredith, eds., *Te Mātāpunenga*.
21. Waitangi Tribunal, *Report on the Mohaka River*, 18–19.
22. Matiu and Mutu, *Te Whānau Moana*, 156–57.
23. Borrows, *Canada's Indigenous Constitution*, 46–51.
24. Tomas and Quince, "Māori Disputes and Their Resolution," 212–15.
25. E.T. Durie, *Custom Law*, 8.
26. Best, *Social Usages of the Māori*, 9.
27. Ministry of Justice, *He Hinatore ki te Ao Māori*, 22.
28. The addition of "tino" intensifies of the base concept of "rangatiratanga."
29. Kawharu, ed., *Waitangi*, 319–21.

30. Kawharu, "Introduction," x–xxii, xix.
31. S. Jones, "Consultation with Tangata Whenua," 6, cited in Tomas, *Key Concepts of Tikanga Māori,* 95.
32. See, for example, the comments of missionary Octavius Hadfield in *Native Tenure: Opinions of Various Authorities,* 9: "The Chief of the tribe, since he has no absolute right over the territory of the various *hapu,* nor over the lands of individual freeman of his own *hapu,* cannot sell any lands but his own ... nor can he do so in opposition to the opinion of the Chiefs of the *hapu* of the tribe, if they consider the territory, and thus the independence of the tribe impaired by doing so."
33. Benton, Frame, and Meredith, eds., *Te Mātāpunenga.*
34. Mead, Tikanga *Māori,* 29.
35. Ibid.
36. For example, in one well-known story, Māui tricks his ancestress, Mahuika, the keeper of fire, into giving him nearly all her magical and treasured supply of fire.
37. Ministry of Justice, *He Hinatore ki te Ao Māori,* 24.
38. Harawira (letter to the editor), *Te Puke Ki Hikurangi,* cited in Benton, Frame, and Meredith, *Te Mātāpunenga,* 109.
39. Cowan, "The Gods of the Māori," cited in Benton, Frame, and Meredith, *Te Mātāpunenga,* 111.
40. Marsden, *The Woven Universe,* 67.
41. *Resource Management Act* (New Zealand) 1991, s 2.
42. See Waitangi Tribunal, *Ko Aotearoa Tēnei.*
43. Ibid.
44. Ibid., 23.
45. Matiu and Mutu, *Te Whānau Moana,* 166–68.
46. Ibid.
47. Marsden, *The Woven Universe,* 5.
48. Mead, *Tikanga Māori,* 31–32.
49. Mikaere, *He Rukuruku Whakaaro,* 212.
50. Firth, *Economics of the New Zealand Māori,* 245–79.
51. Ministry of Justice, *He Hinatore ki te Ao Māori,* 23. This is not completely foreign to the common law (consider, e.g., the use of oaths as a means of certifying the veracity of statements).
52. Matiu and Mutu, *Te Whānau Moana,* 159.
53. Metge, *Tuamaka,* 19. In the general context of legal-athropological studies of tribal societies, John McLaren has pointed out that it is unhelpful to focus on the idea of "vengeance" to explain the legal responses to torts or personal injury within these societies (though it may be an appropriate consideration in the context of what might be categorised as "criminal matters"). See McLaren, "The Origins of Tortious Liability," 42.
54. Mead, *Tikanga Māori,* 31.
55. Metge, *Tuamaka.*
56. Patterson, *People of the Land,* 134–35.
57. Metge, *Tuamaka.*
58. Mead, *Tikanga Māori,* 186.
59. Ibid., 342.
60. Ibid., 343–47.
61. Ballara, *Taua,* 101–2.

62. See, for example, *Te Weehi v Regional Fisheries Officer* [1986] 1 NZL.R. 682 (H.C.); *Attorney-General v Ngāti Apa* [2003] 3 NZL.R. 643 (C.A.).
63. See *Public Trustee v Loasby* (1908) 27 NZL.R. 801, and *Huakina Development Trust v Waikato Valley Authority* [1987] 2 NL.R.188 (H.C.). See also *Arani v Public Trustee* [1920] A.C. 198 (P.C.), in which the privy council assumed that Māori society had mechanisms to permit the evolution of Māori custom so that Pākehā as well as Māori children could be the subjects of customary adoptions and entitled to succeed to the property of the adoptive parents. Though this decision may be seen as recognition that self-determined changes to Māori legal traditions may take place, it should be noted that there is also a question as to whether the privy council correctly applied tikanga in this instance.
64. Boast, "Māori Customary Law and Land Tenure," 32–37.
65. New Zealand Law Commission, *Māori Custom and Values.*
66. Ibid., 52–59.
67. *Te Ture Whenua Māori Act* (New Zealand) 1993, s 115.
68. See New Zealand Law Commission, *Māori Custom and Values,* 56–58.
69. *Resource Management Act* (New Zealand) 1991, s 7.
70. *Takamore v Clarke* [2011] NZCA 587.
71. *Takamore v Clarke* [2012] NZSC 116.
72. This is a somewhat crude simplification of the functions of the pōwhiri, though it is sufficient for the purposes of this book.
73. Mead, *Tikanga Māori,* 117.
74. Ibid., 118.
75. Māori Party Constitution, online.
76. Turia, "Operating Māori Values within the System."
77. Ibid.
78. Māori Party Constitution, online, Rule 11.1.
79. Ibid., Rule 11.2.
80. Ibid., Rule 11.3.
81. Ibid.
82. Gower, "Leaked complaint shows extent of Māori Party split."
83. *New Zealand Herald,* "Faith in Harawira lost - caucus."
84. H. Harawira, "Crunch time for Māori grumbles."
85. *New Zealand Herald,* "Faith in Harawira lost - caucus."
86. Ibid.
87. Ibid.
88. Gower, "Leaked complaint shows extent of Māori Party split."
89. New Zealand Press Association, "Māori Party plays down Harawira tensions."
90. Cheng, "Harawira wants to stay with party."
91. New Zealand Press Association, "Māori Party plays down Harawira tensions."
92. Te Aho, "The Tangled Web of Treaty Settlements."
93. *Central North Island Forests Land Collective Settlement Act* (New Zealand) 2008, Schedule 2, s 2.
94. Ibid.
95. Ibid., Schedule 2, s 4.
96. Ibid., Schedule 2, s 5.
97. Ibid., Schedule 2, s 6.

Chapter 4: Treaty Settlements and Māori Law

1. See, e.g., *New Zealand Māori Council v Attorney-General* [1987] 1 N.Z.L.R. 641 at 663 (C.A.); *New Zealand Māori Council v Attorney-General* [1991] 2 N.Z.L.R. 129 (C.A.); *New Zealand Māori Council v Attorney-General* [1994] 1 NZL.R. 513 (P.C.); Waitangi Tribunal, *Muriwhenua Land Report*; Waitangi Tribunal, *The Taranaki Report*; Waitangi Tribunal, *The Ngai Tahu Report 1991*; Waitangi Tribunal, *The Te Roroa Report*.
2. E.T. Durie, "Background Paper," 12.
3. See, e.g., Waitangi Tribunal, *Turangi Township Remedies Report*; Waitangi Tribunal, *Tāmaki Makaurau Settlement Process Report*; Waitangi Tribunal, *East Coast Settlement Report*.
4. Palmer, The Treaty of Waitangi, 264.
5. Ibid., 264–67.
6. *Waikato Raupatu Claims Settlement Act* (New Zealand) 1995.
7. Office of Treaty Settlements, *Ka tika ā muri, ka tika ā mua*, 2nd ed., 35–40.
8. Ibid., 44–51.
9. Ibid., 44.
10. Office of Treaty Settlements, *Ka tika ā muri, ka tika ā mua*, 1st ed., 52.
11. Office of Treaty Settlements, 2nd ed., 54–60.
12. See, e.g., Ngāti Ruahine Terms of Negotiation, para 13.1.
13. Office of Treaty Settlements, 2nd ed., 57.
14. Office of Treaty Settlements, 2nd ed., 54–56.
15. Ibid., 61–68.
16. Following the successful example of the CNI forestry negotiations, it is now common for lawyers not to participate in the actual face-to-face negotiations.
17. Office of Treaty Settlements, 2nd ed., 62–63.
18. Ibid., 64–65.
19. See Ngāti Toa Rangatira Letter of Agreement.
20. See Crown Offer to Ngai Tūhoe.
21. Office of Treaty Settlements, 2nd ed., 69–80.
22. See, e.g., Waitangi Tribunal, *The Te Arawa Mandate Report*.
23. Office of Treaty Settlements, 2nd ed., 80.
24. Ibid., at 96.
25. Note that many Māori communities would also see their relationship with the Crown as being governed by other important agreements (see Boast, "Recognising Multi-Textualism." In some ways at least, the new treaty settlements may start to be seen as the primary relationship instrument.
26. The only treaties signed between First Nations and the Crown in mainland British Columbia are Treaty 8 (1899), which includes parts of northeastern British Columbia, and the Nisga'a Final Agreement (1999).
27. The British Columbia Claims Task Force Terms of Reference (1990).
28. The British Columbia Claims Task Force, *The Report of the British Columbia Claims Task Force*.
29. Graham, *Trick or Treaty?*, 55–64.
30. See Office of Treaty Settlements, 2nd ed., 44–51; and Crown Forestry Rental Trust, *Māori Experiences of the Direct Negotiation Process*, 16–21.
31. Woolford, *Between Justice and Certainty*, 161–65. Although treaty settlements usually include mechanisms designed to establish new, healthier relationships between

Māori and the Crown, these settlements are fundamentally premised on the extinguishment of Māori rights under the Treaty of Waitangi.

32. See ibid., 172–79.
33. Office of Treaty Settlements, 2nd ed., 27–29.
34. The context in which this decision was taken is also significant. In the period leading up to the development of these principles, the Crown was engaged in negotiations with Māori that led to the national settlement of all claims in relation to commercial fisheries. "The Sealords Deal," as this agreement came to be known (because it involved the purchase of a stake in the commercial fishing company, Sealords), was a pre-cursor to these new-style, negotiated settlements.
35. *Treaty of Waitangi Amendment Act* (New Zealand) 2008. The limitation on historical claims is now set out in *Treaty of Waitangi Act* (New Zealand) 1975 s. 6AA.
36. Office of Treaty Settlements, *Crown Proposals for the Settlement of Treaty of Waitangi Claims*, 9–12.
37. Ibid.
38. In the Canadian context, see Tully, "Reconsidering the B.C. Treaty Process," 8–9.
39. Office of Treaty Settlements, 2nd ed., 127.
40. See, e.g., L Te Aho, "Ruruku Whakatupua Te Mana o te Awa Tupua - Upholding the Mana of the Whanganui River."
41. Office of Treaty Settlements, *Crown Proposals for the Settlement of Treaty of Waitangi Claims*, 22.
42. Ward, *An Unsettled History*, 52–54.
43. The Ngai Tūhoe and Whanganui Settlement Offers provide for some novel and innovative forms of redress, yet they only address cultural-symbolic issues to a very limited extent and in a way that does not deviate from the basic Crown framework or challenge the colonial relationship. See Crown Offer to Ngai Tūhoe (2012) and Tōtohu Whakatupua - Whanganui River Agreement (2012).
44. Te Aho, "Corporate Governance," 308.
45. Ibid., 308–9.
46. Freire, *Pedagogy of the Oppressed*, 45–48.
47. Te Aho, "Corporate Governance," 309.
48. See, e.g., *Ngāti Ruanui Claims Settlement Act* (New Zealand) 2003, Preamble; *Ngāti Tuwharetoa (Bay of Plenty) Claims Settlement Act* (New Zealand) 2005, Background; *Ngāti Mutunga Claims Settlement Act* (New Zealand) 2006, Preamble.
49. *Ngāti Awa Claims Settlement Act* (New Zealand) 2005, Schedule 6.
50. Ibid., Schedule 10.
51. Ngai Tamanuhiri Deed of Settlement cl. 5.1 (2011).
52. Rongowhakaata Deed of Settlement cl. 6.15 (2011).
53. *Waikato Raupatu Claims Settlement Act* (New Zealand) 1995, Preamble.
54. This might be seen as parallel to issues relating to the language and concepts used in the treaty of Waitangi. "Kāwanatanga" (government) is used in the Māori text of the treaty as the translation for "sovereignty" and "tino rangatiratanga" is used to express the authority of the chiefs. "Mana" is conspicuously absent from the text of the treaty, despite being used five years earlier in the 1835 Declaration of Independence in the phrase "Ko te Kīngitanga ko te mana" as a translation of "All sovereign power and authority."
55. See T.R. Williams, *Te Mana Motuhake o Tūhoe.*
56. Rongowhakaata Deed of Settlement, cl. 2.18.

57. *Waikato Raupatu Claims Settlement Act* (New Zealand) 1995.
58. Note that the debate about the appropriate interpretation of the Treaty of Waitangi itself has illustrated similar difficulties in relation to the application of the Māori text and meaning ascribed to Māori concepts used in the treaty.
59. Sharp, *Justice and the Māori.*
60. Ibid., 249–318.
61. Ibid., 264.
62. Webber, "Legal Pluralism and Human Agency," 180–81.
63. Ibid., at 179–82.
64. Sharp, *Justice and the Māori*, 265.
65. *New Zealand Māori Council v Attorney-General* [1987] 1 N.Z.L.R. 641 at 663 (C.A.).
66. See Chapter 1.
67. McHugh, *Aboriginal Societies*, 416.
68. Ibid.
69. Sharp, *Justice and the Māori*, 278.
70. Ibid.
71. Ibid., 27–40.
72. Ibid., 34.
73. Ibid., 34–36.
74. Ibid., 35.
75. Ibid.
76. Office of Treaty Settlements, 2nd ed., 87.
77. Ibid., 88.
78. Ibid., 87.
79. Waikato-Tainui Deed of Settlement, 1995, Attachment 9; Ngai Tahu Deed of Settlement, 1997, Section 18.
80. Office of Treaty Settlements, 2nd ed., 28–30, 88.
81. Margaret Mutu, a prominent Māori leader who has acted as chief negotiator for her tribe, has noted the problems this creates for doing justice in each claim, and, consequently, for reaching durable settlements. See Mutu, "Recovering Fagin's Ill-Gotten Gains," 204–5.
82. Office of Treaty Settlements, 2nd ed., 72.
83. Ibid., 75.
84. Ibid.
85. Gover, *Tribal Constitutionalism.*
86. Te Atiawa Manawhenua ki te Tau Ihu Trust: Replacement Deed of Trust, cl. 6 (2000); Ngāti Tama Manawhenua ki te Tau Ihu Deed of Trust, cl. 9.2 (1993); Te Rūnanga o Ngai Tahu Charter (2000).
87. See, e.g., Deed of Trust of the Patiki Trust, cl. 1.1 (2006).
88. See, e.g., Deed of Restatement and Amendment of Trust: Te Kotahitanga o Te Arawa Waka Fisheries Trust Board, cl. 1.1 (2005).
89. See, e.g., Rules of Muaupoko Tribal Authority Inc., cl. 6.1(b) (2005). See also Constitution and Rules of Ngāti Ranginui Iwi Soc. Inc., cl. 1.1 (2005): "[a]ll persons who whakapapa to any of the seven hapu of Muaupoko Iwi."
90. See, e.g., the constitution of Te Rūnanga o Ngāti Awa: "(a) 'Ngāti Awa' is ngā uri o ngā Hapū o Ngāti Awa and: (b) means the collective group composed of individuals referred to in paragraph (b) of this definition; and means: (i) every individual who is descended from a Ngāti Awa Tipuna; (ii) every individual who is a member of a hapū,

group, family or whanau referred to in paragraph (c) of this definition; and (c) includes the Hapū; and any hapū, group, family or whanau composed of individuals referred to in paragraph (b) of this definition" (Charter of Te Rūnanga o Ngāti Awa, cl. 1.1 [2005].)

91. See, e.g., Ngāti Toa Rangatira initialled Deed of Settlement, 2012.
92. Gover, *Tribal Constitutionalism*, 89.
93. See, e.g., Waitangi Tribunal, *The Te Arawa Mandate Report*; and Waitangi Tribunal, *Tāmaki Makaurau Report*.
94. Waitangi Tribunal, *The Ngāti Tuwharetoa ki Kawerau Settlement Cross Claim Report*, 61.
95. Ibid.
96. Waitangi Tribunal, *East Coast Settlement Report*.
97. Ibid., 67.
98. Many of these issues were subsequently addressed by the High Court of New Zealand. See *Port Nicholson Block Settlement Trust v Attorney-General* [2012] NZHC 3181. It is worth noting Justice Williams's comments at para. 95, in which he suggests that one of the difficulties with the cultural redress mechanisms used in modern settlement to recognise customary interests is that these mechanisms "do not reflect the sophisticated hierarchy of interests provided for by Māori custom. They have the effect of flattening out interests as if all are equal, just as the Native Land Court did 150 years ago. In short, modern [Resource Management Act]-based acknowledgements dumb down tikanga Māori."
99. Waitangi Tribunal, *Port Nicholson Block Urgency Report*.
100. See, e.g., Vertongen, "Remedies."
101. Office of Treaty Settlements, 2nd ed., 72.
102. Ibid., 76.
103. Ibid., 76–77.
104. Ibid., 77.

Chapter 5: Post-Settlement Governance and Māori Law

1. *Te Runanga o Ngai Tahu Act* (New Zealand) 1996.
2. Charter of Te Rūnanga o Ngāi Tahu (2012).
3. Ibid.
4. The New Zealand Law Commission was established by the *Law Commission Act* 1985. It has a membership of between three and six commissioners, who are appointed by the Governor-General on the advice of the responsible minister. The functions of the commission are "to take and keep under review in a systematic way the law of New Zealand; to make recommendations for the reform and development of the law of New Zealand; to advise on the review of any aspect of the law of New Zealand conducted by any government department or organisation and on proposals made as a result of the review; and, to advise the Minister of Justice and the responsible Minister on ways in which the law of New Zealand can be made as understandable and accessible as is practicable," (s 5, *Law Commission Act* [New Zealand] 1985). In making its recommendations, the commission is required to take into account "te ao Maori (the Maori dimension)" and "give consideration to the multicultural character of New Zealand society"; it must also "have regard to the desirability of simplifying the expression and content of the law, as far as that is practicable" (s 5, *Law Commission Act* (New Zealand) 1985).

5. New Zealand Law Commission, *Waka Umanga*, 67.
6. Ibid., 68.
7. Ibid.
8. Ibid.
9. Ibid., 67.
10. For general information about the Harvard Project on American Indian Economic Development, see the project's website, http://www.hpaied.org. For an example of the project's work on the importance of culture in relation to governance and economic development, see Cornell and Kalt, "Where Does Economic Development Really Come From? Constitutional Rule among the Contemporary Sioux and Apache."
11. Ibid., 69.
12. Ibid.
13. Sullivan, "Indigenous Governance," 10–12.
14. New Zealand Law Commission, *Waka Umanga*, 69–70.
15. Ibid., 69.
16. Ibid. 70.
17. See, e.g., Waitangi Tribunal, *Tāmaki Makaurau Settlement Process Report.*
18. Ibid., 7–13.
19. In this respect, there are striking parallels between the modern settlement process and the process implemented by the Native Land Court in the 19th century that was aimed at determining who held customary interests in Māori land. See Boast, *Buying the Land, Selling the Land*, 111–17.
20. New Zealand Law Commission, *Waka Umanga*, 71.
21. Ibid.
22. Ibid., 72.
23. See, e.g., Waitangi Tribunal, *Report on the Crown's Foreshore and Seabed Policy.*
24. New Zealand Law Commission, *Waka Umanga*, 72.
25. Ibid.
26. R. Joseph, "Unsettling Treaty Settlements," 155.
27. New Zealand Law Commission, *Waka Umanga*, 73.
28. Ibid., 74.
29. Ibid.
30. Ibid.
31. Ibid., 75–76.
32. Waitangi Tribunal, *Tāmaki Makaurau Settlement Process Report.*
33. Hefferan, "Post-Settlement Dispute Resolution."
34. Waitangi Tribunal, *Tāmaki Makaurau Settlement Process Report*, 6–7.
35. C. Jones, "Māori Dispute Resolution."
36. Ibid., 127.
37. See *Cook v The Minister of Aboriginal Relations and Reconciliation* [2007] BCSC 1722.
38. Woolford, *Between Justice and Certainty*, 122–23.
39. Ibid., 123.
40. Tully, "Reconsidering the B.C. Treaty Process," 426.
41. Woolford, *Between Justice and Certainty*, 122–26.
42. Crown Forestry Rental Trust, *Māori Experiences of the Direct Negotiation Process.*
43. Woolford, *Between Justice and Certainty*, 123.
44. Ibid., 124.
45. Ibid.

46. Crown Forestry Rental Trust, *Māori Experiences of the Direct Negotiation Process*, 44.
47. Woolford, *Between Justice and Certainty*, 54.
48. Sharp, *Justice and the Māori*, 42.
49. Webber, "Legal Pluralism and Human Agency."
50. Sharp, *Justice and the Māori*, 64.
51. Sharp, "The Trajectory of the Waitangi Tribunal," 204–5.
52. Office of Treaty Settlements, *Crown Proposals for the Settlement of Treaty of Waitangi Claims*, 23. This general approach to settlement redress is now reflected in the Office of Treaty Settlements' guide for claimants (see Office of Treaty Settlements, 2nd ed., 28–29), which also sets out the Crown's specific approach to financial and commercial redress.
53. See also *Bidois v Leef* [2015] NZCA 176, a decision of the New Zealand Court of Appeal. In that case, the court was asked to set aside an arbitral award that had been made as part of a process very similar to the tikanga-based dispute resolution process developed in the CNI forestry settlement. The process in question had been agreed in order to establish, for the purposes of the allocation of settlement assets, the relative customary interests of the constituent groups of Ngāti Ranginui (an iwi from the Tauranga region that entered into a deed of settlement with the Crown on June 21, 2012). The High Court had found that the adjudication was not binding because it was outside the scope of the Arbitration Act 1996, as it addressed "mana whenua," an issue that did not arise in respect of a defined legal relationship. The Court of Appeal overturned that decision. Although the court had significant concerns about the way the agreement was framed, it determined that mana whenua did arise as part of a defined legal relationship for the purposes of the Arbitration Act because the issue of mana whenua was directly connected to claims registered with the Waitangi Tribunal.
54. *Te Rūnanga o Ngāti Manawa v Attorney-General*, High Court Wellington CIV-2011-485-1233, 2 November 2011, at para 59.
55. *Tūrāhui v Waitangi Tribunal* [2015] NZHC 1624, at para 61.
56. Note that while it is difficult to remove settlement disputes from the supervision of the state courts in one sense, the courts in both New Zealand and British Columbia have also been reluctant to intervene in settlements, which are viewed as political compacts and consequently non-justiciable in most respects. See, e.g., *Te Rūnanga o Wharekauri Rekohu v Attorney-General* [1993] 2 N.Z.L.R. 301 (C.A.). This presents a double challenge for Māori legal traditions: a state legal system that asserts exclusive legal authority to deal with settlement disputes, and limited practical availability of legal oversight mechanisms within the state system for settlement issues.
57. Gover, *Tribal Constitutionalism*.
58. For recent examples, see Ngāti Manawa Deed of Settlement (2009) cl. 4.8.2; Ngāti Whare Deed of Settlement (2009) cl. 4.7.4; and Deed of Settlement in Relation to the Waikato River (2009) cl. 16.10.2.
59. McKee, *Treaty Talks in British Columbia*, 92–96. Alongside state obsession with certainty, the state has a similar fixation with reaching agreements expeditiously, despite taking over one hundred years to recognise that there existed issues to be resolved.
60. Woolford, *Between Justice and Certainty*, 144–70.
61. Mikaere, "Settlement of Treaty Claims."
62. See, e.g., Ngāti Toa Rangatira initialled Deed of Settlement (2012), cl. 4.4.
63. De Costa, "Treaties in British Columbia," 141.
64. De Costa, "History, Democracy, and Treaty Making in British Columbia," 314.

65. De Costa, "Treaties in British Columbia," 146.
66. The British Columbia Claims Task Force, *The Report of the British Columbia Claims Task Force*, 63–65.
67. De Costa, "Treaties in British Columbia," 141.
68. Ibid.
69. Mikaere, "Settlement of Treaty Claims," 454.
70. Ibid., 443.
71. Ibid., 444.
72. New Zealand Government, 7 *Ideas to Accelerate the Settlement Process.*
73. Gover, *Tribal Constitutionalism*, 160.
74. Ibid., 161.
75. Ibid., 165–66.
76. Ibid., 165.
77. Borrows, *Canada's Indigenous Constitution*, 23–58.
78. Gover, *Tribal Constitutionalism*, 165.
79. Ibid., 166.
80. See D. Williams, '*Te Kooti Tango Whenua*,' 187–89.
81. Office of Treaty Settlements, 2nd ed., 44–51.
82. Iorns Magallanes, "Reparations for Māori Grievances in Aotearoa New Zealand," 563.
83. Graham, *Trick or Treaty?*, 90.
84. Office of Treaty Settlements, *Ka tika ā muri, ka tika ā mua*, 2nd ed., 47–48. For recent examples, see Ngāti Manawa Deed of Settlement (2009) cl. 13.1 and cl. 13.4; Ngāti Whare Deed of Settlement (2009) cl. 12.1 and cl. 12.3.
85. For example, Waikato-Tainui signed one agreement in 1995, which settled their claims in relation to land confiscations, and in December 2009 concluded another settlement, this time in relation to the Waikato River.
86. Office of Treaty Settlements, 2nd ed., 44.
87. Ibid.

Chapter 6: New Stories and Old Stories Re-Told

1. Office of Treaty Settlements, 2nd ed., 28.
2. Ibid., 30.
3. Ibid., 28.
4. See, e.g., Regan, *Unsettling the Settler Within.*
5. Ibid., 58.
6. Ngāti Raukawa Deed of Settlement (2012), para 3.17.
7. Te Rarawa Deed of Settlement (2011), para 3.44.
8. Taranaki Whānui o te Upoko o te Ika Deed of Settlement (19 August 2008), para 3.2, para 3.3.
9. Waitangi Tribunal, *The New Approach Revisited,* 1.
10. Ibid.
11. Finlayson, "Address by the Minister for Treaty of Waitangi Negotiations."
12. Sharples, "Post-Settlement Crown–Iwi Relationships." Note that Pita Sharples, Minister for Māori Affairs at the time of this meeting, is also a member of Ngāti Kahungunu and, like Timi Kara (Sir James Carroll), has attained high office in the New Zealand government.
13. Key, "Towards 2014."

14. See, e.g., Waitangi Tribunal, *Tāmaki Makaurau Settlement Process Report.*
15. Tully, *Public Philosophy in a New Key,* 237–38.
16. Ibid., 225–28.
17. See Woolford, *Between Justice and Certainty.*
18. Tully, *Public Philosophy in a New Key,* 234.
19. Mikaere, "The Treaty of Waitangi and Recognition of Tikanga Māori."
20. Tully, *Public Philosophy in a New Key,* 226–28.
21. Woolford, *Between Justice and Certainty,* 172–79.
22. See Tully, *Public Philosophy in a New Key,* 234.
23. Ibid., 229.
24. See Webber, "Legal Pluralism and Human Agency."
25. Tully, *Public Philosophy in a New Key.*
26. G. Smith, "Research Issues Related to Māori Education," cited in L. Smith, *Decolonizing Methodologies,* 85.
27. Christie, "Indigenous Legal Theory," 206.
28. Webber," Legal Pluralism and Human Agency."
29. Tamanaha, "Understanding Legal Pluralism: Past to Present, Local to Global."
30. Gover, *Tribal Constitutionalism.*
31. See Napoleon and Friedland, "An Inside Job."
32. See E.T. Durie, "Will the Settlers Settle?"
33. See J. Williams, *He Aha te Tikanga Māori?*
34. See Napoleon and Friedland, "An Inside Job."
35. New Zealand Law Commission, *Māori Custom and Values.*
36. Ministry of Justice, *He Hinatore ki te Ao Māori.*
37. See Hart, *The Concept of Law,* 87–88.
38. Napoleon and Friedland, "An Inside Job," 8.

Epilogue: Māui and the People of the North

This epilogue was inspired by my participation in a workshop on Indigenous Legal Traditions held in Fort St John, BC, in 2011. I would like to acknowledge the generosity of the peoples of the Treaty Eight territory for sharing their stories with all of us who were privileged to participate in that workshop.

"Pinepine te Kura"

In Māori traditions, songs or waiata are usually performed at the end of speeches to support what has been said. "Pinepine Te Kura" is a famous song from Ngāti Kahungunu. It is an oriori, a chant composed for young children.

Bibliography

New Zealand legislation is available at: http://www.legislation.govt.nz. Deeds of settlement and most other settlement instruments are available at the website of the Office of Treaty Settlements: http://www.ots.govt.nz. Offer letters and related material are available at the website of the New Zealand Government: http://www.beehive.govt.nz. Decisions of the New Zealand courts are available at the Courts of New Zealand website: http://www.courtsofnz.govt.nz. Waitangi Tribunal reports are available at the Waitangi Tribunal website: http://www.justice.govt.nz/tribunals/waitangi-tribunal. Te Mātāhauariki Institute: http://lianz.waikato.ac.nz/publications-internal.htm.

LEGISLATION

Central North Island Forests Land Collective Settlement Act (New Zealand) 2008
Conservation Act (New Zealand) 1987
Local Government Act (New Zealand) 2002
New Zealand Public Health and Disability Act (New Zealand) 2000
Ngāti Awa Claims Settlement Act (New Zealand) 2005
Ngāti Mutunga Claims Settlement Act (New Zealand) 2006
Ngāti Ruanui Claims Settlement Act (New Zealand) 2003
Ngāti Tuwharetoa (Bay of Plenty) Claims Settlement Act (New Zealand) 2005
Resource Management Act (New Zealand) 1991
State Owned Enterprises Act (New Zealand) 1986
Te Runanga o Ngai Tahu Act (New Zealand) 1996
Te Ture Whenua Māori Act (New Zealand) 1993
Treaty of Waitangi Act (New Zealand) 1975
Treaty of Waitangi Amendment Act (New Zealand) 2008
Waikato Raupatu Claims Settlement Act (New Zealand) 1995

Waikato-Tainui Raupatu Claims (Waikato River) Settlement Act (New Zealand) 2010
Whanganui Iwi (Whanganui (Kaitoke) Prison and Northern Part of Whanganui Forest) On-account Settlement Act (New Zealand) 2011

SETTLEMENT AND GOVERNANCE INSTRUMENTS

Charter of Te Rūnanga o Ngāti Awa (2005)
Charter of Te Rūnanga o Ngāi Tahu (2012)
Constitution of Ngāti Kahungunu Iwi Incorporated (2006)
Constitution and Rules of Ngāti Ranginui Iwi Soc. Inc. (2005)
Crown Offer to Ngai Tūhoe (2012)
Deed of Restatement and Amendment of Trust: Te Kotahitanga o Te Arawa Waka Fisheries Trust Board (2005)
Deed of Settlement in Relation to the Waikato River (2009)
Deed of Trust of the Patiki Trust (2006)
Ngai Tahu Deed of Settlement (1997)
Ngai Tamanuhiri Deed of Settlement (2011)
Ngāti Manawa Deed of Settlement (2009)
Ngāti Raukawa Deed of Settlement (2012)
Ngāti Ruahine Terms of Negotiation (2008)
Ngāti Tama Manawhenua ki te Tau Ihu Deed of Trust (1993)
Ngāti Toa Rangatira initialled Deed of Settlement (2012)
Ngāti Toa Rangatira Letter of Agreement (2009)
Ngāti Whare Deed of Settlement (2009)
Rongowhakaata Deed of Settlement (2011)
Rules of Muaupoko Tribal Authority Inc. (2005)
Taranaki Whānui o te Upoko o te Ika Deed of Settlement (2008)
Te Atiawa Iwi Authority and Te Atiawa (Taranaki) Settlements Trust Registration Form (undated)
Te Atiawa Manawhenua ki te Tau Ihu Trust: Replacement Deed of Trust (2000)
Te Rarawa Deed of Settlement (2011)
Te Rūnanga o Ngai Tahu Application for Registration (undated)
Te Rūnanga o Ngai Tahu Charter (2000)
Te Rūnanga o Ngāti Whare Iwi Trust, Beneficiary Registration Form (undated)
Te Rūnanga o Rangitane o Wairarapa Registration Form (undated)
Tōtohu Whakatupua – Whanganui River Agreement (2012)
Waikato Raupatu Lands Trust Registration Form (undated)
Waikato-Tainui Deed of Settlement (1995)

JURISPRUDENCE

Arani v Public Trustee [1920] A.C. 198 (P.C.)
Attorney-General v Ngāti Apa [2003] 3 NZL.R. 643 (C.A.)
Barton-Prescott v Director-General of Social Welfare [1997] 3 NZL.R. 179 (H.C.)
Bidois v Leef [2015] NZCA 176
Cook v The Minister of Aboriginal Relations and Reconciliation [2007] BCSC 1722

Haronga v Waitangi Tribunal [2011] NZSC 53
Hoani Te Heuheu Tukino v Aotea District Maori Land Board [1941] AC 308
Huakina Development Trust v Waikato Valley Authority [1987] 2 NZL.R. 188 (H.C.)
Koia v Waitangi Tribunal [2011] CIV-2010-485-1519 (H.C.)
Leef v Bidois [2012] NZHC 2631
Mabo v Queensland (No 2) (1992) 175 C.L.R. 1
New Zealand Māori Council v Attorney-General [Lands case] [1987] 1 NZL.R. 641 (H.C. and C.A.)
New Zealand Māori Council v Attorney-General [1989] 2 NZL.R. 142 (C.A.)
New Zealand Māori Council v Attorney-General [1991] 2 NZL.R. 129 (C.A.)
New Zealand Māori Council v Attorney-General [1994] 1 NZL.R. 513 (P.C.)
Ngai Tahu Māori Trust Board v Director-General of Conservation [1995] 3 NZL.R. 534 (C.A.)
Port Nicholson Block Settlement Trust v Attorney-General [2012] NZHC 3181
Public Trustee v Loasby (1908) 27 NZL.R. 801
R. v. Sparrow [1990] 1 S.C.R. 1075
R. v. Symonds (1847) NZPCC 387
Taiaroa and Others v Attorney-General [1994] (H.C.) 4 October, unreported, CP No 99/94
Takamore v Clarke [2011] NZCA 587
Takamore v Clarke [2012] NZSC 116
Te Rūnanga o Ngāti Manawa v Attorney-General, High Court Wellington CIV-2011-485-1233, 2 November 2011
Te Rūnanga o Wharekauri Rekohu v Attorney-General [1993] 2 NZL.R. 301 (C.A.)
Te Weehi v Regional Fisheries Officer [1986] 1 NZL.R. 682 (H.C.)
Tūrāhui v Waitangi Tribunal [2015] NZHC 1624
Wi Parata v Bishop of Wellington (1877) 3 NZ Jur. (NS) 72 (S.C.)

WAITANGI TRIBUNAL REPORTS

East Coast Settlement Report (Wai 2190) (Wellington, NZ: Legislation Direct, 2010).
He Whakaputanga me te Tiriti - The Declaration and the Treaty: The Report on Stage 1 of the Te Paparahi o Te Raki Inquiry (Wellington: Legislation Direct, 2014).
Ko Aotearoa Tēnei: A Report into Claims Concerning New Zealand Law and Policy Affecting Māori Culture and Identity (Wellington, NZ: Legislation Direct, 2011).
Māori Electoral Option Report (Wai 413) (Wellington, NZ: Brooker's, 1994).
The Mohaka ki Ahuriri Report (Wai 201) (Wellington, NZ: Legislation Direct, 2004).
Muriwhenua Land Report (Wellington, NZ: GP Publications, 1997).
The Ngai Tahu Report 1991 (Wellington, NZ: Brooker and Friend, 1991).
Ngāi Tahu Sea Fisheries Report (Wellington, NZ: Brooker and Friend, 1992).
The Ngāti Tuwharetoa ki Kawerau Settlement Cross Claim Report (Wellington, NZ: Legislation Direct, 2003).
Ngāwhā Geothermal Resources Report (Wai 304) (Wellington, NZ: Brooker and Friend, 1993).
Port Nicholson Block Urgency Report (Wellington, NZ: Legislation Direct, 2012).
Prcliminary Report on the Te Arawa Representative Geothermal Resource Claims (Wai 153) (Wellington, NZ: Brooker and Friend, 1993).
Report on the Crown's Foreshore and Seabed Policy (Wai 1071) (Wellington, NZ: Legislation Direct, 2004).

Report on the Mohaka River (Wellington, NZ: Department of Justice, 1992).
Report of the Waitangi Tribunal on the Manukau Claim (Wellington, NZ: Government Printer, 1985).
Report of the Waitangi Tribunal on the Muriwhenua Fishing Claim (Wai 22) (Wellington, NZ: Department of Justice, 1988).
Report of the Waitangi Tribunal on the Orakei Claim (Wai 9) (Wellington, NZ: GP Publications, 1987).
Tamaki Makaurau Settlement Process Report (Wai 1362) (Wellington, NZ: Legislation Direct, 2007).
The Taranaki Report: Kaupapa Tuatahi (Wellington, NZ: GP Publications, 1996).
The Te Arawa Mandate Report – Wahanga Tuarua (Wai 1150) (Wellington, NZ: Legislation Direct, 2005).
Te Arawa Representatives Geothermal Resources Report (Wellington, NZ: Brooker and Friend, 1993).
The Te Roroa Report (Wellington, NZ: Brooker and Friend, 1992).
Te Whānau o Waipareira Report (Wai 414) (Wellington, NZ: GP Publications, 1998).
Te Whanganui-a-Orotu Report (Wai 55) (Wellington, NZ: Department of Justice, 1995).
Turangi Township Remedies Report (Wellington, NZ: GP Publications, 1998).

OTHER PRIMARY MATERIAL

7 Ideas to Accelerate the Settlement Process (draft produced by New Zealand Government for discussion at Kōkiri Ngātahi – Treaty Settlements Hui, Auckland, NZ, April 22, 2009).
British Columbia Claims Task Force, *The Report of the British Columbia Claims Task Force* (Victoria, BC: The Government of British Columbia, Treaty Negotiations Office, 1991).
The British Columbia Claims Task Force Terms of Reference (Victoria, BC: The Government of British Columbia, 1990).
Cheng, D., "Harawira wants to stay with party," *New Zealand Herald* (February 8, 2011).
Gower, P., "Leaked complaint shows extent of Māori Party split," *3 News* (February 4, 2011), online: 3 News, http://www.3news.co.nz.
Māori Affairs Select Committee, *Report on the Ngāti Porou Claims Settlement Bill* (New Zealand Parliament, 2011).
Māori Party Constitution (2010), online: The Māori Party, http://www.maoriparty.org/.
Ministry of Justice, *He Hinatore ki te Ao Māori – A Glimpse into the Māori World* (Wellington, NZ: Ministry of Justice, 2001).
Native Tenure: Opinions of Various Authorities (1861) AJHR, E No. 1, Appendix A.
New Zealand Herald, "Faith in Harawira lost – caucus," *New Zealand Herald* (February 7, 2011).
New Zealand Law Commission, *Māori Custom and Values in New Zealand Law* (Wellington, NZ: New Zealand Law Commission, 2001).
–, *Treaty of Waitangi Claims: Addressing the Post-Settlement Phase* (Wellington, NZ: New Zealand Law Commission, 2002).
–, *Waka Umanga: A Proposed Law for Māori Governance Entities* (Wellington, NZ: New Zealand Law Commission, 2006).
New Zealand Press Association, "Māori Party plays down Harawira tensions," *National Business Review* (January 25, 2011).

Office of Treaty Settlements, *Crown Proposals for the Settlement of Treaty of Waitangi Claims* (Wellington, NZ: Department of Justice: Office of Treaty Settlements, 1994).

–, *Ka tika ā muri, ka tika ā mua – Healing the Past, Building a Future: A guide to Treaty of Waitangi claims and negotiations with the Crown,* 1st ed. (Wellington, NZ: New Zealand Ministry of Justice: Office of Treaty Settlements, 1999).

–, *Ka tika ā muri, ka tika ā mua – Healing the Past, Building a Future: A guide to Treaty of Waitangi claims and negotiations with the Crown,* 2nd ed. (Wellington, NZ: New Zealand Ministry of Justice: Office of Treaty Settlements, 2002).

Waitangi Tribunal, *The New Approach Revisited: A Discussion Paper on the Waitangi Tribunal's Current and Developing Practices* (Wellington, NZ: Waitangi Tribunal, December 2005).

SECONDARY MATERIAL

Absolon, Kathy, and Cam Willett. "Putting Ourselves Forward: Location in Aboriginal Research." In *Research As Resistance: Critical, Indigenous, and Anti-oppressive Approaches,* edited by Leslie Brown and Susan Strega (Toronto: Canadian Scholars Press, 2005).

Alfred, Taiaiake. *Peace, Power, Righteousness: An Indigenous Manifesto,* 2nd ed. (Don Mills, ON: Oxford University Press, 2009).

–. "Warrior Scholarship: Seeing the University as a Ground of Contention." In *Indigenizing the Academy: Transforming Scholarship and Empowering Communities,* edited by Devon A. Mihesuah and Angela Cavender Wilson (Lincoln and London: University of Nebraska Press, 2004).

–. *Wasase: Indigenous Pathways of Action and Freedom* (Peterborough, ON: Broadview Press, 2005).

Anaya, James. "Indigenous Law and Its Contribution to Global Pluralism" (2007) 6 Indigenous L.J. 3.

Archibald, Jo-ann. *Indigenous Storywork: Educating the Heart, Mind, Body, and Spirit* (Vancouver: UBC Press, 2008).

Attwood, B. *Telling the Truth about Aboriginal History* (Crows Nest, NSW: Allen and Unwin, 2005).

Awatere, Donna. *Māori Sovereignty* (Auckland, NZ: Broadsheet, 1984).

Ballara, Angela. *Iwi: The Dynamics of Māori Tribal Organisation from c.1769 to c.1945* (Wellington, NZ: Victoria University Press, 1998).

–. *Taua: "Musket Wars," "Land Wars" or Tikanga?* (Auckland, NZ: Penguin Books, 2003).

Bargh, Maria, ed. *Māori and Parliament: Diverse Strategies and Compromises* (Wellington, NZ: Huia, 2010).

–. "The Post-settlement World (So Far): Impacts for Māori." In *Treaty of Waitangi Settlements,* edited by Nicola R. Wheen and Janine Hayward (Wellington, NZ: Bridget Williams Books, 2012).

–. *Resistance: An Indigenous Response to Neoliberalism* (Wellington, NZ: Huia, 2007).

Barzilai, Gad. "Beyond Relativism: Where Is Political Power in Legal Pluralism?" (2008) 9 Theoretical Inq. L. 395.

Belgrave, Michael. *Historical Frictions: Māori Claims and Reinvented Histories* (Auckland, NZ: Auckland University Press, 2005).

Belgrave, Michael, Merata Kawharu, and David Williams, eds. *Waitangi Revisited: Perspectives on the Treaty of Waitangi* (Auckland, NZ: Oxford University Press, 2005).

Bell, Derrick. *And We Are Not Saved: The Elusive Quest for Racial Justice* (New York: Basic Books, 1987).

Bennett, Mark, and Nicole Roughan. "Rebus Sic Stantibus and the Treaty of Waitangi" (2006) 37 Victoria U. Wellington L. Rev. 505.

Bennion, T. "The Lands Reports." In *The Waitangi Tribunal – Te Roopu Whakamana i te Tiriti o Waitangi*, edited by J. Hayward and Nicola R. Wheen (Wellington, NZ: Bridget Williams Books, 2004).

Benton, Richard, Alex Frame, and Paul Meredith, eds. *Te Mātāpunenga: A compendium of references to the concepts and institutions of Māori customary law* (Wellington, NZ: Victoria University Press, 2013).

Berman, H. *Law and Revolution: The Formation of the Western Legal Tradition* (Cambridge, MA: Harvard University Press, 1983).

Best, Elsdon. *Social Usages of the Māori* (Wellington, NZ: Maoriland Worker Printing and Publishing, 1918).

Birdling, M. "Healing the Past or Harming the Future? Large Natural Groupings and the Treaty Settlement Process" (2004) 2 NZ J. Public and Intl. L. 259.

Bishop, Russell. "Initiating Empowering Research?" (1994) 29 *New Zealand Journal of Educational Studies* 175.

–. *Whakawhanaungatanga: Collaborative Research Stories* (Palmerston North, NZ: Dunmore Press, 1996).

Bishop, Russell, and Ted Glynn. "Researching in Māori Contexts: An Interpretation of Participatory Consciousness" (1999) 20 *Jnl. Intercultural Studies* 167.

Boast, R. *Buying the Land, Selling the Land: Governments and Māori Land in the North Island 1865–1921* (Wellington, NZ: Victoria University Press, 2008).

–. "Māori Customary Law and Land Tenure." In *Māori Land Law*, 2nd ed., edited by R. Boast, Andrew Erueti, Doug McPhail, and Norman Smith (Wellington, NZ: LexisNexis, 2004).

–. "Recognising Multi-Textualism: Rethinking New Zealand's Legal History" (2006) 37 VUWLR 547.

Boast, R., and R. Hill, eds. *Raupatu: The Confiscation of Māori Land* (Wellington, NZ: Victoria University Press, 2009).

Bohm, David. *Wholeness and the Implicate Order* (London: Routledge, 1980).

Borrows, John. *Canada's Indigenous Constitution* (Toronto: University of Toronto Press, 2010).

–. "Creating an Indigenous Legal Community, John Tait Memorial Lecture" (2005) 50 McGill L.J. 153.

–. *Drawing Out Law: A Spirit's Guide* (Toronto: University of Toronto Press, 2010).

–. "Ground-Rules: Indigenous Treaties in Canada and New Zealand" (2006) NZ Universities L. Rev. 188.

–. "Indigenous Legal Traditions in Canada Contemporary and Comparative Perspectives on the Rights of Indigenous Peoples" (2005) 19 Wash. U. J.L. and Pol'y 167.

–. "Physical Philosophy: Mobility and the Future of Indigenous Rights." In *Indigenous Peoples and the Law: Comparative and Critical Perspectives*, edited by Benjamin J. Richardson, Shin Imai, and Kent McNeil (Oxford /Portland, OR: Hart, 2009).

–. *Recovering Canada: The Resurgence of Indigenous Law* (Toronto: University of Toronto Press, 2002).

Bradford, W. "With a Very Great Blame on Our Hearts: Reparations, Reconciliation, and an American Indian Plea for Peace with Justice," (2002–2003) 27(1) Am. Ind. L.R. 1.

Brookfield, F.M. *Waitangi and Indigenous Rights: Revolution, Law and Legitimation*, 2nd ed., (Auckland, NZ: Auckland University Press, 2006).

Brown, Leslie, and Susan Strega, eds. *Research As Resistance: Critical, Indigenous, and Anti-oppressive Approaches* (Toronto: Canadian Scholars Press, 2005).

Burton, Lloyd, and David Ruppert. "Bear's Lodge or Devils Tower: Intercultural Relations, Legal Pluralism, and the Management of Sacred Sites on Public Lands" (1999) 8 Cornell J. L. and Pub. Pol'y. 201.

Byrnes, G. *The Waitangi Tribunal and New Zealand History* (Oxford: Oxford University Press, 2004).

Cain, Patricia A. "Feminist Jurisprudence: Grounding the Theories" (1990) 4 Berkeley Women's L. J. 191.

Christie, Gordon. "A Colonial Reading of Recent Jurisprudence: *Sparrow, Delgamuukw* and *Haida Nation*" (2005) 23 Windsor Y.B. Access Just. 17.

–. "Culture, Self-Determination and Colonialism: Issues around the Revitalization of Indigenous Legal Traditions" (2007) 6 Indigenous L.J. 13.

–. "Developing Case Law: The Future of Consultation and Accommodation" (2006) 39 U.B.C. L. Rev. 139.

–. "Indigenous Legal Theory: Some Initial Considerations." In *Indigenous Peoples and the Law: Comparative and Critical Perspectives,* edited by Benjamin J. Richardson, Shin Imai, and Kent McNeil (Oxford/ Portland, OR: Hart, 2009).

–. "Judicial Justification of Recent Developments in Aboriginal Law" (2002) 17 Can. J.L. and Soc. 41.

–. "Justifying Principles of Treaty Interpretation" (2000) 26 Queen's L.J. 143.

–. "Law, Theory and Aboriginal Peoples" (2003) 2 Indigenous L.J. 67.

Coates, K.S., and P.G. McHugh. *Living Relationships – Kōkiri Ngātahi: The Treaty of Waitangi in the New Millennium* (Wellington, NZ: Victoria University Press, 1998).

Cooke, Sir Robin. "Introduction" (1990) 14 New Zealand Universities L. Rev. 1.

Cornell, S. *Five Myths, Three Partial Truths, A Robust Finding and Two Tasks* (Cambridge, MA: Harvard Project on American Indian Economic Development, John F. Kennedy School of Government, Harvard University, 1994).

Cornell, S. and J. Kalt. "Where Does Economic Development Really Come From? Constitutional Rule Among the Contemporary Sioux and Apache," (1995) 33 *Economic Inquiry* 402.

Corntassel, J. "Toward Sustainable Self-Determination: Rethinking the Contemporary Indigenous-Rights Discourse" (2008) 33 *Alternatives* 105.

Corntassel, J., and Cindy Holder. "Who's Sorry Now? Government Apologies, Truth Commissions, and Indigenous Self-Determination in Australia, Canada, Guatemala, and Peru." (2008) 9(4) *Human Rights Review* 465.

Corntassel, J., Chaw-win-is, and T'lakwadzi. "Indigenous Storytelling, Truth-telling, and Community Approaches to Reconciliation' (2009) 35(1) *English Studies in Canada* 137.

Cover, Robert. "Foreword: *Nomos* and Narrative" (1983) 97 Harv. L. Rev. 4.

Cowan, J. "The Gods of the Māori: Some Curious Beliefs." *Otago Witness,* December 23, 1903.

Coxhead, C. "Where Are the Negotiations in the Direct Negotiations of Treaty Settlements?" (2002) 10 Waikato L.R. 13.

Crocker, D.A. "Reckoning with Past Wrongs: A Normative Framework." In *Dilemmas of Reconciliation: Cases and Concepts,* edited by C.A.L. Prager and T. Govier (Waterloo, ON: Wilfrid Laurier University PressP, 2003).

Crown Forestry Rental Trust. *Māori Experiences of the Direct Negotiation Process* (Wellington, NZ: Crown Forestry Rental Trust, 2003).

Daes, E-I. A. "Some Considerations on the Right of Indigenous Peoples to Self-Determination" (1993) 3 Transnat'l L. and Contemp. Probs. 1.

Dawson, J. "The Remedies Reports." In *The Waitangi Tribunal – Te Roopu Whakamana i te Tiriti o Waitangi,* edited by J. Hayward and Nicola R. Wheen (Wellington, NZ: Bridget Williams Books, 2004).

de Costa, Ravi. "History, Democracy, and Treaty Making in British Columbia." In *The Power of Promises: Rethinking Indian Treaties in the Pacific Northwest,* edited by Alexandra Harmon (Seattle: University of Washington Press, 2008).

–. "Treaties in British Columbia: comprehensive agreement making in a democratic context." In *Honor among Nations? Treaties and Agreements with Indigenous People,* edited by Marcia Langton, Maureen Tehan, Lisa Palmer, and Kathryn Shain (Carlton, AU: Melbourne University Press, 2004).

Delgado, Richard. "Storytelling for Oppositionists and Others: A Plea for Narrative" (1989) 87 Mich. L. Rev. 2411.

Denzin, Norman K., and Yvonna S. Lincoln. "Introduction." In *Handbook of Critical and Indigenous Methodologies,* edited by Norman K. Denzin, Yvonna S. Lincoln, and Linda Tuhiwai Smith (Los Angeles: Sage, 2008).

Denzin, Norman K., Yvonna S. Lincoln, and Linda Tuhiwai Smith. *Handbook of Critical and Indigenous Methodologies* (Los Angeles: Sage, 2008).

Durie, E.T. "Background Paper." In *Treaty Settlements: The Unfinished Business,* edited by Geoff McLay (Wellington, NZ: Institute of Policy Studies and Victoria University of Wellington Law Review, 1995).

–. "Custom Law" (unpublished paper prepared for Waitangi Tribunal members and later referred to the Law Commission, 1994).

–. "Will the Settlers Settle? Cultural Conciliation and Law" (1996) 8 Otago L. Rev. 449.

Durie, Mason. *Te Mana, te Kāwanatanga: The Politics of Māori Self-determination* (Auckland, NZ: Oxford University Press, 1998).

–. "Tino Rangatiratanga." In *Waitangi Revisited: Perspectives on the Treaty of Waitangi,* edited by Michael Belgrave, Merata Kawharu, and David Williams (Auckland, NZ: Oxford University Press, 2005).

–. *Whaiora: Māori Health Development,* 2nd ed. (Auckland, NZ: Oxford University Press, 1998).

Dwyer, S. "Reconciliation for Realists." In *Dilemmas of Reconciliation: Cases and Concepts,* edited by C.A.L. Prager and T. Govier (Waterloo, ON: Wilfrid Laurier University Press, 2003).

Fanon, Frantz. *Black Skin, White Masks* (New York: Grove Press, 1982).

Finlayson, C. "Address by the Minister for Treaty of Waitangi Negotiations." Speech at Te Kōkiri Ngātahi: Treaty Settlements Hui, October 2010, http://www.ots.govt.nz.

Firth, R. *Economics of the New Zealand Māori* (Wellington, NZ: Government Printer, 1959).

Foster, Hamar, Benjamin Berger, and A.R. Buck, eds. *The Grand Experiment: Law and Legal Culture in British Settler Societies* (Vancouver: UBC Press, 2008).

Fox, Caren. "Change, Past and Present." In *Weeping Waters: The Treaty of Waitangi and Constitutional Change*, edited by M. Mulholland and Veronica Tawhai (Wellington, NZ: Huia, 2010).

Frame, Alex. *Grey and Iwikau: A Journey into Custom / Kerei Raua Ko Iwikau: Te Haerenga me nga Tikanga* (Wellington, NZ: Victoria University Press, 2002).

–. "Te Heuheu's Case in London 1940–41: An Explosive Story" (2006) 22 New Zealand Universities L. Rev. 148.

Freire, Paulo. *Pedagogy of the Oppressed*, 30th anniversary ed. (New York: Continuum, 2000).

Glenn, H. Patrick. *Legal Traditions of the World: Sustainable Diversity in Law*, 3rd ed. (Oxford/New York: Oxford University Press, 2007).

Goldstone, R. "Exposing Human Rights Abuses – A Help or Hinderance to Reconciliation?" (1995) 22 Hastings Const. L. Q. 607.

–. "Justice as a Tool for Peacemaking: Truth Commissions and International Criminal Tribunals" (1996) 28 N.Y.U.J. Int'l & Pol 485.

Gover, K. *Constitutionalizing Tribalism: States, Tribes and Membership Governance in Australia, Canada, New Zealand and the United States* (JSD book, New York University, unpublished, 2008).

–. "Tribal Constitutionalism and Membership Governance in Australia and New Zealand: Emerging Normative Frictions" (2009) 7 NZJPIL 191.

–. *Tribal Constitutionalism: States, Tribes, and the Governance of Membership* (Oxford: Oxford University Press, 2010).

Gover, K., and N. Baird. "Identifying the Māori Treaty Partner" (2002) 52 U. Toronto L.J. 39.

Graham, D. *Trick or Treaty?* (Wellington, NZ: Institute of Policy Studies, Victoria University of Wellington, 1997).

Greenhouse, Carol J. "Legal Pluralism and Cultural Difference – What Is the Difference? A Response to Professor Woodman Part II: Urban Normative Fields: Concepts, Theories and Critiques" (1998) 42 J. Legal Pluralism and Unofficial L. 61.

Griffiths, John. "What Is Legal Pluralism?" (1986) 24 J. Legal Pluralism and Unofficial L. 1.

Hall, D. "Māori Governance and Accountability." In *The Waitangi Tribunal – Te Roopu Whakamana i te Tiriti o Waitangi*, edited by J. Hayward and Nicola R. Wheen (Wellington, NZ: Bridget Williams Books, 2004).

Hampton, Eber. "Memory Comes Before Knowledge: Research May Improve If Researchers Remember Their Motives." (unpublished paper presented at the First Biannual Indigenous Scholars' Conference, University of Alberta, Edmonton, Canada, 1995).

Harawira, A. Letter to the editor: "Te Puke Ki Hikurangi." Vol. 5, No. 15, 3 (January 30, 1903).

Harawira, H. "Crunch time for Māori grumbles." *Sunday Star Times* (January 16, 2011).

Harmon, A., ed. *The Power of Promises: Rethinking Indian Treaties in the Pacific Northwest* (Seattle: University of Washington Press, 2008).

Hart, H.L.A. *The Concept of Law* (London: Oxford University Press, Ely House, 1961).

Havemann, Paul. "Perspectives on Māori Rights and Pākehā Duties'" (1993) 1 Waikato L. Rev. 53.

Hayward, Janine, and Nicola R. Wheen, eds. *The Waitangi Tribunal – Te Roopu Whakamana i te Tiriti o Waitangi* (Wellington, NZ: Bridget Williams Books, 2004).

Hazlehurst, Kayleen M., ed. *Legal Pluralism and the Colonial Legacy: Indigenous Experiences of Justice in Canada, Australia, and New Zealand* (Aldershot, UK/ Brookfield, VT: Avebury, 1995).

Hefferan, Gina. "Post-Settlement Dispute Resolution: Time to Tread Lightly" (2004) 10 Auckland U. L. Rev. 212.

Henderson, James (Sakej) Youngblood. *First Nations Jurisprudence and Aboriginal Rights: Defining the Just Society* (Saskatoon, SK: Native Law Centre, University of Saskatchewan, 2006).

–. *Indigenous Diplomacy and the Rights of Peoples: Achieving UN Recognition* (Saskatoon, SK: Purich Publishing, 2008).

Hill, Richard S. *Māori and the State: Crown–Māori Relations in New Zealand/Aotearoa, 1950–2000* (Wellington, NZ: Victoria University Press, 2009).

–. *State Authority, Indigenous Autonomy: Crown–Māori Relations in New Zealand/ Aotearoa, 1900–1950* (Wellington, NZ: Victoria University Press, 2004).

Hond, Mereana. "Resort to Mediation in Māori-to-Māori Dispute Resolution: Is It the Elixir to Cure All Ills?" (2002) 33 Victoria U. Wellington L. Rev. 155.

hooks, bell. *Teaching to Transgress: Education as the Practice of Freedom* (New York: Routledge, 1994).

Iorns Magallanes, C.J. "Reparations for Māori Grievances in Aotearoa New Zealand." In *Reparations for Indigenous Peoples: International and Comparative Perspectives,* edited by Federico Lenzerini (Oxford/ New York: Oxford University Press, 2008).

Irwin, Kathy. "Māori Research Methods and Processes: An Exploration" (1994) 28 *SITES* 24.

Jackson, Moana. "Comment Treaty of Waitangi: Special Issue" (1995) 25 Victoria U. Wellington L. Rev. 245.

–. "Criminality and the Exclusion of Māori" (1990) 20 Victoria U. Wellington L. Rev. 23.

–. "The Face Behind the Law: The United Nations and the Rights of Indigenous Peoples" (2005) 8 Y.B. NZ Juris. 10.

–. "Justice and Political Power: Reasserting Māori Legal Processes." In *Legal Pluralism and the Colonial Legacy: Indigenous Experiences of Justice in Canada, Australia, and New Zealand* , edited by Kayleen M. Hazlehurst (Aldershot, UK/ Brookfield, VT: Avebury, 1995).

–. *The Māori and the Criminal Justice System: A New Perspective – He Whaipaanga Hou* (Wellington, NZ: Department of Justice, 1988).

–. "Tipuna Title as a Tikanga Construct re: the Foreshore and Seabed" (March 2010), online: Peace Movement Aotearoa, http://www.converge.org.nz/pma/mjtipuna.htm.

–. "The Treaty and the Word: The Colonization of Māori Philosophy." In *Justice Ethics and New Zealand Society,* edited by G. Oddie and R. Perrett (Auckland, NZ: Oxford University Press, 1992).

Jones, Carwyn. "Māori Dispute Resolution: Traditional Conceptual Regulators and Contemporary Indigenous Processes." In *Mediating Across Difference: Indigenous, Oceanic and Asian Approaches to Conflict Resolution,* edited by M. Brigg and R. Bleiker (Honolulu: University of Hawaii Press, 2010).

–. "Whakaeke i ngā ngaru – riding the waves: Māori legal traditions in New Zealand public life." In *Between Indigenous and Settler Governance,* edited by Lisa Ford and Tim Rowse (Oxford/New York: Routledge, 2013).

Jones, Shane. "Consultation with Tangata Whenua" (1992, unpublished).

Joseph, P. *Constitutional and Administrative Law in New Zealand,* 3rd ed. (Wellington, NZ: Brookers, 2007).

Joseph, Robert. "Unsettling Treaty Settlements: Contemporary Māori Identity and Representation Challenges." In *Treaty of Waitangi Settlements*, edited by Nicola R. Wheen and Janine Hayward (Welington, NZ: Bridget Williams Books, 2012).

Kawharu, I.H. "Introduction." In *Waitangi: Māori and Pākehā Perspectives of the Treaty of Waitangi*, edited by I.H. Kawharu (Auckland, NZ: Oxford University Press, 1989).

–, ed. *Waitangi: Māori and Pākehā Perspectives of the Treaty of Waitangi* (Auckland, NZ: Oxford University Press, 1989).

Key, J. "Towards 2014: Speech at Te Kōkiri Ngātahi National Hui to Progress Treaty Settlements." Speech given at Te Kōkiri Ngātahi: Treaty Settlements Hui (April 22, 2009), http://www.ots.govt.nz.

Kimpson, Sally A. "Stepping off the Road: A Narrative (of) Inquiry." In *Research As Resistance: Critical, Indigenous, and Anti-oppressive Approaches*, edited by Leslie Brown and Susan Strega (Toronto: Canadian Scholars Press, 2005).

King, Michael. *Te Ao Hurihuri: Aspects of Maoritanga* (Auckland, NZ: Reed, 1992).

King, Thomas. *The Truth about Stories: A Native Narrative* (Toronto: House of Anansi Press, 2003).

Kingsbury, B. "Competing Conceptual Approaches to Indigenous Group Issues in New Zealand Law" (2002) 52 U. Toronto L.J. 101.

Kleinhans, Martha-Marie, and Roderick A. Macdonald. "What Is a *Critical* Legal Pluralism?" (1997) 12 Can. J.L. and Soc. 25.

Kovach, Margaret. *Indigenous Methodologies: Characteristics, Conversations, and Contexts* (Toronto: University of Toronto Press, 2009).

Kymlicka, W. *Multicultural Citizenship: A Liberal Theory of Minority Rights* (Oxford: Oxford University Press, 1995).

Langton, Marcia, Maureen Tehan, Lisa Palmer, and Kathryn Shain, eds. *Honor Among Nations: Treaties and Agreements with Indigenous People* (Melbourne, AU: Melbourne University Press, 2004).

Lederach, J.P. *The Journey Toward Reconciliation* (Scottdale, PA: Herald Press, 1999).

Lederach, J.P., and A.J. Lederach. *When Blood and Bones Cry Out: Journeys through the Soundscape of Healing and Reconciliation* (Oxford: Oxford University Press, 2010).

Lee, Jenny. "Māori Cultural Regeneration: Pūrākau as Pedagogy" (unpublished paper presented to Centre for Research in Lifelong Learning International Conference, June 24, 2005).

Lenzerini, Ferderico, ed. *Reparations for Indigenous Peoples: International and Comparative Perspectives* (Oxford: Oxford University Press, 2008).

Maaka, Roger. "A Relationship, Not a Problem." In *Kōkiri Ngātahi: Living Relationships*, edited by K.S. Coates and P.G. McHugh, (Wellington, NZ: Victoria University Press, 1998).

Macklem, P. "The Māori Experiment" (2002) 52 U. Toronto L.J. 1.

Mahuika, Api."Leadership: Inherited and Achieved." In *Te Ao Hurihuri: Aspects of Māoritanga*, edited by Michael King (Auckland, NZ: Reed Books, 1992).

Marsden, Māori. *The Woven Universe: Selected Writings of Rev. Māori Marsden*, edited by Te Ahukaramū Charles Royal (Otaki, NZ: Estate of Rev. Māori Marsden, 2003).

Matiu, M., and Margaret Mutu. *Te Whānau Moana: Ngā* Kaupapa *me ngā* Tikanga – *Customs and Protocols* (Auckland, NZ: Reed, 2003).

McCan, David. *Whatiwhatihoe: the Waikato Raupatu Claim* (Wellington, NZ: Huia, 2001).

McHugh, P.G. *Aboriginal Societies and the Common Law: A History of Sovereignty, Status, and Self-determination* (Oxford: Oxford University Press, 2004).

–. *The Māori Magna Carta: New Zealand Law and the Treaty of Waitangi* (Oxford: Oxford University Press, 1991).
–. "Tales of Constitutional Origin and Crown Sovereignty in New Zealand" (2002) 52 U. Toronto L.J. 69.
McHugh, Paul G., and Andrew Sharp. *Histories, Power and Loss: Uses of the Past – A New Zealand Commentary* (Wellington, NZ: Bridget Williams Books, 2001).
McKee, Christopher. *Treaty Talks in British Columbia: Negotiating a Mutually Beneficial Future*, 2nd ed. (Vancouver: UBC Press, 2000).
McKenzie, Colin, and Amster Reedy. "A Treaty of Waitangi, Overlapping Claim Mediation: 'A Prospective Hindsight,'" *Resource Management Journal* 9 (2001).
McLaren, John. "The Origins of Tortious Liability: Insights from Contemporary Tribal Societies" (1975) 25 U. Toronto L.J. 42.
McLaren, John, and Hamar Foster. "Hard Choices and Sharp Edges: The Legal History of British Columbia and the Yukon." In *Essays in the History of Canadian Law, Vol. 6: British Columbia and the Yukon,* edited by John McLaren and Hamar Foster (Toronto: Osgoode Society for Canadian Legal History, 1995).
McLay, G., ed. *Treaty Settlements: The Unfinished Business* (Wellington, NZ: Institute of Policy Studies and Victoria University of Wellington Law Review, 1995).
Mead, Hirini M. *Tikanga Māori: Living by Māori Values* (Wellington, NZ: Huia, 2003).
Melissaris, Emmanuel. "The More the Merrier? A New Take on Legal Pluralism" (2004) 13:1 Social Legal Studies 57.
–. *Ubiquitous Law: Legal Theory and the Space for Legal Pluralism* (Farnham, UK/ Burlington, VT: Ashgate , 2009).
Merry, Sally Engle. "Legal Pluralism" (1988) 22 Law and Soc'y Rev. 869.
Metge, J. *New Growth from Old: The Whānau in the Modern World* (Wellington, NZ: Victoria University Press, 1995).
–. *Tuamaka: The Challenge of Difference in Aotearoa/New Zealand* (Auckland, NZ: Auckland University Press, 2010).
Michaels, Ralf. "Re-State-ment of Non-State Law: The State, Choice of Law, and the Challenge from Global Legal Pluralism, the Symposium" (2005) 51 Wayne L. Rev. 1209.
Mihesuah, Devon A. *Natives and Academics: Researching and Writing about American Indians* (Lincoln: University of Nebraska Press, 1998).
–. *So You Want to Write About American Indians?: A Guide for Writers, Students, and Scholars* (Lincoln: University of Nebraska Press, 2005).
Mihesuah, Devon A., and Angela Cavender Wilson. *Indigenizing the Academy: Transforming Scholarship and Empowering Communities* (Lincoln/ London: University of Nebraska Press, 2004).
Mikaere, Ani. "Cultural Invasion Continued: The Ongoing Colonisation of Tikanga Māori" (2005) 8 Y.B. NZ Juris. 134.
–. *He Rukuruku Whakaaro – Colonising Myths, Māori Realities* (Wellington, NZ: Huia, 2011).
–. "Māori Critic and Conscience in a Colonising Context – Law and Leadership as a Case Study" (unpublished paper presented at the 27th Annual Conference of the Law and Society Association of Australia and New Zealand, Victoria University of Wellington, December 10, 2010).
–. "Māori Women: Caught in the Contradictions of a Colonised Reality" (1994) 2 Waikato L. Rev. 125.

–. "Settlement of Treaty Claims: Full and Final, or Fatally Flawed?" (1997) 17 New Zealand Universities L. Rev. 425.

–. "The Treaty of Waitangi and Recognition of Tikanga Māori" in *Waitangi Revisited: Perspectives on the Treaty of Waitangi,* edited by Michael Belgrave, Merata Kawharu, and David Williams (Auckland, NZ: Oxford University Press, 2005).

Mitira, Tiaki Hikawera (J.H. Mitchell). *Takitimu,* facsimile of 1944 ed. (Wellington, NZ: A.H. and A.W. Reed, 1972).

Monture-Angus, Patricia. *Journeying Forward: Dreaming First Nations' Independence* (Halifax, NS: Fernwood, 1999).

Moore, Sally Falk. *Law as Process: An Anthropological Approach* (Hamburg: LIT Verlag and James Curry, 2000).

Morse, B. "Indigenous Peoples of Canada and Their Efforts to Achieve True Reparations." In *Reparations for Indigenous Peoples: International and Comparative Perspectives,* edited by F. Lenzerini (Oxford/New York: Oxford University Press, 2008).

Mulholland, M., and V. Tawhai, eds. *Weeping Waters: The Treaty of Waitangi and Constitutional Change* (Wellington, NZ: Huia, 2010).

Mutu, M. "Constitutional Intentions: The Treaty of Waitangi Texts." In *Weeping Waters: The Treaty of Waitangi and Constitutional Change,* edited by M. Mulholland and Veronica Tawhai , (Wellington, NZ: Huia, 2010).

–. "Recovering Fagin's Ill-Gotten Gains: Settling Ngāti Kahu's Treaty of Waitangi Claims Against the Crown." In *Waitangi Revisited: Perspectives on the Treaty of Waitangi,* 2nd ed., edited by Michael Belgrave, Merata Kawharu, and David Williams (South Melbourne, AU/New York: Oxford University Press, 2005).

Nadasdy, P. "The Antithesis of Restitution? A note on the dynamics of land negotiations in the Yukon, Canada." In *The Rights and Wrongs of Land Restitution,* edited by D. Fay and D. James (Kentucky: Routledge- Cavendish, 2009).

Napoleon, V. *Ayook: Gitksan Legal Order, Law and Legal Theory* (PhD diss., University of Victoria, 2009).

–. "Who Gets to Say What Happened? Reconciliation Issues for the Gitxsan." In *Intercultural Dispute Resolution in Aboriginal Contexts,* edited by C. Bell and D. Kahane (Vancouver: UBC Press, 2004).

Napoleon, V., and Hadley Friedland. "An Inside Job: Developing Scholarship from an Internal Perspective of Indigenous Legal Traditions" (unpublished paper prepared for An Exploratory Workshop: Thinking About and Practicing with Indigenous Legal Traditions, Fort St. John, 30 September-2 October, 2011) .

Nelken, David. *Comparing Legal Cultures* (Aldershot, UK/ Brookfield, VT: Dartmouth, 1997).

–. "Towards a Sociology of Legal Adaption." In *Adapting Legal Cultures,* edited by David Nelken and Johannes Feest (Oxford/Portland, OR: Hart, 2001).

Nelken, David, and Johannes Feest. *Adapting Legal Cultures* (Oxford /Portland, OR: Hart, 2001).

O'Malley, V. *Agents of Autonomy: Māori Committees in the Nineteenth Century* (Wellington, NZ: Huia, 1998).

Oddie, Graham James, and Roy W. Perrett. *Justice, Ethics and New Zealand Society* (Auckland, NZ: Oxford University Press, 1992).

Orange, C. *The Treaty of Waitangi,* 2nd ed. (Wellington, NZ: Bridget Williams Books, 2011).

Palmer, Matthew S.R. *The Treaty of Waitangi in New Zealand's Law and Constitution* (Wellington, NZ: Victoria University Press, 2008).

Patterson, John. *Exploring Māori Values* (Palmerston North, NZ: Dunmore Press, 1992).

–. *People of the Land: A Pacific Philosophy* (Palmerston North, NZ: Dunmore Press, 2000).

Phelps, T.G. *Shattered Voices: Language, Violence, and the Work of Truth Commissions* (Philadelphia: University of Pennsylvania Press, 2004).

Pihama, Leonie. *Tihei Mauri Ora – Honouring Our Voices: Mana Wahine as Kaupapa Māori Theoretical Framework* (PhD diss., University of Auckland, 2001).

Pohatu, Taina. *I Tīpu ai Tātou i ngā Turi o o Tātau Mātua Tīpuna: Transmission and Acquisition Processes within Kāwai Whakapapa* (master's thesis, University of Auckland, 1996).

Reeves, W.P. *The Long White Cloud: Ao Tea Roa*, 4th ed. (London: Allen and Unwin, 1950).

Regan, P. *Unsettling the Settler Within: Indian Residential Schools, Truth-Telling, and Reconciliation in Canada* (Vancouver: UBC Press, 2010).

Rigby, A. *Justice and Reconciliation: After the Violence* (Boulder, CO: Lynne Rienner Publishers, 2001).

Roughan, Nicole. "The Association of State and Indigenous Law: A Case Study in 'Legal Association'" (2009) 59 U. Toronto L. J. 135.

–. "Democratic Custom vs International Customary Law" (2007) 38 Victoria U. Wellington L. Rev. 403.

–. "Te Tiriti and the Constitution: Rethinking Citizenship, Justice, Equality and Democracy" (2005) 3 NZJPIL 285.

Royal, Te Ahukaramū Charles. "Mātauranga Māori: Paradigms and Politics" (unpublished paper presented at Ministry for Research, Science and Technology Hui, Wellington, January 13, 1998).

Santos, Bonaventura de Sousa. *Toward a New Common Sense: Law, Science, and Politics in the Paradigmatic Transition* (New York: Routledge, 1995).

Schneiderman, David. "Pluralism, Disagreement, and Globalization: A Comment on Webber's Legal Pluralism and Human Agency Commentary," (2006) 44 Osgoode Hall L.J. 199.

Shahar, Ido. "State, Society and the Relations between Them: Implications for the Study of Legal Pluralism," (2008) 9 Theoretical Inq. L. 417.

Sharafi, Mitra. "Justice in Many Rooms Since Galanter: De-Romanticizing Legal Pluralism through the Cultural Defense Galanter-Influenced Scholars" (2008) 71 Law and Contemp. Probs. 139.

Sharp, Andrew. "Blood, Custom, and Consent: Three Kinds of Māori Groups and the Challenges They Present to Governments" (2002) 52 U. Toronto L.J. 9.

–. *Justice and the Māori: The Philosophy and Practice of Māori Claims in New Zealand Since the 1970s*, 2nd ed. (Auckland, NZ: Oxford University Press, 1997).

–. "The Trajectory of the Waitangi Tribunal." In *The Waitangi Tribunal – Te Roopu Whakamana i te Tiriti o Waitangi*, edited by Janine Hayward and Nicola R. Wheen (Wellington, NZ: Bridget Williams Books, 2004).

Sharples, P. "Post-Settlement Crown-Iwi Relationships" (speech at Te Kōkiri Ngātahi: Treaty Settlements Hui, October 2010, http://www.ots.govt.nz.

Smith, Graham. "Research Issues Related to Māori Education" (paper presented to NZARE Special Interest Conference, Massey University, reprinted in 1992, *The Issue of Research and Māori*, Research Unit for Māori Education, University of Auckland), cited in Linda Tuhiwai Smith, *Decolonizing Methodologies*.

–. "Transforming Leadership: A Discussion Paper" (unpublished paper presented to the Simon Fraser University Summer Institute, Burnaby, BC, (6 July, 2009).

Smith, Linda Tuhiwai. *Decolonizing Methodologies: Research and Indigenous Peoples* (London/ Dunedin: Zed Books/University of Otago Press, 1999).

–. "Kaupapa Māori Research." In *Reclaiming Indigenous Voice and Vision,* edited by M. Battiste (Vancouver: UBC Press, 2000).

Stevens, Michael J. "Settlements and 'Taonga': A Ngai Tahu Commentary." In *Treaty of Waitangi Settlements,* edited by Nicola R. Wheen and Janine Hayward (Wellington, NZ: Bridget Williams Books, 2012).

Sullivan, Patrick. "Indigenous Governance: The Harvard Project, Australian Aboriginal Organisations and Cultural Subsidiarity" Working Paper 4, Desert Knowledge CRC Working Paper Series, Alice Springs, (2007).

Tamanaha, Brian Z. "The Folly of the Social Scientific Concept of Legal Pluralism" (1993) 20 J.L. and Soc'y 192.

–. "A Non-Essentialist Version of Legal Pluralism" (2000) 27 J.L. and Soc'y 296.

–. "Understanding Legal Pluralism: Past to Present, Local to Global" (2008) 30 Sydney L. Rev. 375.

A Taranaki Veteran. "The Great Muru" (1919) 28 *Jnl. Polynesian Soc.* 97.

Tau, Te Maire. "Matauranga Māori as an Epistemology." In *Histories, Power and Loss: Uses of the Past – A New Zealand Commentary,* edited by Paul G. McHugh and Andrew Sharp (Wellington, NZ: Bridget Williams Books, 2001).

Te Aho, L. "Corporate Governance: Balancing Tikanga Māori with Commercial Objectives" (2005) 8 YB of N.Z. Juris 300.

–. "Ruruku Whakatupua Te Mana o te Awa Tupua - Upholding the Mana of the Whanganui River," (2014) May Māori LR 12.

–. "The Tangled Web of Treaty Settlements: Emissions Trading, Central North Island Forests, and the Waikato River" (2008) 16 Waikato L. Rev. 229.

Te Ahu Poata-Smith, E.S. "The Changing Contours of Māori Identity and the Treaty Settlement Process." In *The Waitangi Tribunal – Te Roopu Whakamana i te Tiriti o Waitangi,* edited by J. Hayward and Nicola R. Wheen (Wellington, NZ: Bridget Williams Books, 2004).

Teubner, Gunther. "Two Faces of Janus: Rethinking Legal Pluralism, the Closed Systems and Open Justice: The Legal Sociology of Niklas Shumann" (1991) 13 Cardozo L. Rev. 1443.

Tomas, Nin. *Key Concepts of Tikanga Māori (Māori Custom Law) in Tai Tokerau Past and Present* (PhD diss., University of Auckland, 2006).

Tomas, N., and Khylee Quince. "Māori Disputes and Their Resolution." In *Dispute Resolution in New Zealand,* edited by P. Spiller (Oxford: Oxford University Press, 1999).

Tully, James. *Public Philosophy in a New Key: Vol. 1. – Democracy and Civic Freedom* (Cambridge: Cambridge University Press, 2008).

–. "Reconsidering the B.C. Treaty Process." In *Speaking Truth to Power* (Vancouver: British Columbia Treaty Commission and Law Commission of Canada, 2001).

–. *Strange Multiplicity: Constitutionalism in an Age of Diversity* (Cambridge: Cambridge University Press, 1995).

Turcotte, Kellinde. "Why Legal Flexibility Is Not a Threat to Either the Common Law System of England and Australia or the Civil Law System of France in the Twenty-first Century" (2005) 1 Hanse L. Rev. 190.

Turia, T. "Operating Māori Values Within the System" (unpublished paper presented to Māori Customary Law class, Victoria University of Wellington, December 8, 2007).
Turner, Dale A. *This Is Not a Peace Pipe: Towards a Critical Indigenous Philosophy* (Toronto/Buffalo/London: University of Toronto Press, 2006).
Twining, William L. *Globalisation and Legal Theory*, Northwestern University Press ed. (Evanston, IL: Northwestern University Press, 2001).
–. *Legal Theory and Common Law* (Oxford: Basil Blackwell, 1986).
Vanderlinden, Jacques. "Return to Legal Pluralism: Twenty Years Later" (1989) 28 J. Legal Pluralism and Unofficial L. 149.
Vertongen, Baden. "Remedies – *The Mangatū Remedies Report* – analysis" (2014) April Māori LR 10.
Verwoerd, W. "Toward a Response to Criticisms of the South Africa Truth and Reconciliation Commission." In *Dilemmas of Reconciliation: Cases and Concepts*, edited by C.A.L. Prager and T. Govier (Waterloo, ON: Wilfrid Laurier University Press, 2003).
Von Benda-Beckmann, Franz. "Who's Afraid of Legal Pluralism?" (2002) 47 J. Legal Pluralism and Unofficial L. 37.
Waldron, J. "Redressing Historic Injustice" (2002) 52 U. Toronto L.J. 135.
Walker, Ranginui. "The Relevance of Māori Myth and Tradition." In *Te Ao Hurihuri: Aspects of Maoritanga*, edited by Michael King (Auckland: Reed, 1992).
Warbrick, Paerau. "'O ratou wenua': Land and Estate Settlements." In *Treaty of Waitangi Settlements*, edited by Nicola R. Wheen and J. Hayward (Wellington, NZ: Bridget Williams Books, 2012).
Ward, Alan. *An Unsettled History: Treaty Claims in New Zealand Today* (Wellington, NZ: Bridget Williams Books, 1999).
Waziyatawin. *What Does Justice Look Like? The Struggle for Liberation in Dakota Homeland* (St. Paul, MN: Living Justice Press, 2008).
Webber, Jeremy. "Culture, Legal Culture, and Legal Reasoning: A Comment on Nelken" (2004) 29 Austl. J. Leg. Phil. 27.
–. "Legal Pluralism and Human Agency" (2006) 44 Osgoode Hall L.J. 167.
Wheen, Nicola R., and Janine Hayward, eds. *Treaty of Waitangi Settlements* (Wellington, NZ: Bridget Williams Books, 2012).
Wickliffe, Caren. "A Māori Criminal Justice System in the Context of Rethinking Criminal Justice." In *Re-thinking Criminal Justice, Vol. I: Justice in the Community*, edited by F. McElrea (Auckland, NZ: Legal Research Foundation, 1995).
Williams, David V. "He Aha Te Tikanga Māori." Revised draft as at November 10, 1998, of Joe Williams, cited by New Zealand Law Commission, *Māori Custom and Values*.
–. *"Te Kooti Tango Whenua": The Native Land Court, 1864–1909* (Wellington, NZ: Huia, 1999).
Williams, Joe. "He Aha te Tikanga Māori?" (unpublished paper presented to the Mai i Te Ata Hāpara Hui, Te Wananga o Raukawa, Otaki, New Zealand, 2000).
–. "Quality Relations: The Key to Māori Survival." In *Kōkiri Ngātahi: Living Relationships*, edited by K.S. Coates and P.G. McHugh (Wellington, NZ: Victoria University Press, 1998).
Williams, Robert A. Jr. "Documents of Barbarism: The Contemporary Legacy of European Racism and Colonialism in the Narrative Traditions of Federal Indian Law" (1989) 31 Arizona L. Rev. 237.
–. *Linking Arms Together: American Indian Treaty Visions of Law and Peace, 1600–1800* (New York/Oxford: Oxford University Press, 1997).

–. “Vampires Anonymous and Critical Race Practice” (1997) 95 Michigan L. Rev. 741.
Williams, Te Rangimarie. *Te Mana Motuhake o Tūhoe* (LLM thesis, Victoria University of Wellington, 2011).
Wilson, Margaret. “A Path to Constitutional Change.” In *Kōkiri Ngātahi: Living Relationships*, edited by K.S. Coates and P.G. McHugh (Wellington, NZ: Victoria University Press, 1998).
Wilson, Shawn. *Research Is Ceremony: Indigenous Research Methods* (Black Point, NS: Fernwood, 2008).
Woodman, Gordon R. “Ideological Combat and Social Observation – Recent Debate about Legal Pluralism Part II: Urban Normative Fields: Concepts, Theories and Critiques” (1998) 42 J. Legal Pluralism and Unofficial L. 21.
Woolford, Andrew. *Between Justice and Certainty: Treaty Making in British Columbia* (Vancouver: UBC Press, 2005).

Index

Printed and bound in Canada by Friesens
Set in MinionPro and Calibri by Apex CoVantage, LLC
Copy editor: Jillian Shoichet
Proofreader: Dianne Tiefensee
Indexer: Margaret de Boer